# EDWARDIAN CIVIC BUILDINGS AND THEIR DETAILS

Edwardian Civic Buildings and their Details

Richard Fellows

Architectural Press
OXFORD AUCKLAND BOSTON JOHANNESBURG MELBOURNE NEW DELHI

Architectural Press
An imprint of Butterworth-Heinemann
Linacre House, Jordan Hill, Oxford OX2 8DP
225 Wildwood Avenue, Woburn, MA 01801-2041
A division of Reed Educational and Professional Publishing Ltd

℞ A member of the Reed Elsevier plc group

First published 1999

© Richard Fellows 1999

All rights reserved. No part of this publication may be reproduced in any material form (including photocopying or storing in any medium by electronic means and whether or not transiently or incidentally to some other use of this publication) without the written permission of the copyright holder except in accordance with the provisions of the Copyright, Designs and Patents Act 1988 or under the terms of a licence issued by the Copyright Licensing Agency Ltd, 90 Tottenham Court Road, London, England W1P 9HE. Applications for the copyright holder's written permission to reproduce any part of this publication should be addressed to the publishers

British Library Cataloguing in Publication Data
Fellows, Richard A.
   Edwardian Civic Buildings and their Details
   1. Architecture, Edwardian
   I. Title
   724.6

Library of Congress Cataloguing in Publication Data
A catalogue record for this book is available on request

ISBN 0 7506 2887 1

Composition by Scribe Design, Gillingham, Kent
Printed and bound in Great Britain

Contents

Acknowledgements vii

Introduction ix

1 Edwardian architecture 1
2 Civic expansion 7
3 Building and context 22
4 Integration of the arts – external enrichment 39
5 Space and organization 51
6 The art of entering 68
7 Space and character 79
8 Integration of the arts – internal enrichment 93
9 Technology 111
10 Conclusion 121

Notes and references 123
Bibliography 125
Index 127

University Libraries
Carnegie Mellon University
Pittsburgh, PA 15213-3890

Acknowledgements

I would like to thank all those who have helped and encouraged me in the writing and production of this book. In particular I must mention the library staff at the University of Huddersfield, and Keith Parker, formerly librarian at the Institute of Advanced Architectural Studies, University of York. Margaret Richardson provided invaluable commentary on my work, as did Neil Warnock-Smith at Architectural Press. Also at the publishers, I must thank Mike Cash and Marie Milmore.

My thanks also go to Richard Buxton, who has prepared the index and Bill Ellis who read the proofs.

As far as illustrations are concerned, the following have provided help: Vasilieos Balampanos, Craig Whittingham-Ball, Albert Booth, Rebecca Hammersley, Lynne Jackson, Caroline Nicholl and Simon J. Roberts. Above all, Susan Pritchard has given time and energy in dealing with my own efforts. Those who have allowed illustrations to be reproduced are acknowledged in the figure legends; all photographs are by the author unless otherwise stated.

With regard to particular buildings, I have reason to thank the following: Bristol Central Library – Mrs J. Bradley; Colchester Town Hall – Annie Hammerton; Deptford Town Hall – Mr J. Coulter (Lewisham local studies); Lancaster Town Hall – Charles Wilson and Peter Williamson; County Hall Northallerton – Tony Webster and North Yorkshire County Council; Oxford Town Hall – John Ashdown, Robin Edwards, Mr D. Clark and Dr M. Graham; County Buildings Stafford – Mr P. Owen; County Hall Wakefield – Tom Hickin and Melanie Reeves; Wesleyan Central Hall – Peter Tudor.

Finally, my wife's help, patience and support have been invaluable in the production of this book.

R.F.

Introduction

Edwardian Civic Buildings and their Details was chosen as the title and theme of this book, following on from Dan Cruickshank's *Georgian Buildings and Their Details*, which has been a popular and successful work. Initially conceived as part of a crusade to prevent the wholesale demolition of unassuming but valuable street architecture, Cruickshank's book documents subtle variations played upon a fairly basic theme. In the case of Edwardian civic buildings there is, in the main, no threat to their continued existence, except that reorganization in local government has reduced the importance of some and has made one or two redundant, putting them in need of new uses. In addition, restrictions in maintenance budgets have lead to some deterioration of what are expensive and lavish buildings that are often still heavily used and require continuous detailed attention in order to remain in good condition. The fact that most are now around one hundred years old is, perhaps, a milestone that demands recognition. They have served their communities unstintingly during this time and have become accepted as major landmarks within towns and cities.

Civic buildings are, in themselves, diverse and interesting. They fulfil a variety of functions, express themselves in a range of architectural languages and incorporate the works of artist and craftsmen. Those built in the Edwardian period display some of the characteristics of that fascinating era, which was a time of transition between Victorian and modern values, when the art of building reached a peak, but also when techniques and materials associated with the later twentieth century were beginning to prove their value. In the main, they extended what the building was able to achieve and introduced a range of possibilities which was seized upon by architects.

Certainly large Edwardian buildings are very different from Georgian town houses. In the case of the latter, various related plan forms were developed over a range of sizes, and there was almost a standardization of approach. It was possible to achieve refinement across a limited palette of architectural elements, and the joy of studying the type is related to the subtlety of variation. Concentration is upon the proportion and treatment of similar internal spaces and, normally, one main façade facing on to the street. It therefore allows a comparative study of detail which is relatively straightforward, but is rewarding in that it shows that character and individuality can be achieved within a limited framework. In Edwardian buildings diversity is the order of the day. Any one of a number of styles may have been chosen as the most appropriate means of expression by the architect, and within this, the work of craftsmen and artists, employed to add individual touches, expands a terrific range of detail in buildings that are as little standardized as possible. In addition, each building has a particular programme of internal accommodation that produces a significant and distinctive form. Not only this, but, unlike Georgian town houses, which are usually disposed in a continuous row forming the wall of the corridor street, Edwardian civic buildings may be built within existing urban blocks, on fringe urban sites or on new sites. There is little consistency. In summary, then, the building types and the conditions of their construction are almost as different as it is possible to be.

In preparing a book with ostensibly the same agenda as Cruickshank's, it has certainly not been possible to follow the same analytic examination of detail. Instead, different categories have been chosen which are appropriate to the subject matter but which still, hopefully, are in the spirit of the original. In selecting the categories, there has been an attempt to capture some of the major architectural issues related to Edwardian civic buildings. For instance, their role in the hierarchy of the town or city in which they are located is always of great importance. How the building makes its presence felt through the use of landmarks like clock towers, or symbols associated with important public buildings such as pedimented entrances, is of significance. The interaction between the work of artists and the architect, both internally and externally, is of consequence in a period when such collaboration reached its zenith. In addition, the propriety of how to enter the building, and distinctions internally based on usage by different classes of occupants is part of a fascinating view of a period, long gone, when such problems assumed an importance now almost impossible to comprehend. New technology, on the other hand, was of great advantage in helping the architect to achieve his ends, but the extent to which it should be expressed or how to integrate it within existing canons of detail and ornamentation seems to have been something that was cheerfully addressed.

All of these issues make a fascinating study, but cannot be contained easily within a convenient temporal envelope. Boundaries must be drawn, however. In terms of the need for buildings of this type, the opening of the last decade of the nineteenth century seems to be a good starting point. County councils had recently come into being, and adjustments in the running and scope of local government gave an impetus to the development of new local authority buildings. Libraries and other cultural buildings were increased in number by changes in allowances within the system of rates which provided money to be spent on these purposes, and the advent of philanthropic bequests which enabled the provision of new premises. After about 1910, the pace of development seemed to slow generally, although the construction of the great headquarters of the London County Council had only recently begun.

Stylistically, too, to set the limits of the period in 1890 at one end and 1910 at the other seems suitable. At the outset, the eclectic style of Richard Norman Shaw and Sir Ernest George, based on picturesque details and outlines derived from a variety of sources, was at its height. As the last decade of the nineteenth century wore on, however, this was overtaken by a style largely derived from the work of Christopher Wren and his contemporaries – at once national and capable of expansion to a large scale – which was much more consistent in its architectural palette. This continued with certain variations through the early years of the new century, but was gradually superseded by a style owing much to the influence of the Franco-American *beaux-arts* approach, which used a classical grammar, but which was completely different to theoretically to what had gone before.

From within the twenty-year period, labelled as Edwardian for convenience, though having at least half its span in the last years of Victoria's reign, a number of examples have been selected. In the first place, they exemplify types: town and city council buildings, county buildings and libraries. Wesleyan Central Hall, Westminster, has been included because of its appropriateness, despite the fact that it is not, strictly, a civic building. Within these broad categories the issue of size and complexity has been addressed, as has stylistic development. These buildings are used throughout the book as the basis for description and discussion, although other examples are drawn in to amplify points.

CHAPTER ONE

Edwardian architecture

The upsurge in the construction of civic buildings at the end of the nineteenth century and the beginning of the twentieth gave an excellent opportunity to architects to demonstrate their skills. Because of their importance in establishing an identity for sprawling new towns and cities, and enshrining local democracy, these buildings were all afforded architectural importance and great efforts were made to ensure that they represented the status of the borough's and counties of which they were the physical manifestations.

The outcome of this effort has sometimes been scorned as pompous, unrestrained and inelegant. The use of historical styles was derided by the architects of the modern movement, who dominated succeeding generations. The tenor of the twentieth century has been such that the florid work of the Edwardians has taken a long time to come back into favour with designers, and many still find it indigestible. This is not usually the case amongst those who identify with their local surroundings, and for whom these buildings are inseparable from the images and mental maps of their towns. The visual characteristics of the buildings are usually strong enough or idiosyncratic enough to leave a permanent impression.

Edwardian civic architecture has a number of strengths which have marked it out from later efforts. Its rich variety is a product of the personal approaches of its architects, in an age of individualism, when the concept of the artist–architect predominated. These designers went out of their way to ensure that what was created was public art, producing landmarks for locals and powerful images of the building and its purpose. In addition, they felt strongly that their work should include contributions by other artists: sculptors, carvers, modellers, mural painters, stained glass designers, plasterworkers and so on, each working towards a unified concept by making an individual statement. The craft of building reached a high point, and many of those employed internally also contributed externally, for instance, to the design of rainwater pipes and heads in lead, the carving of cornices and the application of sculpture and modelled decoration enhancing window and door openings and parapets. Excellent craftsmanship and first rate materials are usually found throughout. Perhaps one of the great achievements of the arts and crafts movement is realized in these buildings. Too often only domestic work is thought of as belonging to the movement – something that is essentially private and specific to the individual. In fact, the houses of Voysey, Prior and all the other famous domestic architects of the turn of the century are only part of the arts and crafts picture.

In seeking to define the period to be covered, the influence of the arts and crafts movement and the era of the 'artist–architect' have been strongly influential.

The starting point for this survey of Edwardian civic buildings is 1890. There are good reasons to make it a few years earlier or later, but nothing that is potent enough to prevent the choice of a round number. The year, in any case, marks the beginning of the construction of the Hall of the Institute of Chartered Accountants. Designed by John Belcher with Arthur Beresford Pite, it most clearly symbolizes the origins of Edwardian baroque, and the arts and crafts influence that made it different from other classical revivals. The close of the period is more problematic, but few buildings are mentioned that were built after about 1908. It may be thought that the outbreak of the First World War might be a more convenient termination, or, perhaps the death of Edward VII himself, in 1910. Yet before that date, there is no doubt that the influence of full time architectural education and the change in fashion towards the Franco-American *beaux-arts* style was already making work from just a few years earlier seem outmoded. Although the new style used classical precedent, the approach to design – theoretical and systematic

– was completely different. It spawned what might be called for civic and government buildings the George V style, dignified and well mannered, but cold and lacking individuality.

At the beginning of the period, the intense, heavy, uncomfortable, spiky and aggressive manner of High Victorianism had given way to a more pleasant and humane architecture of the last three decades of the nineteenth century. This trend was represented, and to a large extent introduced, by Richard Norman Shaw and his colleague W. Eden Nesfield, together with architects less fond of publicity like Philip Webb. Although Webb was concerned with the art of building, and was one of the first generation to be influenced by William Morris, the trend primarily was towards a referential architecture based on the visual characteristics of appropriate sources. Domestic work, in particular, was reinvigorated by this approach, espousing the 'olde English' of late medieval and sixteenth century manor houses and farmsteads. Local vernacular crafts were, in some cases, employed or copied. In larger scale work for urban locations with the exception of churches, the 'Queen Anne' style was usually in evidence. This title was very largely inappropriate, but served as a heading for an eclectic mix of any styles or details which the architect felt picturesque enough to serve his purpose. Many of its practitioners had been brought up within the 'gothic revival' tradition and their buildings consequently have some three-dimensional vigour and a strong sense of massing. By and large, though, there was a lack of theory and the architectural success of the building relied upon the artistic qualities of the architect. Sir Ernest George, for example, a foremost member of the profession in the last decades of the century, was an excellent draughtsman and watercolourist. He filled sketchbooks full of details, some of which he reinterpreted for use later in his designs. Indeed, it was the golden age of the sketch book, and architects commonly took sketching holidays or tours at home or on the Continent, both to hone their visual sensibilities and to acquire a catalogue of references.

As the period discussed in this book begins, this type of approach was in full flood. Interesting developments were beginning to occur, however, but these represent a maturing process, rather than the change of outlook which was to happen around the end of the first decade of the new century. What is generally known as *Edwardian Baroque* began to emerge, most commonly based on late seventeenth century English work, and known popularly as the 'Wrenaissance'. It took Wren's Hampton Court palace as a cue for large buildings, or the more modest output of provincials working in the same style for smaller works. Details of Wren's churches occur in many buildings of different types, particularly in the treatment of internal space. Other influences come from the designs of Hawksmoor, Vanbrugh and Gibbs. Some architects, however, succumbed to continental inspiration, Lanchester Stewart and Rickards, one of the most sophisticated Edwardian practices, basing their buildings on French and Viennese baroque.

What caused the shift away from the eclectic bittiness of what the architectural critic H.S. Goodhart-Rendel called the bric-à-brac[1] style towards the consistency of the 'Wrenaissance' is superficially explained as a change of fashion, but is really the result of a number of reasons. In the first place, the bric-à-brac style could not be developed. It relied upon quaintness, very often taking its detail from curiosities, or from periods of architecture where style was distorted or imperfectly understood. That is why Elizabethan and Jacobean styles tended to predominate. In the hands of a good architect, who was also an excellent draughtsman or painter, the result could be charming. This is probably best illustrated by the work of Ernest George, whose sketches of burghers' houses in the low countries and northern Germany provided a starting point for some excellent and imaginative picturesque designs, such as his houses in Harrington Gardens, Kensington, constructed in the early 1880s. In the hands of weak architects, such eclecticism was usually doomed to disaster, and any thread of consistency, or architectural qualities such as unity or rhythm were lost in a welter of meaningless detail. In addition, if the scale of the building was large, the preoccupation with ornament or what Sir Reginald Blomfield called the 'entanglements of detail', meant that it was difficult to compose on a suitable civic scale or to give the building the qualities of dignity and repose demanded of important structures. The restlessness of the bric-à-brac style tended to defeat the architects' very real desire to create work in the grand manner. The earlier use of the gothic revival for secular buildings and of Italian palazzo-inspired civic piles first pioneered by Charles Barry, had long since gone, and so the movement was towards the more appropriate and well-founded architecture represented by the 'Wrenaissance'.

English Renaissance architecture became a subject for serious study, and architects wrote scholarly books which gave a historical and theoretical background, as well as drawing the attention of the reader to various useful examples. Chief amongst these publications was Reginald Blomfield's *A History of Renaissance Architecture in England, 1500–1800*, which was published in 1897. Also popular was John Belcher and Mervyn Macartney's *Later Renaissance Architecture in England* (1901) and J. Alfred Gotch's *Architecture of the Renaissance in England* (1894). Blomfield's praise of Christopher Wren gives a good idea why the work of the latter was chosen as an example for large buildings. He says, 'the special strength of Wren's genius lay in this largeness of idea, in this power of conceiving a great architectural scheme as a whole ... and keeping his purpose proof against all the temptations of unnecessary detail'.[2]

Figure 1.1
Kirby Hall. Reginald Blomfield's drawing of Kirby Hall (1570–75), which, together with similar Elizabethan and Jacobean examples, provided inspiration for architects of the bric-à-brac school

These publications were bolstered by the advent of the *Architectural Review*, a periodical which began publication in 1896 and in which both Blomfield and Macartney had a hand. The *Review* appealed to the artist–architect and contained items of interest to those involved with craft revivals, scholarly articles on historical topics, reviews of books and coverage of new buildings designed by architects largely untainted by commercial practice or whose principles were espoused by the readership.

Despite the scholarly nature of the investigation and appraisal of seventeenth century design, the approach to architecture was still primarily visual. The best architects were often also very good draughtsmen, and had a grasp of the sweep, flow and rhythm of buildings which was usually intuitive, but was enhanced by the visual exercise of continual sketching. There was no slavish adherence to any particular model, and it was up to the designer to interpret details and motifs and to use them as and when required. The extent to which baroque detail was used was a matter of taste; how and where it was placed a question of artistic judgement. Externally, at least, architecture from this period was judged in a similar manner to the other visual arts. Unlike work from earlier and later periods, no heavy body of theory informed what was good or bad.

Many of the practitioners of Edwardian baroque were closely allied to the arts and crafts movement. It may be imagined that the architects of those ravishing and sometimes idiosyncratic country residences which are closely tied to their location by architectural character, materials and form were a breed apart from the men who created urban palaces for huge commercial enterprises or municipal authorities. In the main, this is not the case. First class architects practised in both styles, using whatever was most appropriate. Their urban buildings are no less 'arts and crafts' than their country houses. Even those at the extremes, like Edward Prior, found a version of the Wren style most suitable when called upon to design in the city. The best known exception to this is probably C.F.A. Voysey, whose major output was domestic, and who did few large buildings. Even Voysey's clothes

Figure 1.2

The Ashmolean Museum, Oxford. Reginald Blomfield's drawing of the Ashmolean Museum at Oxford, showing many of the features that 'Wrenaissance' architects found irresistible

followed arts and crafts principles and were designed by himself, but by and large, there is no difference between the man wearing the Norfolk jacket and the man wearing the frock coat: one worn in the country, the other in town, and there is a direct analogy with the buildings he designed.

Roger Scruton has talked about 'an honest appropriation of the past',[3] and this was perfectly natural to the Edwardians. Even architects like Reginald Blomfield, who was one of the chief advocates of the use of a large scale, 'grand manner' classicism would use different styles when necessary; for instance, in his work for Major Edgar Lubbock, Caythorpe Court in Lincolnshire (1899), which is late sixteenth century in style. Henry Hare enjoyed designing in a 'free Tudor', seen to best effect in his scheme for the Westminster Presbyterian College at Cambridge (1897). When he moved almost exclusively to baroque precedents after the turn of the century, University College, Bangor, one of his major works (1907) reverts to 'Tudorbethan'. A later generation heaped opprobrium upon what was seen as a lack of morality in flitting from style to style. It was as though the architect was not satisfied with his wife, and dallied with all sorts of wanton women.

Although not all baroque was based on English precedent, a theme that ran through all architecture of the time, and many of the other arts, was nationalism. It scarcely needs saying that Imperial Britain required grand buildings to house the institutions that ran the Empire. What could be better than to appropriate the swagger of the Restoration, a great period in British history for both the arts and the sciences. At the same time, the arts and crafts movement expressed a much more particular nationalism. The movement identified with both history and locality. The use of local crafts and materials to construct buildings was something that was considered very desirable to those most committed to the movement, and may be seen particularly in domestic work. Although seemingly innocent, it is not hard to see how an extension of this kind of thinking could lead to the more destructive nationalism that pervades the twentieth century. Essentially, it saw distinctions between different places as an interesting and valuable part of human experience. It was opposed to what would come later, the internationalism of the *beaux-arts* and modern movements.

Edwardian buildings, therefore, are usually laden with visual messages about history, site, context and importance, within the hierarchy of the city. They reach out to the public, speak an essentially popular language, and can be 'read' by users or passers-by. They avoid the elitism of later work. They therefore fulfil some of the essential tasks of civic architecture. At the same time, they respond to functionalism in a modern way.

During the nineteenth century, the need for new building types tended to overthrow conventions of form. In addition, a new construction technology was developed and the range of what it was possible to build expanded. The interaction between these two factors led to many interesting configurations not previously seen in the western tradition. The determinism that one associates with functionalism in the twentieth century can be seen, for instance, in the pavilion plan hospital or the Victorian prison as well as in buildings designed by engineers or used for industrial purposes. Progress in environmental technology such as mechanically aided ventilation, central heating using water or air, the development of efficient gas and then electric light enabled deep plan forms to be used. The availability of a relatively safe form of elevator meant that multi-storey building was possible.

Edwardian architecture inherited these developments, and although some buildings may have had the appearance of traditionally disposed classical ranges they were often 'programme' buildings, generated by the need to fulfil complicated functional requirements. In civic buildings, in particular, one might find a number of mixed spatial types and sizes: large spaces such as council chambers which had specific formal and locational requirements; suites of offices for borough officials; ranges of offices for clerks; grand ante rooms, landings and staircases; assembly rooms and concert halls; entertainment suites and committee rooms. The organization of such a diversity of accommodation, often within a very tight urban straitjacket, was achieved by great skill in planning together with the assistance of, for instance, the plenum system of heating and ventilation, electric light and power which enabled the space to be internal. Steel and concrete floors allowed the achievement of large spans carrying heavy loads, and lightweight steel trusses meant that roofs could fly over large spaces without intermediate support. Typically, in Edwardian buildings, though, structural issues do not determine the design of the building, and it is not a techtonic architecture. The architect willingly used technology as a means to an end. This scandalized the succeeding generation, who felt that the character of a building should in large part be a product of its structural system.

The cosy world of the artist–architect could not last for long, however, within a century that would see constant violent change and upheaval affecting all levels of society. Pressure came not only from within, but from outside the country also. Over all loomed the shadow of the skyscraper. Britain was very much subject to the influence of the burgeoning United States at this time, particularly in terms of business and investment. American methods had grown pragmatically as the country developed, without the trammels of European convention, elaborated over many centuries. In terms of building construction, a level of efficiency had been reached which the British could only wonder at. Pressure to build quickly within cities, and to optimize density of development had produced distinctive multi-storey buildings which presented new challenges and opportunities to designers. These were swiftly met and surmounted. Multi-disciplinary offices grew up where engineers, architects and building technologists solved common problems. The great steel mills set up by magnates like Carnegie churned out quantities of standard steel sections, which, in the form of columns and beams of known properties, could be rapidly bolted together to form a skeleton frame which grew by the day. Capital was tied up for a minimum length of time before a return on investment was begun. Inside these enormous buildings mechanical services threaded their way between floors providing heating, lighting, ventilation, circulation and communication.

British architects were somewhat in awe of these achievements when seen from a distance, but American practice began to infiltrate the British Isles themselves. The best known instance of this is probably the construction of Selfridges department store in Oxford Street, London (1908–09). Built for an American client, it blew apart existing building regulations, opening up big spaces to allow for browsing shoppers, circulating unhindered from one floor to another. It was a triumph for United States' money, practice and technology. Well before this time, however, American steelwork practice had begun to find its way into English buildings. By mid-Edwardian times, there was no doubt that irreversible changes were taking place, and that the role of the artist–architect was being supplanted or marginalized.

Pressure also came from the Continent, where advances made in the use of reinforced concrete exceeded those in the United Kingdom. In France, in particular, the theory and practice of reinforced concrete construction was very well developed by the 1890s and various patented systems were established. These gained something of a stronghold as the realization of the freedom of planning given by the new technology became apparent in Great Britain. Certainly, by about 1908 several important public and commercial buildings were being constructed, taking full advantage of the new material, and both French and American systems were popular. Only a few years before, reinforced concrete was confined to industrial buildings and civil engineering works.

Consequently, the first decade of the twentieth century was a period of rapid change in the architectural scene. New methods, materials, opportunities and practices were coming to the fore, and in addition, full time architectural education began in earnest. A scholarly approach, based on knowledge of existing precedent and influenced to some extent by the French *beaux-arts* system, via the United States, meant that the spontaneity of Edwardian architecture was lost, and was replaced by the cold, intellectual and in certain cases overbearing George V style. By Edward VII's death, if not earlier, the change of mood was very apparent, and this, more than the advent of the First World War, marks the end of the period which is the subject of this book. A graphic illustration may be provided by comparing the initial competition designs for the London County Council's new headquarters with the elements of the work as it proceeded to the hiatus caused by the war and then beyond into the 1920s.

The subject of this study, therefore, is civic architecture produced between 1890 and 1910. Many of these Edwardian buildings have functioned well for around one hundred years. They have withstood constant hard wear, polluted environments and the neglect engendered by two periods of national emergency. During this time they have retained popularity with the public, if not with the architectural profession. Their importance to generations cannot be underestimated. Examples included in the study are town and county halls and public libraries, buildings that represent a town or city and its cultural life, places where citizens could gather for formal and ceremonial meetings, to observe the workings of democracy, or, more humbly, to gain access to knowledge and opinion. The public library, it is not too far-fetched to say, was the tool through which for many decades earlier in the century, those from poor backgrounds could reach out for knowledge, begin to refine their education and take advantage of great, life enhancing literature for no charge. This book focuses on buildings which speak loud of their civic importance, but has omitted types such as fire stations and public baths, which, for all their virtues, are often dominated by large functional elements, albeit with external elaboration. Art galleries are, of course, of the lofty type under discussion, but were often incorporated into public libraries in smaller towns. Gallery spaces were highly specialized from an architectural point of view.

What follows is partial, but enough to show a wonderful heritage of buildings which still speak to their public, even if the original message has been changed or superseded.

Chapter Two

Civic expansion

The splendid civic buildings constructed at the close of the nineteenth century were representative of the maturing of municipal life at the end of decades of very rapid growth engendered by the Industrial Revolution, and characterized by the change from a rural to an urban population. The old methods of local government, administered by justices and boards overseen by the gentry and the aristocracy, were replaced by new corporations, initially established by the Municipal Corporations Act of 1835. These bodies quickly began to realize their powers and to collect rates not just for the implementation of services, but for the construction of town halls, redolent of civic pride, and buildings as various as public baths, wash houses and libraries. These buildings celebrated the new spirit of great towns, the industrial wealth that had created them, and the councillors and aldermen who were masters of that wealth. A prime example is Leeds Town Hall. It most forcefully speaks of the power of Victorian England. Opened in 1858 by the Queen herself, it had been designed by a young Yorkshireman, Cuthbert Brodrick, who was winner of a competition which had been judged by Charles Barry, architect of the Houses of Parliament. In preceding generations, a building of this size and quality would have been initiated by the aristocracy, or the Church, but Leeds Town Hall was home to manufacturers and merchants. In its great assembly hall, the citizens could experience the spiritual uplift of the works of the most celebrated composers or listen to first class oratory.

Whereas Leeds Town Hall was dominated by the inclusion of a large public auditorium, the town hall at Manchester, designed by the prolific and talented Alfred Waterhouse in 1868, reflected more clearly what was to happen with Edwardian municipal buildings. Long ranges of offices defined the edges of a roughly triangular site, the public hall contained within. These single-banked cellular spaces, served by a corridor running around the inside, overlooking internal courts, were where the business of municipal life was transacted. This pattern became more common as the century progressed.

Money could be borrowed from central government, and improvements were made to the urban fabric: new streets, parks, lighting and paving. Not only were the essentials of water supply and gas provided, but local tramways (Huddersfield, 1880) and electricity generation and distribution (Bradford, 1889) were also undertaken. Further local government acts in 1888 and 1894 paved the way for more efficient organization and for extra responsibilities to be vested in Councils, as well as creating new authorities. The Technical Instruction Act of 1889 allowed the establishment of municipal technical schools, which the council could finance, and following the 1902 Balfour Education Act responsibilities for children's education passed from school boards to the local authority education committees. What was later called the 'nanny role', the council's impingement on the citizens' everyday life, was further increased by the establishment of offices such as that of the health visitor. In 1890, the Housing of the Working Classes Act meant that council housing could be built. Although the first schemes were started in London in the 1890s, those in the provinces did not begin until after the turn of the century.

From mid-century on, rates could be levied for facilities designed to promote the physical, mental and spiritual well-being of the populace. The Public Baths and Wash Houses Act of 1846 enabled the allocation of rate money for construction of suitable buildings, and the Public Libraries Act of 1850 allowed a half-penny rate to be levied for libraries and art galleries.

Everywhere in big industrial towns the council was busy. Municipal enterprise equalled that of burgeoning business. Thus, not only were new civic buildings required, but the administration of the extensive range of services provided by local authorities necessitated large town halls and grander civic offices.

Town halls

Prior to the Edwardian period, town halls usually consisted of a public hall, rooms for council business and, quite likely, court rooms. Older buildings such as pre-incorporation town halls were found to be quite inadequate from the point of view of transacting all the business now necessary, and in many instances ad hoc extra accommodation had to be found. Civic pride, strengthened by the enhanced range of responsibilities, favoured the establishment of new buildings where scattered services could be brought together on one site. Achieving the practical improvements that provision of a new building would bring, however, was only part of the picture. Town halls which had been built in the mid-Victorian period were required to impress very forcibly the power and importance of the new corporations, and the ponderous classicism or frenetic gothicism of the time gave architects powerful languages with which this could be achieved. By the last decade of the Queen's reign the earnestness of earlier years had changed first to a picturesque eclecticism and then to the sumptuousness of baroque. There was still a need to give the buildings a character that would emphasize their importance within the urban fabric, as well as a greater desire to respond to contextual and historic references.

Some town halls were built anew, particularly in the London area where antiquated systems of local government were replaced. By and large what was usually called for, though, was either replacement of an existing building which could no longer cope with the demands made upon it, or considerable extensions to inadequate accommodation. In the first instance, and at the hub of the town hall's purpose, was the requirement for a council chamber specifically designed for the number of representatives in the borough and conducive in plan and form to the kind of debates which were to be held. Press facilities and a public gallery were normally incorporated so that democracy could be seen at work. Nearby, committee rooms were located, often fitted out with specially designed furniture, so that delegates could meet to discuss and resolve issues. These, together with the mayor's parlour and other reception rooms were generally treated to lavish finishes – with hardwood panelling to walls, marble fireplaces, ceilings with ornate plasterwork and specially designed light fittings. They were given this treatment because they were at the heart of the civic process and were symbolically important. Senior council officers, the borough surveyor, perhaps, had rather more modest rooms, and then the offices for various functionaries and clerks were often quite plain. If a public meeting hall was included, however, this too was accorded lavish treatment. In most cases, halls were multi-purpose and could accommodate concerts, by virtue of having a platform for performers at one end of the space, public meetings, dances or banquets.

Many town halls incorporated different kinds of accommodation in a portmanteau fashion, including police stations, fire stations, art galleries, public libraries and magistrates' courts. This, perhaps, harks back to the idea of the town's justices being closely involved in municipal administration, and the historic role of the local constable. Fire stations were, in the main, originally manned by policemen. However, it was just as likely to be the result of tidy-minded decision making, coupled with economy in keeping all municipal functions together within one new building envelope. Over the years, these buildings have usually retained their primary purpose, but the libraries, police stations and fire stations have been re-established in large scale, purpose-built premises elsewhere in the town or city.

Oxford Town Hall, from the beginning of the period, is a good example of one of the 'portmanteau' town halls. Its role was formulated well before the demands of increased administration necessary at the turn of the century were properly understood. In fact, discussions about the need for a new building exercised the City Council from as early as 1873. Oxford's existing town hall dated from the mid-eighteenth century, but incorporated parts of an older building. By the time that replacement was discussed it contained committee rooms, a mayor's parlour, council chamber, public library and part of a post office. It seems that the council could not break away from the thinking that the new civic building should contain as many functions as possible. When proposals for the new hall were crystallized, it was decided that all the existing types of accommodation, with the exception of the post office, should be retained and, in addition, administrative offices, a police station, sessions court and a large public hall with organ and gallery should also be provided. This would present the architect with an immense challenge in terms of organization and planning, particularly because the site was of urban significance, located at the corner of a city block and hemmed in by existing buildings. Furthermore it was bounded by the major thoroughfare of St Aldate's and narrow Blue Boar Street on its other sides.

A competition was announced in 1891 for the design of the new building. At first the City Surveyor was appointed to judge the entries, but he was soon replaced by T.E. Collcutt (1840–1924), who was a native of Oxford, and who had made a great success in architectural practice, designing large and important public and commercial buildings. He won the competition for

Wakefield Town Hall in 1877 and for the Imperial Institute in South Kensington in 1886, and had recently been engaged on the construction of Wigmore (Bechstein) Hall in the west end of London, when he was asked to adjudicate. The schedule of accommodation produced by the council which the contestants had to satisfy was demanding, and could be divided into at least five categories: the town hall itself, police, administration of justice, municipal offices and public library. Each of these categories could be sub-divided, and the schedule is very particular as to the floor areas to be allocated to functions as diverse as 'dormitories for sixteen constables' in the police accommodation or rooms for 'Medical Officer and Inspector of Nuisances' in the municipal offices section. In addition, it was insisted that the library should be positioned on the south-west corner of the site.

The reason for the combination of these diverse functions in town halls of the period has already been speculated upon, but in Oxford there were, perhaps, additional circumstances. The city, itself, though ancient, was quite modest at the time and the vast expansion in wealth and size engendered by William Morris (Lord Nuffield) was yet to come. In addition, it was dominated by the University, which was a law unto itself. Furthermore, the County of Oxford was run from separate premises. All in all, then, a complex civic centre must have seemed an attractive proposition, reinforcing the corporation's importance.

The project was obviously seen as prestigious, and a great opportunity for those wishing to gain a reputation, for the competition attracted no fewer than 390 applicants, but few 'big names'. In the event, it was won by a young architect at the start of a career that was to bring great success in the design of civic and municipal buildings. Henry T. Hare was 30 years of age and Oxford Town Hall was the first of a number of competition successes in a busy professional life that was to occupy him for the next three decades up to his relatively early death. Hare's win was confirmed by Colcutt in May 1892 and his winning scheme was published in July of that year. Various alterations were made to his design prior to construction, but this seems to have been normal practice with competition winners. The site was cleared early in 1893, with the removal of existing municipal buildings and the demolition of houses in St Aldate's and Blue Boar Street. Evidence of late medieval construction, three bays of vaulted cellar, were allowed to remain, and were incorporated into Hare's scheme. The foundation stone was laid in July of that year, and work proceeded for nearly another four years. The original contractor, a local builder, who had submitted a tender of £51,000, close to the council's cost limit, soon went bankrupt and was replaced by Messrs Parnell and Son of Rugby, whose final account was for £81,683. Although

Figure 2.1

Oxford Town Hall. Henry Hare's design is the epitome of the bric-à-brac style. It is also an accomplished solution to very difficult spatial and architectural problems. This is the main façade to St Aldate's

this seems a considerable increase over the initial expectation, few of the buildings discussed in this book came anywhere close to the original cost estimates. Invariably, extra funds were found, often by creative use of monies outside the building budget, and delight was expressed at the result. This was certainly the case when on 12 May 1897 the Prince of Wales arrived to open the new Town Hall, amidst processions of worthies, and the wielding of a ceremonial key. Emotions ran so high that the event provided an excuse for 'town and gown' skirmishes in the evening. Reporting, the *Oxford Times* noted, 'Mr. Henry T. Hare, the architect of the new City Buildings, is a young man who is progressing rapidly in his profession ... It is very rare indeed for a work of such magnitude ... to be received with such cordial and unanimous favour. Everybody testifies to the taste and success of the structure as a whole and in its multifarious details.'

Oxford Town Hall is representative of development in a historic city, as are two other examples considered in

Figure 2.2
Colchester Town Hall. One of the most satisfying and representative 'Wrenaissance' designs, John Belcher's building is both exuberant and dignified, occupying an important but severely restricted site in the ancient borough. (© Colchester Museums)

this book: Colchester Town Hall and Lancaster Town Hall. Colchester comes from the middle of the period under scrutiny, and Lancaster from near the end.

Colchester, like Oxford, was built anew on a tight, inconvenient, but historically important site. In fact, the town had been administered from the same place from the Middle Ages. The medieval Moot Hall was located in High Street from the time of its construction in the twelfth century until 1843, when it was replaced by a rather undistinguished building in the classical style. This was found to be too small for the council's burgeoning responsibilities, and there were doubts about structural stability. After little more than fifty years of operation it was demolished in 1897 to make way for its successor. It had contained an assembly hall, called the Moot Hall to maintain the old tradition, and this was something that was continued when John Belcher's fine new design was planned. In addition, there was a court room and police station as well as committee rooms for the council. These were all provided in the replacement building, but the number of court rooms was increased to two, and ranges of administrative offices included in the scheme.

Lancaster is similar to Colchester and Oxford, in that it is an ancient city. Its original town hall was sited in Market Square, but was replaced by a new one in 1783 on the same site. By 1897, 'the work of the Corporation had for some time ... so materially increased'[1] that a loan was applied for from central government to finance a new building on a new site. The money eventually arrived from other quarters, but it was not until 1906 that the building was begun, being opened to the public just before Christmas 1909. A completely new site was provided in Dalton Square, which allowed the construction of a municipal headquarters containing the usual administrative areas, committee rooms, entertainment suites, council chambers, court room and substantial police station, and also a public hall to seat 1700. Along with this was sufficient land to create a handsome public square to complement the new building.

The extent and magnificence of the work at Lancaster was due to the munificence of Lord Ashton. Ashton's family, the Williamsons, had made a substantial fortune from the linoleum industry that was centred in the town in the late nineteenth century. His father had laid out a splendid park for the citizens in the 1870s, partly as a project to mitigate against industrial recession by providing employment. Ashton, himself, continued this philanthropy by paying for the town hall, a gift of approximately £150,000, and, in a parallel expression of generosity, built the functionally useless, but impressive Ashton Memorial in Williamson Park, designed by John Belcher and opened two months before the town hall. This first class example of Edwardian baroque, which dominates the town, cost no less than £87,000. Both the memorial and the town hall were constructed by the local firm of Waring and Gillow, noted furniture manufacturers, whose subsidiary, the Waring-White Company, was at the leading edge of advanced building construction practice.

Deptford and Stockport town halls were built to serve areas of unrestricted urban sprawl generated during the nineteenth century. In Deptford, the aim was to provide 'some building which should be the centre of local life ...',[2] and also accommodate the council in a suitably dignified manner. The erection of a focus for council activity had been discussed as early as 1891, but decisions were delayed whilst the acquisition of the site for a new public baths and wash house was undertaken, and then the negotiations for adjacent property to make a plot large enough for the municipal headquarters in New Cross Road. In these circumstances, council business continued to be transacted in four rooms on the first and second floors above shop premises in Tanners' Hill. These rooms were used as offices during the day but doubled as committee and meeting rooms during the evening. It was not until 1905 that the situation was remedied and the councillors and aldermen could disport themselves in their marble halls.

Although Deptford's elected representatives chose wisely in terms of their architects, there was not enough room on site to provide a public assembly hall, but this seems to reflect the halting way in which they went about acquiring property and deciding on a suitable location. The same could not be said quite about Stockport, which seems to have had grandiose ideas from the outset. The town had not only grown itself during the preceding decades, but, as a borough, had incorporated several of the smaller urban areas round about. It may have been this overall patchiness, or the fact that the town itself was of a poor urban quality with no great buildings or public spaces, that encouraged the development of a large and showy town hall on Wellington Road South. Here there appears to have been plenty of room to suit Brumwell

Figure 2.3

Lancaster Town Hall. This handsome building was made possible by Lord Ashton's philanthropy. It reflects Georgian restraint, at a time when architectural fashions were beginning to change

Thomas's civic palace. Like the other examples mentioned, it took some time to come to fruition, having been discussed as a possibility in the early 1890s. A competition was held in 1903, and the building was completed five years later. Thomas's scheme contained a fine public hall, which accommodates 1250, seated, for concerts. It is clear that a grand, if somewhat overstated building like this was necessary to help to bind together the disparate community that the borough council served.

Smaller civic buildings received the same kind of attention as their bigger brothers – a kind of scaled-down grandeur. Henry Hare's Henley Town Hall must be one of the finest of these lesser works. Architecturally, it strikes the right note in terms of scale, relative to both its location and importance, its degree of elaboration and its quality. Built of red facing bricks with Bath stone dressings and occupying a block in the little town, it conjures up visions of old fashioned country town market halls with the council chamber located over the sales stalls, whilst conveying a restoration cheerfulness and dignity. Within the simple rectangle of the plan, three main levels contain offices for civic officials on the lower

Figure 2.4

Henley Town Hall. Small civic buildings were treated as seriously as larger buildings in terms of quality of materials, details and overall design effort. (Photo: E Dockree. Reproduced courtesy of *Architectural Review*)

ground floor, committee rooms and council chamber on the principal floor and a public hall over. The council chamber was designed to double as a court room. Despite its modest size, Hare designed the building as carefully as any one of his larger and more expensive works.

Where entirely new buildings were not provided, some very distinguished extensions were undertaken. One of the earliest of note, and a precursor of the 'Wrenaissance' style, was J.M. Brydon's addition to the Guildhall at Bath, won in competition in 1891. The original building, dating from 1776, contained the old court room, magistrates' room, banqueting and committee rooms. The extension added a council chamber, a mayor's parlour, new court rooms and offices for important council officials. In 1897 an art gallery and library were also added. Another interesting extension was that appended to Bradford Town Hall (1905–09). Richard Norman Shaw was appointed consultant to the city architect, F.E.P. Edwards. Edwards was responsible for planning, on a basically triangular site, an extension to the gothic revival building designed in the late 1860s by local architects Lockwood and Mawson. The accommodation includes a large dining room with minstrels' gallery, and a council chamber in 'Wrenaissance' style. The importance of this building, though, lies in Norman Shaw's manipulation of style and his attempts to use motifs that are very much his own, whilst fitting in with the gothic revival and attempting 'the appearance of one complete building under one roof'.

Perhaps the greatest extension, a huge building in its own right, in fact, is from the end of the period. Designed by H.V. Ashley and Winton Newman, the Birmingham Council House extension occupied an island site some 320 feet (97.5 m) by 270 feet (82.3 m). It incorporated four major administrative departments, art galleries and provision for future extensions. Each department could be accessed separately from the surrounding streets: the education department, facing Margaret Street, had committee rooms and a library as well as clerks' offices; the health department was entered from Congreve Street, as was the tramways department; the gas department with its committee rooms, offices and substantial fittings showroom was associated with a huge rates office. The art galleries and natural history museum were an extension of the existing galleries, and a bridge across Edmund Street linked the old and new. This handsome provision for the fine collection of paintings was covered by the Feeney bequest.

County halls

Despite the growth of municipal corporations in urban areas during Victoria's reign, and the establishment of county boroughs, counties themselves, mainly rural, were governed in a rather disparate way. This must have seemed increasingly old fashioned as the century progressed and new means of speedy communication spread across the land affecting previously isolated communities. In addition, acts of parliament concerned with welfare and education had increased the number of administrative bodies required to implement them across the counties. The Local Government Act of 1888, establishing elected county councils, did not come before time, therefore.

Before the new Act much of the supervision work in local government had been undertaken by Justices of the Peace, who attended quarter sessions and looked after the maintenance of roads and the provision of the police force amongst other things. These gentlemen were drawn from the aristocracy and squirearchy, and even after democratic councils were instituted, formed the backbone of the new organization. This, no doubt, is why despite the implied need for modesty in new council buildings, they often have the aura of a sumptuous gentlemen's club.

The justices, school and local health board members and poor law guardians all had places in which to meet, but these were inadequate for the new councils and were often scattered. The need to provide council chambers for sometimes more than one hundred members, in itself demanded new structures. Increased administrative responsibilities around the turn of the century also required more space. At its inception, the North Riding of Yorkshire County Council employed around fourteen people, most of whom were principal officers, with a small number of clerical assistants. These officers were largely men in private professional practice who worked part time for the county. By 1903, however, the number had risen to twenty-five and at the outbreak of the First World War stood at fifty. These were occupants of the county hall; many more staff were employed by the council, working on roads or teaching children.

It became clear that English counties were powerful political units, particularly those that had industrial towns and villages within their boundaries. They were no longer the Borsetshires of the landed gentry, dominated solely by the nobility and the church, even though they continued to have influence. The Marquess of Ripon, in his *Chairman's Statement as to the Work of the Council,* asserted that 'There are many counties that do not have the population or turnover of the West Riding'.[3] Of course, the West Riding of Yorkshire was an area that had benefited from the Industrial Revolution, and no doubt those counties that were purely rural were feeling less self-satisfied because of the results of agricultural depression. However, the development of industrial and commercial might did give problems to the Yorkshire councillors early in the council's existence. Leeds had grown to be the most prominent city within the county, a place of power and influence. There was a question as to whether it should be the centre of county government rather than the ancient city of Wakefield. After much debate, Wakefield was chosen, ostensibly for sound practical reasons, but perhaps, also, because of historical sentiment. It was shown that it was marginally more accessible than Leeds and that building was going to be cheaper in a place where land values were lower, and the council already owned property.

As early as 1890, two years before Wakefield was finally chosen, a detailed analysis of spatial requirements had been prepared. It omitted the need for a police headquarters, because one already existed, close to the other council property in the city. This was, primarily, the Rishworth House estate, and the house itself was already used for council business. It became clear, though, that extensions to the existing property would not be an adequate response to the council's needs. The new requirements were on an altogether grander scale than could be provided by the house and its adjuncts. A decision was taken to demolish the property and to replace it by a completely new building designed to accommodate a total of about 700 square metres of meeting rooms, including a council chamber 18 m by 12 m, and 2555 square metres of administrative accommodation. In addition there were to be a variety of other spaces, including a law library. There was to be a completely new parliament house and centre of government for a

Figure 2.5

County Hall, Wakefield. Wakefield rather than Leeds was chosen for the headquarters of the West Riding of Yorkshire County Council and little effort was spared to provide a palace for the government of a wealthy and powerful province. (Photo: Albert Booth)

county that was as rich and populous as many of the sovereign states of the world.

After its establishment, the first meetings of the county council took place in Wakefield's fine Town Hall. It took some time, though, for a final decision to be taken to site County Hall in the city, and a competition was organized the following year, 1893, which was won by James Gibson and Samuel Russell. Their practice was one of thirty-eight entrants. As well as stating the complicated spatial requirements, the competition conditions rather unhelpfully noted, 'The style of architecture will be left to the competitors, but the Queen Anne or Renaissance School of architecture appears suited to an old town like Wakefield'.[4] These styles were, of course, the acceptable architectural language of the day, one on the way out, the other about to begin its ascendancy. To execute the substantial works, a Leeds contractor was appointed, with a tender of £76,824, well above the architects' estimate of £64,424. Construction took place between 1894 and 1898.

Despite a rather delayed completion, congratulations abounded. The Vice Chairman of the General Purposes Committee said that it had reason to be proud of the architects and that the building was 'admirably executed, the decoration superb, the best building of its kind in the land'. The contractor praised the architects for the way in which they 'pushed on with work' and the architects praised the 'capable and practical General Purposes

Committee'. Opening the building, after a procession from the Town Hall, the Marquess of Ripon used a golden key taken from a beautiful case designed by the architects. County Hall, he said, was a 'building perfectly adapted to their [the County Council's] purposes, and an ornament to the City of Wakefield'.[5] County Hall was extended twice before the century was two decades old, such was the growth of the council's work.

Although not as mighty as the West Riding, Staffordshire presented a similar picture, but with a greater mixture of the rural and the industrial. In the north of the county were the Potteries, and in the south, the Black Country with its host of small metal-working industries. Elsewhere were extensive rural areas. The driving force behind the provision of a new building to accommodate county activities and to serve the requirements of more than a hundred councillors was Lord Harrowby, chairman of the General Purposes Committee. As in all the cases discussed, there was never a clear or simple request for a new building followed by immediate construction. A strong and committed body of people, usually with a determined leader, was required to push proposals through.

The Shire Hall in Stafford looking onto the Market Place, was the original county headquarters, but was too small for the new democratically elected body. Nevertheless, it was next to the substantial Judge's House, and the Chief Constable's office was in nearby St. Martin's Place. The council met in the Borough Hall from time to time, in its early days, like West Riding Council, using the facilities provided by the host town. Clearly this was not adequate, and there was a plan to convert Shire Hall and the Judge's House into a new county hall. In the event, this did not prove feasible, but there was a desire that the Shire Hall should remain as the public face of the council. The council acquired properties on Eastgate Street and Martin Street and the seventeenth century Eastgate House. It was then able to use the site for the new building, thereby linking the Shire Hall, the Judge's House and Eastgate House into a complex at once relating the council's new image to a historical context. Lord Harrowby may have thought that this neatly avoided the need for 'a grand stately palace' and have modestly required 'good, thoroughly businesslike offices for county work',[6] but what transpired was a rich building with its own character, probably more representative of the council than the worthy but dull Shire Hall.

At Northallerton, a modest market town, there was little urban or historical context to which a new county hall for the North Riding of Yorkshire could relate. There was office space in the Court House, and extensions were proposed in 1892, only to be rejected the following year in favour of a new building. This was a wise decision, because County Hall has subsequently expanded throughout the twentieth century and has absorbed a great area of land. It would have swallowed up most of Northallerton, if allowed to grow. This was not evident at first though, and a decision for a new building was shelved from 1894 until a new building

Figure 2.6
County Hall, Northallerton. Designed for the administration of a large but mainly rural county, Brierley's grand building stands at the edge of the small and unassuming town, but close to the railway station. (Photo: T Lewis. Reproduced courtesy of *Architectural Review*)

committee was formed in 1901, and a revised scheme proposed. By now, there was no attempt to relate the hall to the town. Instead it was positioned close to the railway station, on open fields that belonged to the chairman of the council and his brother. The original ownership of the site does not seem to have caused embarrassment, and the site's relationship to the main limb of the transport network was no doubt sensible, given that the North Riding of Yorkshire was large and mainly rural.

Although the North Riding County Hall is from relatively late in the period, and an example of architectural restraint, some county halls were started even further into the new century. The great London County Council building comes into this category. The preliminary competition was held in 1907, but it was well after the Great War by the time the original scheme was completed. Immense as it was, it was added to throughout succeeding decades. Most of the competition drawings show baroque palaces fronting the Thames, but by the time the first phase of the County Hall had been completed, a Franco-American severity had taken over. The gradual increase in influence of the *beaux-arts* manner can also be seen in works such as Glamorgan County Hall, designed by one of the rising stars of municipal architecture, E. Vincent Harris, in conjunction with Thomas A. Moodie. Harris and Moodie won a competition in 1908 with a cool and refined design which contrasts interestingly with the other great civic building in Cathay's Park, Cardiff – the City Hall, designed exuberantly by Lanchester, Stewart and Rickards a decade earlier.

At Berkshire County Hall, in Reading, won in competition by Warwick and Hall in 1909, the Wrenaissance style was continued. This building is almost an extension to adjoining assize courts, rather like a grand house in appearance, it contained accommodation for the clerk to the peace; general offices; the education secretary's office; the county treasurer and the surveyor's department. Its relationship to the adjoining buildings in terms of the location of both vertical and horizontal circulation seems crucial.

One of the latest county buildings in the period was the Middlesex Guildhall, begun in 1910, and designed

Figure 2.7

Glamorgan County Hall, Cardiff. Built towards the end of the period, this building has some of the austerity of the Franco-American *beaux-arts* style, which was becoming *de rigueur* amongst younger architects. The parkland setting enhances the building's monumentality. (Reproduced courtesy of *Architectural Review*)

by Gibson, Skipwith and Gordon. Gibson had designed West Riding County Hall at Wakefield in conjunction with S.B. Russell before becoming associated with new partners. Oddly, but presumably because of the proximity of Westminster Abbey and the Houses of Parliament, the hall was designed in the gothic style, one of the last major secular buildings to be so treated. Although the details are gothic – quite relaxed and without the fidgety spikiness of the Victorian gothic revival – the massing of the building is almost classical.

Public libraries

The responsibility of councils to cater for the academic, intellectual, cultural and even spiritual welfare of citizens was recognized relatively early on. Public libraries, museums, art galleries and technical schools were built in large numbers. The development of these amenities is often intertwined, and, in several instances, buildings housed lending and reference libraries, galleries and lecture rooms. Generically, however, the public library as a type seems to sum up the civic pride invested in what was both a social and cultural centre for all classes of citizens; indeed the hope and salvation of some of the poorest.

The Public Libraries Act of 1850 allowed towns of over 10,000 inhabitants to impose a half-penny rate for the establishment of libraries. This was not really enough to provide for the establishment of the facility and the running costs. As a result, many boroughs did not adopt the Act and it was not until between 1890 and 1909 that the great upsurge in construction took place. There were four reasons for this: improvements in legislation, such as the 1894 Local Government Act, which made the provision of libraries easier to achieve and more widespread; the increasing maturity of local authorities which were now professionally run and could take management responsibilities; pressure to provide facilities for a population that had become literate due to compulsory primary education; a number of philanthropists who made capital funds available. Chief amongst the philanthropists were John Passmore Edwards (1823–1911) and Andrew Carnegie (1835–1918). Edwards was the son of a Cornish tradesman, who rose to become a proprietor of newspapers and magazines. He was a progressive social reformer with many interests, but is chiefly remembered for the money he gave for over twenty libraries in London and the west of England.

Carnegie was a Scot who had emigrated to America and made his fortune in the iron and steel industry. His first donation was £8,000 to his home town of Dunfermline. Two hundred and thirteen towns in England and Wales received grant aid from his organization, fifty in Scotland and forty-seven in Ireland. He also gave money for library buildings in the United States. The Carnegie Corporation in America eventually came to see the library as a community centre with an auditorium and provision for other leisure activities. In the United Kingdom, his benefactions, dependent upon a free site and a guarantee that money for running the service should be available, led to the erection of both central and branch libraries, the latter to service expanding suburbs.

The basic provision in most libraries consisted of three types of accommodation. First, there was a newsroom, usually near to the entrance and often patronized by the poorer sections of society, and a reading or magazine room. These were heavily, though casually used. In addition there was sometimes a children's room. Secondly, there was a lending library. Initially, access was closed, and borrowers had to select their choice of books from indicator boards set in a lobby. The order was placed over a counter and only library staff had access to the book stacks from which the desired volumes were retrieved. At the beginning of the Edwardian period, this system was changing in favour of open browsing, albeit closely monitored. In libraries of this type, shelving was sometimes arranged radially in a 'panopticon'-like fashion from the desk of the eagle-eyed librarian. Thirdly, there would be a reference library for serious students, which often housed important local collections. In addition to all of this there were, of course, public lobbies, staircases and circulation areas, book storage and administrative offices. Optionally, there may have been lecture rooms, meeting rooms or galleries for the display of works of art or curiosities.

Perhaps one of the finest public libraries of the period was constructed during the early years of the century in Bristol. Designed by the firm of Adams, Holden and Pearson, it is usually regarded as one of Charles Holden's outstanding early works. During a time when first class architectural work was produced, this particular scheme stands out for its originality and the creativity of its designer.

Bristol had adopted the Public Libraries Act in 1877, which was well before the period of rapid growth at the end of the nineteenth century, and the city library had been established even earlier, in 1856, when the subscription library was replaced. In 1899 a bequest was received. It came from the estate of a wealthy local man, Vincent Stuckey Lean, and amounted to £45,000 after tax. Of this, £41,000 was allocated for the library building and equipment and £4,000 for the site. Lean, a member of a Bristol banking family, was a library enthusiast who had travelled the world, noting examples of libraries and collections. He also left a substantial sum for the improvement of the reading rooms in the British Museum. The bequest allowed the construction of a completely new building on a new site. The council

Figure 2.8
Bristol Central Library. A view of the library taken from Lower College Green, enhancing Holden's blocky massing. The main entrance front to Deanery Road is much less dramatic

settled on one of historical significance, that of the Canon's House and Old Deanery near the Cathedral, adjoining the Norman Abbey Gateway. The schedule of accommodation for the new premises, prepared by the chief librarian after a survey of most important existing provincial libraries, included book and newspaper stores, unpacking room, patents room and staff facilities to be located in a basement; a newsroom with stands for one hundred papers, a lending department for 20,000 volumes and a magazine and general reading room on the ground floor, whilst on the first floor was a reference library with shelving for 100,000 volumes and seating for 150. In addition, there was a space for the *Bristol Collection*, which had to be fitted out with a Grinling Gibbons chimney piece, presses and panelling inherited from a former library building.

There is little doubt that the library building was regarded as an extremely prestigious project, from the choice of its site through to the quality of the architecture. Although the building has been extended during its life, essentially it is the same as it was when built, and the wisdom of providing this facility, underpinned with the philosophy of making knowledge and literary art available to all, has stood the citizens of Bristol in good stead throughout the century.

Although not all libraries constructed during the period were as lavish or imaginative as Holden's project at Bristol, most were accomplished and, in many respects, delightful. Henry Hare was responsible for many of these, notably Islington Central Library, where Carnegie contributed £20,000 towards the cost, Hammersmith Central Library and Wolverhampton Public Library.

Thus a variety of civic buildings began to grow as the nineteenth century gave way to the twentieth. The greatest of all, as has been noted, was County Hall of the London County Council. Begun in 1909 it did not open until 1922. Ironically, its life was short. It was through a competition that the design of this and many of the other new buildings considered here was chosen. Although there were sometimes problems in the conduct of competitions, as there was in the case of County Hall, it did mean that young architects of considerable ability, such as H.T. Hare, were able to begin long and successful careers.

Competitions and commissions

The competition system for selecting the designers of important public buildings was the norm at the time. Its advantages were that the client body – perhaps the general purposes committee of a council – was able to specify not only spatial requirements but also matters of style and character, and, most importantly to many, the maximum cost, and could then be assured of a large number of designs from which to choose. As noted above, the profession of architecture, itself, was enhanced by the bringing forward of young or hitherto neglected talent. A large number of the leaders of the subsequent generation of architects first came to prominence through the competition system.

Competitions had been held for important public buildings during the nineteenth century. In many cases there were problems in the conduct of the competition, in the choice of winner, in the design of the chosen scheme or in all three. Indeed, there were *causes célèbres*, such as the infamous Foreign Office competition of 1857–58, which are remembered to this day. Despite attempts to provide a sound basis for the running of these events, such as the RIBA's *General Rules for the Conduct of Architectural Competitions* (1871), fiascos continued throughout the remainder of the nineteenth century and into the early years of the twentieth century. However, no matter what problems were encountered, there always seems to have been a desire to use the competition system for significant buildings. This may have had something to do with the general ethos of the Victorian period: capitalism, free market economies, natural selection and the survival of the fittest. M.H. Port has pointed out that the failures to produce satisfactory results may be set down to the poor framing of instructions where stringent conditions were imposed. These conditions, often in the cause of economy, were virtually impossible to fulfil. In addition it was felt that those assessing entries were not clear about what they wanted – an architect or a design. In some instances, this lack of clarity lead to fudging of results, to the re-running of the competition, the award of the commission to other than first prizewinner, or the insistence upon the award winner receiving guidance. It was virtually unheard of for a winning scheme to be built without revision, in most cases to quite a substantial degree. Variants upon the basic system of advertising a competition to all and sundry, were tried. Sometimes a limited number of prominent architects were selected, sometimes a two-stage event was held. A shortlist was produced from stage one, so that the number of entries could be reduced for the proper consideration of those that fulfilled the brief best or were of better architectural quality. In addition, it was proposed that a jury system would produce a fairer result than the usual provision of a sole assessor. In this case, competitors could work in a way that would be likely to please the assessor should his identity be known.

Although competitions for government buildings may have been fraught, for smaller civic buildings upsets were less frequent. Commonly, a sole assessor was appointed, usually a senior and well-known architect who had, himself, been a successful competitor for a major project. The decision of the assessor was final, except that, in some cases, the sub-committee responsible for the competition had a veto. In a small number of competitions, the existing borough surveyor or architect acted as assessor.

Alfred Waterhouse (1830–1905) was the doyen of assessors in the 1890s, having designed a wide range of famous buildings varying from Manchester Town Hall to the Natural History Museum in Kensington and Strangeways Gaol. Of the architects and projects mentioned in this book, he chose Walter Brierley for North Riding County Hall (although it was eight years before the building was started) and Henry T. Hare for Wolverhampton Public Library. Also of the Waterhouse generation, Richard Norman Shaw (1831–1912) and John MacVicar Anderson (1835–1915) chose John Belcher for Colchester Town Hall and Henry Hare for Staffordshire County Council Buildings, respectively. Shaw was appointed as the best known and most successful architect of the late nineteenth century, Anderson as he happened to be President of the RIBA.

Beyond this, assessors were often participants in the Edwardian building scene, men still very active and vigorously pursuing their careers. Thomas E. Collcutt, furthering his early success with notable buildings like Lloyd's Registry of Shipping and the Savoy Hotel, awarded first prize to A. Brumwell Thomas at Stockport and Plumstead, and Henry Hare at Oxford. John Belcher (1841–1913), victor at Colchester, chose Lanchester, Stewart and Rickards for Deptford Town Hall, and Henry Hare for Islington Central Library. Aston Webb (1849–1930), best known for the Victoria and Albert Museum extension and the refacing of Buckingham Palace, was responsible for the appointment of Lanchester, Stewart and Rickards to design Wesleyan Central Hall in a two stage competition, although, somewhat embarrassingly, he recommended one of his assistants, Ralph Knott, for London County Hall. Independent to the last, the West Riding of Yorkshire decided to rely upon its own employee, the

County Architect and Surveyor J. Vickers Edwards, to adjudicate the competition won by Gibson and Russell for the splendid building in Wakefield. He was obviously highly regarded, being described as 'our Yorkshire Vanbrugh'.[7]

It may seem that this method was cosy and too close-knit. The fact is, however, that for the most part the assessors were men of excellent judgement. They chose wisely, although it was sometimes argued that schemes that were flashily presented caught the judge's eye. It is difficult to see, though, how Belcher's design for Colchester Town Hall could have been improved upon and the continuing success of Henry Hare is surely due to that architect's mastering of economical spatial organization and architectural appropriateness.

Some architects remained aloof from the competition system. It was rare to find devoted arts and crafts men like Charles Voysey or Edward Prior entering competitions. At the other extreme, some architects entered into partnership specifically to undertake competitions. Even the celebrated firm of Lanchester, Stewart and Rickards began with the idea of competitive practice and progressed through a number of successes. Gibson and Russell won at Wakefield, but after 1900 the partnership ended and James Gibson won the Walsall Municipal Buildings competition with William Wallace; Samuel Russell was successful in two further partnerships, of which that with Edwin Cooper is best known, resulting in fine civic buildings in Hull. Even artist–architects, like Reginald Blomfield, who kept away from commercial practice and designed mainly for the 'squirearchy', were tempted into competitions on some occasions.

Despite its short comings, the system produced some excellent buildings, even if architects were not always satisfied. Quite often they were called upon to compromise or alter their designs or to take external advice; many did not even receive a prize, as the money was subsumed into the percentage paid for undertaking the commission.

Architects' remuneration, in general, was usually based on the receipt of a percentage of the cost of the work undertaken. Walter Brierley, winner of the competition to design North Riding County Hall was subsequently appointed County Architect with an annual salary of £100 per year, but it was assumed that he would continue with his own private practice at the same time. He received £1,000 for carrying out work on County Hall, based on the estimated original cost of £20,000, but was forced to ask for an extra £250, to take account of the increase in value up to £25,000, exclusive of external works and furnishings. He noted, 'I have done my very best for the work, regardless of time and money, and have studied the Council's interests very much more than my own in my desire to produce a really good and fine building ...'.[8] His effort was recognized, by the chairman of the Council at the first meeting of 1906, when he stated, 'I think you will agree with me that great credit is due to our architect, Mr. Brierley, for designing and carrying out such a stately, suitable and convenient building'.[9]

Henry Hare received £4,200 for more than four years' work on Oxford Town Hall, though this equated approximately to Brierley's 5 per cent for Northallerton. Construction contracts did not always run smoothly, and in most cases more money was called for before buildings were completed. In addition, labour relations were sometimes poor at this time, both between workers and employers and between various unions. Contractors were not always financially secure. Hare lost the selected builder of Oxford Town Hall to bankruptcy in 1893, and the building itself was completed for £81,683, excluding furniture and fittings, which brought the final total to over £91,000. Concurrently, at Stafford, a tender of £26,840 was accepted for the construction of County Buildings, and Hare was able to exercise economies which brought this figure down by a few hundred. Nevertheless, poor quality ground conditions were encountered, and by the time the first phase of building was completed in Spring 1895, it had cost £45,000 including site, furniture and fittings. The council's resources were here supplemented by money allocated to the technical education budget from a government tax on spirits known as 'whisky money'. Fortuitously, local authorities were responsible for the implementation of the Technical Instruction Act of 1889, and, no doubt, Staffordshire's accountants were equal to the task of allocating money to where it could be most effectively used.

Nearly all of the buildings discussed here exceeded original estimates quite considerably, and although they are all of quality and by well-known architects, the variations in cost are huge. Wolverhampton Central Library, complete with furniture and fittings, cost well short of £20,000, Bristol more than twice as much. Colchester Town Hall, at £55,000, although £20,000 more than Deptford, was £100,000 less than Lancaster, including its associated square, adjoining buildings and Victoria Memorial. Lancaster was thus in the same league as Cardiff City Hall and the Wesleyan Central Hall. The cost of London County Hall was measured in millions. Despite these vicissitudes, a vast amount of pride was shown in the finished buildings and they were opened with appropriate ceremonies and congratulations.

Wakefield County Hall was well received by its clients, and there were plaudits all round, as we have seen. The opening, by the Marquess of Ripon, was a grand occasion, following a procession from the town hall. A reception held later was a 'brilliant affair'.

The ceremony with which the building was opened was reflected in many of the examples discussed. Staffordshire adopted a discreet approach, but, by and large, pomp and circumstance was something that was welcomed in this period. From the cynical dying years of the century, it is with nostalgia that one looks back to a time when there was a genuine, if naïve, pride in the achievements of town and county councils. Certainly in the latter case, the new bodies were also celebrating the beginning of an improved kind of local government, one that was to have a vital and expanding role throughout most of the century.

Certainly the construction of civic buildings around the turn of the century gave great opportunities to architects to establish their careers. Because the prevalent architectural philosophy of the time saw architecture as the 'mistress art', an inclusive discipline which drew in examples of many kinds of other arts and crafts, it also gave employment to sculptors, modellers, mural painters, and metal workers. The new works were representative of the public espousal of the arts as a symbol of municipal being, and the buildings in which they were incorporated were the physical embodiment both of the organs of government and the communities which they served.

CHAPTER THREE

Building and context

Edwardian civic buildings, more often than not, were considered to be instrumental in bringing about urban improvement. They provided a keynote in the artistic redevelopment of the city, the nineteenth century city in particular, which was seen as a product of *laissez-faire* economic growth and unrestricted physical change. The new buildings demonstrated the power of local democracy and its attendant facilities on one hand, civic pride and pretension on the other. Their influence in focusing the civic spirit, in providing an identity for a place and in delineating a mental map for the town's inhabitants was paramount.

There was a perception, voiced by many commentators, that Britain lagged well behind both the Continent and America when it came to civic design. Thomas Mawson, for instance, in his *Civic Art*, ruefully notes, 'others have accomplished far more than we; they have proceeded upon a settled policy, and their designs and methods have been systemized from the outset'.[1] A shining example, for some, was provided by the 'City Beautiful' movement in the United States. This was essentially a *beaux-arts* vision of the regular and the orderly; the rational planning of grand spaces and vistas, with pure, marble-clad buildings rising above broad avenues, or enclosing squares, piazzas and 'places'. It was a reaction to the rapid development of the country and a celebration of its arrival as a unified, mighty industrial and commercial nation, soon to be the most powerful in the world. Charles M. Robinson crystallized some of its ideals in his *Modern Civic Art, or the City Made Beautiful*; 'The tall façades glow as the sun rises; their windows shine as topaz ... Whatever was dingy, coarse and ugly, is either transformed or hidden in shadow ...'.[2]

There was also a vision in England, which was somewhat restricted, though similarly prompted by the great urban explosion of the nineteenth century. It was not, like America, set in a vast area where nature was on a massive scale, but was nostalgically related to the gentle countryside which was falling into decay and declining during the agricultural depression of the century's dying decades. Here the most persuasive view was backwards, to an age of a smiling landscape, peopled with happy and fulfilled craftsmen. The longing to return to a golden age was nothing new, of course, and had been a theme throughout Queen Victoria's reign. It was given added impetus by the genius of William Morris, who allied it to his socialist ideals. *News from Nowhere* (1890) is a study set in an England of the future where greed is long forgotten and the abolition of capitalism has lead to a society in which free of stress, everyone is unremittingly pleasant. The social ambience is of a rather jolly tea party given by 'artistic' upper crust liberals at a country house weekend. Although it may seem infuriatingly naïve, the images conjured up by Morris are persuasive, and must have been even more so to his own generation who witnessed the squalor of the Victorian city. In his description of Hammersmith, the narrator of *News from Nowhere* says,

> I thought I knew the Broadway by the lie of the roads that still met there. On the north side of the road was a range of buildings and courts, low, but very handsomely built and ornamented ... while above this lower building rose the steep lead-covered roof and the buttresses and higher part of the wall of a great hall, of a splendid exuberant style of architecture, of which one can say little more than it seemed to me to embrace the best qualities of the gothic and northern Europe with those of the Saracenic and Byzantine, though there was no copying of any one of these styles ...[3]

These images of the future, one cloyingly nostalgic, the other, though based on classical precedent, rather chillingly portentous of the least attractive aspects of twentieth century modernism, no doubt filtered through to even the least cerebral of Edwardian architects, producing, on one hand, the gilded weather vane and on the other, the great white portico.

Most Edwardian architects rose splendidly to the challenge with new buildings. In some cases entirely new sites were developed on land not previously occupied, in others, buildings were removed in order to make way for additions, or yet again, the new structures rose on infill plots. Whatever their situation, few are positioned merely to satisfy the pragmatic needs to allow access and to admit light. These buildings are, in fact, notable for the way in which they respond to their context. Most importantly, the typical Edwardian civic building sought to relate itself to the existing layout and structure of the town in which it was located in order to establish itself within the urban hierarchy. A town hall, for instance, had to adopt the right scale and manner relative to other buildings so that its importance was signified and so that its function as a public amenity, a ceremonial centre and an administrative headquarters was clearly signalled. The choice of site was also crucial in this context, but the disposition of the building on the site and its dialogue with its neighbours had to be clearly established. Edwardian architects seemed capable of undertaking this complicated and exacting task in a way that has been forgotten or ignored by later generations. A fire station, police station, public library or court house would be treated according to its standing within the urban hierarchy: scale and materials were chosen; sculpture and carving added and the building set to dominate its neighbours or made more reticent as appropriate.

A related issue was the question of self-advertisement. Town halls had to make their presence obvious and many possess clock towers, turrets or domes which pierce the skyline and can be seen where any prospect of the area may be enjoyed or from larger spaces within the town. Where streets are narrow, projections such as porticoes or sculptural features draw the eye to the building. In some cases, spaces were newly created around important buildings, so that the whole was designed so that a grand impression was made – perhaps a square conceived with a central axis, running into the centre line of the building, through the main entrance.

It has nearly always been difficult to achieve grand manner urban planning in Britain, and even the location of public squares is limited in its effect by the extent to which surrounding property boundaries can be violated. It has been pointed out, for instance, in Spiro Kostof's *The City Shaped*,[4] that without a degree of absolutism, and in the modern democratic situation, it is difficult to achieve large scale co-ordinated urban schemes. Nevertheless, even where it has been impossible to accomplish grandeur, Edwardian buildings respond to their immediate physical context by addressing the street. The building may be in a situation where its appreciation as an in-the-round object is impossible and effort may have to be put into one façade; if the building is on a corner site the question is how it turns the corner, and whether both façades are of equal importance, or whether there is a major–minor relationship. Consideration must be given to the scale of the building and its relationship to the adjacent fabric, and, indeed, to passers-by in the street and vehicles. In addition, the direction of approach is noted and related to the signs with which the building announces its presence.

Edwardian buildings respond quite often to the historical context of the city, sometimes in a direct, literal way, by quoting appropriate features or materials; the addition of sculpture of symbolic local relevance is quite common. At other times, vaguer references are used as a summary. All of this is dependent upon the artistic skill, sense and taste of the architect. Internationalism, in terms of *beaux-arts* classicism, arrived at the end of the Edwardian period and was then continued throughout the modern movement, where references to local context, both architectural and historical, were eschewed or studiously ignored.

Finally, of considerable contextual importance, was the way in which the architect solved the problem of demarcating zones within and around the building; into those which were public, private, semi-public and so on. Most Edwardian buildings have a sophisticated language for effecting the transition between these zones – for introducing the public into a building for instance. The range of architectural elements with which this was accomplished usually included changes in wall and floor materials, the degree and nature of decoration, the use of steps, porticoes, porches, the cutting-back of the building's skin or the crossing of bridges.

There was plenty of scope for architectural invention and delight in these contextual issues. Edwardian civic buildings are, perhaps, the most interesting of any from this point of view. It may be pointed out that much of this was the result of stultifying social hierarchy and the need for proprieties which have now been consigned to history for very good reasons. However, it may also be suggested that the popularity of Edwardian buildings has something to do with the direct use of architectural language to which the public can respond, in a way that it cannot in modern buildings where there are large areas of anonymous glazing.

The building within the city

Edwardian civic buildings seem to have been constructed in three kinds of locations: within existing areas of the town or city with their own strong character and usually with historical importance; in non-descript and run-down fringe areas; or on green field sites. In the first case, the architect was faced with problems of fitting-in those to do with scale, materials, massing, detail and historical reference. Civic buildings usually need a 'presence', and a further problem was to make the building sufficiently obvious or attractive without compromising its context. In the second and third cases, the design had to act as a means of upgrading the area in which it found itself and possibly acting as an example for further development. Within these contexts it also had to advertise its presence fairly forcefully. Sometimes it was constrained to occupy an existing street pattern, and reinforce the 'grain' of the urban context; in other cases, new and complementary urban features were constructed to match the style and ambition of the civic building.

Kostof notes the importance of urban skylines, and the way in which, during the nineteenth century, these had been degraded by the construction of large scale buildings. The skylines, he says, were reinstated by the use of towers, previously associated with religious edifices, on large and important secular buildings. Most significantly, these were used to advertise the presence of town halls. He also mentions the conflict between public and commercial monuments. In the United States the verticality of the latter was challenged by the horizontal planes and lines of civic buildings 'rendered in classical envelopes of marble, ... that defined urban space and monumentalized pedestrian perspectives ...'.[5] Although this point of view is relative to the situation in the United States, it is not without validity in the British context.

The building of the new County Hall for the West Riding of Yorkshire, in Wakefield, in the mid-1890s exemplifies many of the issues so far discussed. Wakefield, not Leeds, was the county town of the West Riding of Yorkshire. As already noted, when it was decided to build the new county hall there, the site chosen was that of the Rishworth estate. Rishworth House was already used by the county council for offices and committee rooms, but was too small in scale to provide the basis for extensions of the type and size the new accommodation required. The estate was located immediately to the north-west of an area comprising substantial and important buildings, and formed a continuation of a group which already contained the town hall, the court house and Mechanics' Institute. This conglomeration of high quality buildings helped to reinforce Wakefield's status, for there is an ambivalence in the city, brought about by its function not only as an administrative and diocesan centre but also as an industrial area with extensive mining nearby. The city's fabric seems to fall between two extremes of quality.

There appears to have been no grand plan to create such a group and, indeed, the buildings that form it were constructed over a period of ninety years. The Court House dates from 1806, the Mechanics' Institute (formerly a 'music salon') from 1822 and the town hall

Figure 3.1

County Hall, Wakefield. County Hall, in the foreground, is at the top of a slope rising from the town centre. To the left is the portico of the courthouse, with the tower and roof of Collcutt's Town Hall beyond. Originally the façade was to be in local brick with stone dressings, but sandstone was eventually used throughout

was begun in 1877. Therefore there is no consistency of style or detail, although stone is used throughout. There is dialogue, however, and the new county hall could scarcely fail to respond to its neighbours, particularly the town hall. This was designed by T.E. Collcutt (1840–1924), a well-known architect of considerable ability who continued to practise throughout the Edwardian period despite having made his name much earlier. Collcutt's building had a powerful presence, and although its style may best be described as Queen Anne (a delightfully vague label) or, in Goodhart-Rendel's phrase, 'bric-à-brac', its designer clearly inherited a sense of muscularity and powerful massing from his exposure to the gothic revival, although the style was in decline by the time Collcutt's project was begun. There is a thrusting verticality to the building, a four-storey main block being emphasized in height by oriels which run up beyond the façade, forming dormers in front of the steeply pitched roof. There are powerful chimney stacks and behind the main block and to one side is a rather austere campanile which is nearly 60 metres high. This is, therefore, a building which is very dominant. However, the line of Wood Street is such that the tower is well set back, and the Doric portico of the courthouse pushes forwards, catching the eye of passers-by journeying in either direction.

Faced with such a powerful physical context, the architects of the new County Hall, James G.S. Gibson (1861–1951) and S.B. Russell (1864–1955) had a difficult design task. They had to produce a building that spoke for itself, that had sufficient 'presence' to emphasize its importance, but which did not clash with what was already there. Moreover, although the existing Wood Street buildings demanded a response, there was very little to respond to to the north and west.

The architects' solution was to emphasize the length of the building's ranges, whilst providing variety in terms of the roofline and the treatment of the façade's surface. Vertical features contrast with the rhythm of the bays of fenestration, columns and arches, and the long runs of cornice and balustrading. There is a tower, which, no doubt, the architects felt compelled to provide, given the importance of the building. It is octagonal and stands at the corner of the building, at the junction of Bond Street and Cliff Parade, above the entrance, facing towards the city centre and its illustrious neighbours. It does not read as a detached element, but rises from within the body of the building to a height of about 40 metres. It terminates in a cupola and lantern, and is in complete contrast to the forcefulness of the town hall tower, almost a masculine–feminine difference. Again, this is well judged, for while it is sufficiently pronounced to mark out the presence of the building within the townscape of Wakefield, and to advertise the position of the entrance, it does not compete with the older building. Although further from the town centre, it is at a greater height than the other buildings.

Both the Town Hall and County Hall contribute greatly to the skyline of Wakefield, and as one moves from the shopping areas, views of profuse skyline details lead to expectations of rich and important structures. This is not confined to relatively close-up views, however. From outside Wakefield the ridge upon which the buildings stand rises high above the surrounding landscape, and it is possible to see the silhouette of both the tower and cupola from many miles away to the west of the city; not nearly as impressive as the skyline of Oxford, of course, but the mark of an important place.

In general terms, therefore, the architectural treatment of the building reinforces and consolidates its contextual relationships. The architectural language through which it communicates and seeks to achieve these criteria is far from simple. When Gibson and Russell designed the West Riding County Hall, the instructions in the competition documents noted 'the style of architecture will be left to the competitors but the Queen Anne or Renaissance school of architecture appears suited to an old town like Wakefield'. The assessor, J. Vickers Edwards, noted that the winning scheme was 'of superiority and in the Queen Anne style'.[6] Such was the slackness of this terminology and the all encompassing nature of a phrase that sounds specific, that the architects, in their own commentary submitted with the drawings, stated, 'The style of architecture adopted is the Renaissance, with distinctly English detail as exemplified in such buildings as Kirby and Wollaton halls. We believe this type especially recommends itself to Wakefield and the buildings as shown would group with those adjoining.'

The architects sought to display the style, or at least the stylistic elements which they considered appropriate to this class of building, on the façade to Bond Street, an extension of Wood Street which runs from the city centre, Cliff Parade, and the corner angle between. Although still clad in stone, the building lapses into a quieter and less detailed language on the long façade to the less important Burton Street. There are three main floors, with an extra 'attic' floor in the roof space on the Bond Street front. The tower is located above the entrance where, at the corner of the building, the angle is cut, or chamfered. At the other end of the block is a much smaller tower with a tall, polygonal roof, gothic in inspiration, or deriving from early sixteenth century French work. In between the towers is a six-bay range with a projecting gabled block near each end rising up to the ridge line of the main roof with a finial projecting beyond. The gables are stepped with a segmental head, broken by an obelisk, a feature made fashionable by Richard Norman Shaw, the most successful architect of the period. In addition, there are curved oriel windows at first floor level, another Shaw feature, but related also to Collcutt's town hall.

In effect, the gables act as end pavilions with a symmetrical range between. The ground floor bays consist of paired window openings. Above at first floor level, the wall is recessed, with round-headed nine-light windows subdivided by stone mullions and transoms. Rising out of the wall to the ground floor, and in front of the first floor window, is an arcade with mouldings around the tops of the arches, and statue niches to the piers. A balustrade runs between each pier. The plane of the wall is taken up beyond a cornice to form another, solid balustrade to the floor above, which is also recessed, but comprises twelve smaller bays of round-headed windows with engaged columns between. The balustrade to this floor is carved with early renaissance ornament.

The façade to Cliff Parade continues to be ornate with the second floor set back, as on Bond Street. At first and

Figure 3.2

County Hall, Wakefield. The tower with its cupola rises from the corner of the building above the entrance. It forms a landmark, visible from a distance, but complements rather than competes with Collcutt's tower. (Photo: Albert Booth)

second floor level there are changes, however: arched openings run at ground floor level, whilst above them are five separate oriels, the heads terminating against the underside of the second floor balcony. All of this is contained between two end pavilions similar to those on the main front. The 'chamfered' corner has a heavily moulded arched opening with a balcony above, and over that the wall again becomes a gable.

The octagonal tower itself rises up from the entrance vestibule, through the height of the building. It projects out, first as plain wall surfaces with narrow windows, but soon acquires more decoration, with gargoyles at the angles, beads of modelling, and corner piers. These turn into columns at the top level where the wall surface is pierced by arched openings with alternately emphasized voussoirs and quoins. This vertical progression is topped by a cornice, on which sits, in ascending order, a cupola, a lantern and weather vane. There is no clock; telling the time is a privilege preserved for the town hall along the road.

Much more could be written about the County Hall's external expression and adoption of style. Later in the Edwardian period, it is less laborious to describe buildings, as the vagaries of bric-à-brac give way to more regular Wrenaissance, neo-Georgian or *beaux-arts* styles.

Contextually, both in terms of the stylistic nature of the surroundings and in a broader sense of identifying with Wakefield's past, there is no reason why the architects should have chosen this style. It used fashionable elements, a baroque tower, growing out of a shaft which is more gothic in expression; 'Queen Anne' gables and oriels, motifs made fashionable by Richard Norman Shaw; round-headed windows reminiscent of the French chateau architecture of the time of François I. Oddly, all of these features seem to blend together and this decorative style contrasts well with the austerity of the court house and Collcutt's clock tower nearby. The curves of domes, arches and pediments complement the rectilinearity of the town hall, and the horizontal emphasis of cornices and balustrades balances the town hall's verticality.

Despite its variety of treatment, the result is a dignified and interesting building that sits well at the summit of the gradual slope from the town centre. Perhaps the rather dour Grindleford sandstone helps to calm down the excitement of too much incident, and, in any case, the rhythms and proportions of the building are well judged.

Strong contexts; tight sites

The County Hall at Wakefield was built on an expandable site, at the fringe of central civic development. Some buildings have had to fit in with very strong local contexts, often on tight and difficult sites. The town hall at Oxford and the county buildings at Stafford – both built to the designs of Henry T. Hare in the early years of his successful career, are cases in point. The Oxford

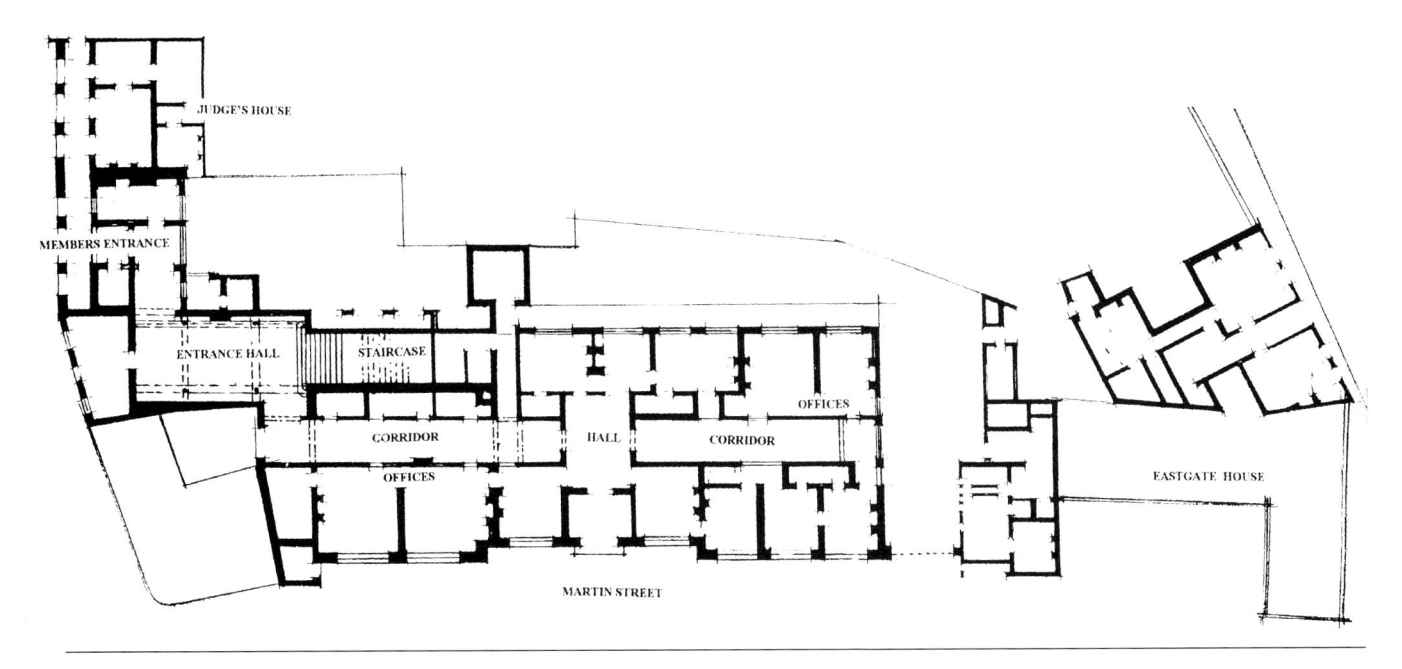

Figure 3.3
County Buildings, Stafford. Site plan. This ground floor plan of Hare's original scheme shows how it knits into a tight site which is surrounded by buildings of variable quality

Figure 3.4

County Buildings, Stafford. The main façade lines narrow Martin Street in the city centre. Hare's early use of the 'Wrenaissance' style was probably prompted by Eastgate House, a property owned by the council, adjoining the site

municipal buildings were constructed on a site bounded by St Aldate's and Blue Boar Street – near to, but not on the important junction, Carfax, at the commercial centre of the city. The sensitivity of the site, let alone the problems imposed by the physical constraints, need hardly be elaborated. Although Stafford cannot be said to have Oxford's range of important and beautiful buildings, it is a historic county town. If anything, the site was even more constrained here, with the need to link with the existing Georgian Shire Hall and Judge's House, and the late seventeenth century Eastgate House – all properties owned by the county council, and forming a block in the city centre. Nevertheless, Hare's building had only one major façade, that to the narrow thoroughfare of Martin Street. Hare's excellent planning and clear spatial organization within such difficult circumstances is discussed in Chapter 5. However, he also had to make his buildings communicate within historical contexts whilst speaking for themselves. At Stafford his job was in some ways easier than at Oxford. In fact, the council believed that the existing late Georgian Shire Hall with its elevation to the Market Place would be the public face of the building, and that Hare's contribution in a narrow back street would clearly be subsidiary. What was wanted was 'good, thoroughly businesslike offices for county work', a palace was not required and there was to be 'no clock tower, no grand public hall, no organ'.[7] What Hare produced was much finer than suggested by these quotations, but at least he was given the idea that there was no need to impose his building on Stafford. The new county building therefore forms what was, until it was built, the least important side of a town centre block. Hare let it speak for itself, reflecting, to a large extent, the nature of the internal accommodation in the treatment of the façade. He adopted an architectural language which may best be described as 'Wrenaissance', well in advance of many architects, but Hare was often happy to use any style he considered appropriate, and its use must have been prompted by Eastgate House – part of the council's block of property. There is a ventilation tower, cupola and flèche (a device frequently used by Hare), but little is visible until the narrow alleys leading to Martin Street are penetrated, and the full length of the façade becomes apparent. The red brick and stone walls and the intricacy of the details are framed like pictures by the sides of the dark approaches – but, apart from this, Hare's objective has been to reinforce the property boundaries and the historic form of the urban fabric.

Whilst the buildings in Stafford could be described as a little brash, they add variety, interest and quality to what might otherwise be a dismal area. In Oxford the façade is exposed to public scrutiny. St Aldate's runs down to Christchurch, its tower acting as a focal point, as the road curves slightly – and the buildings on either side, including the town hall, have the urban function of leading the eye towards it without too much distraction. In the opposite direction, they lead up hill towards one of the busiest junctions in Oxford, at the heart of the shopping area. Hare had to make his building conform, but also draw attention to itself as the symbol of the municipality. The chief building of 'town', even though there is a predominance of colleges – 'gown'.

The main 58 metre long façade to St Aldate's is symmetrical with a central entrance, and comes tight up to the pavement. Above, on the centreline of the entrance, is a device often used by Hare – a timber, lantern-like towered vent structure, capped by a cupola and attenuated 'spirelet' with weather vane on top. The roofline is punctured by gables and cupolas with finials and

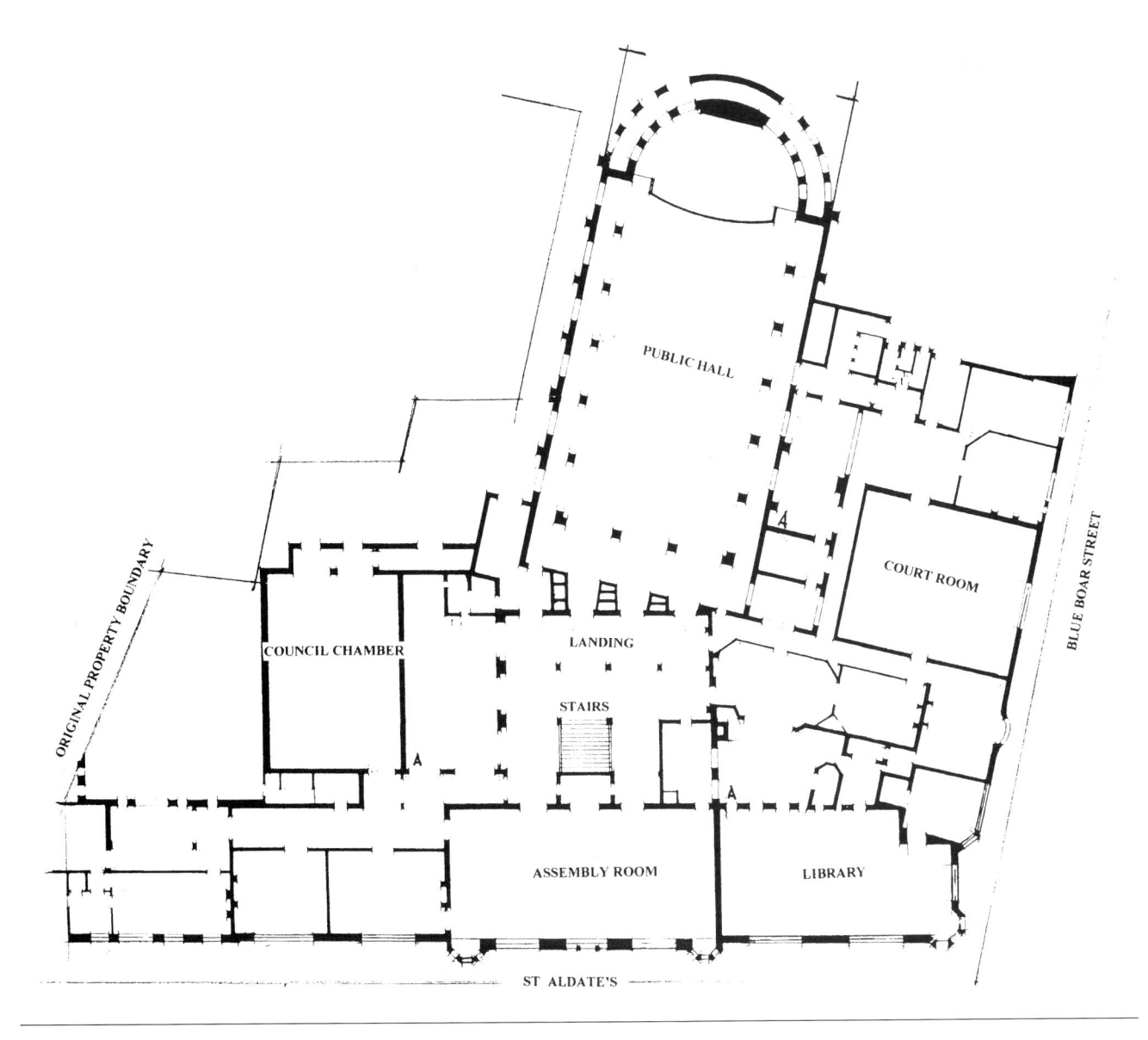

Figure 3.5
Oxford Town Hall. Site plan

chimneys. Although the street slopes, the string courses and parapets remain horizontal, the slope being taken up in a sub-basement.

The other public façade of the building is in narrow Blue Boar Street. Even though St Aldate's is something of a canyon at this point, it is broad enough to afford a view of the building, and is of reasonable proportion, despite being clogged with traffic. Blue Boar Street is very narrow, the town hall rising on one side for a length of about 43 metres, the other side constrained by walled college gardens. The corner of the building is turned with a little three-sided tower projecting out of first floor level, and squeezing in between a dormer gable to St Aldate's, and the end gable to the main roof on Blue Boar Street. This little tower acts as a 'corner post', catching the eye for those walking up the main street, or along the narrow lane. It also marks a change of expression and use of building materials between the two façades.

Hare's use of Clipsham stone with a Colyweston stone roof (originally) and a scale appropriate to its location in this part of Oxford helps the town hall fit in. Two major storeys, with a further storey at dormer level, is probably the correct representation of density on this site, and as one moves north to the commercial hub, it is of a size that is typical of the centre. Hare's building may have helped to establish the scale, because further down St Aldate's a domestic scale of earlier buildings pertains until Christchurch is reached.

Figure 3.6

Oxford Town Hall. The angle turret at the junction of the main front to St Aldate's and the Blue Boar Street façade. The rather festive style follows that already established by architects such as T.G. Jackson, as appropriate for the city

Figure 3.7

Carfax. Part of Hare's scheme was carried out for this important road junction in central Oxford. The style is reminiscent of the Blue Boar Street elevation of the Town Hall

Hare was involved with a project to redesign Carfax, only one block of buildings away from the town hall. St Martin's church was demolished in 1896 and Hare designed a scheme for remodelling the crossroads, including the old church tower which was left standing. In the event his 'gorgeous scheme' did not come off, and he was responsible for only the Midland Bank on the north-west corner and Tower House, beyond the church tower on Queen Street. Despite the picturesque nature of the buildings – the bank has a turret where it turns the corner – this was an attempt at a comprehensive piece of urban design. Amidst the welter of detail, it is interesting to remember that at one stage Hare had been trained in a *beaux-arts* atelier in Paris.

The architectural language used by Hare in the Town Hall has little to do with French sophistication, and the main façade demonstrates the bric-à-brac style at its most showy. It makes Wakefield seem positively reserved. The historical precedents for its use were twofold. First, the Elizabethan style relates to several of the elements of Oxford's colleges. The gables, seemingly derived, however, from those at Kirby Hall in Northamptonshire (1570–75), are of an appropriate scale and importance for a building like this, located in a historic street. The idea of gables running onto a street, rather than a uniform façade and cornice was, of course, something that had been revived and made popular in mid-Victorian times.

Secondly, Hare's design followed a precedent that had begun ten or twenty years earlier with the work of T.G. Jackson, whose style facetiously known as 'Anglo-Jackson' was developed for buildings such as his Examination Schools (1876). Basil Champneys, designer of prominent college buildings, also promulgated the style, and, therefore, it was to be expected that any new building in the centre of the city would speak this language. It was one of Hare's earliest large commissions, and fashion would change as the decade progressed. Had it been built a few years later, it would have looked very different. Indeed, at the almost contemporary county buildings in Stafford, Hare was using an early version of 'Wrenaissance', despite the mullioned windows, and he would go on to use this style or a simplified Tudor, until he broke out into heavy baroque later in the period.

In the design of Oxford Town Hall, there are two types of architectural expression, with a change of style as the building rounds the corner from St Aldate's to Blue Boar Street. The St Aldate's front is extravagant and heavily wrought. Blue Boar Street has something that affects greater simplicity, a more casual vernacular country town style not unlike his Carfax project, rather than the ruffs and frills of the Elizabethan period.

The St Aldate's façade is symmetrical, apart from the projecting tower at the south end which helps it to turn the corner. There is a centrepiece of three bays, with two gables and orieled bays either side. The centre bay is confined either side by three-sided tower features which emerge at first floor level and run up to balustrade level before terminating in little cupolas with finials.

Round-headed windows mark the bays at ground floor: two per bay in the side bays and one per bay, more widely spaced, in the central position. The main changes occur above ground floor level. In the centre portion are three large mullioned and transomed screens, each made up of sixteen lights. Above the centre, an ornate gable rises. In the elements to either side of the centre there are oriels, bracketed up from between the paired arched ground floor openings. Above these oriels are two tiers of columns, the bottom of which is larger and separates three windows, the top supports a round pediment.

The skyline and roofline maintain the hyper-activity defined elsewhere. There is a balustrade across the centre section, and gables to either side, of course, each with its own obelisk-like finial. On the parapet of the centre section are heraldic beasts, and smaller ones lurk at the sides of the pediments. On the centre-line is the elaborate timber framed lantern and 'spirelet'.

The main façade is constructed in Clipsham limestone, but around the corner in Blue Boar Street walling is squared rubble brought to courses in Bladon stone, with ashlar dressings. This emphasizes the contrasting plainness of the façade – rather like a cross between a Tudorbethan manor house and an old market building – particularly where triple arches announce the entrance to the public corridor running through the building, and to the WCs below. The chief feature of the façade, however, is the gable end to the main St Aldate's range, and the other transverse roofs, with oriels below. There is very little surface decoration here, however, but the more domestic treatment is in keeping with the nature of the street.

Figure 3.8

Blue Boar Street. The Town Hall faces narrow, winding Blue Boar Street with humble country Tudor in contrast to the grand front to St Aldate's

Another example of building on a constricted site within a strong historical context is provided by Colchester Town Hall. This was completed a decade after Hare's projects at Oxford and Stafford were begun, however, and the stylistic and formal approach is representative of high Edwardian baroque and far removed from bric-à-brac.

Colchester is one of the most ancient of English towns, and was granted status as a borough in the twelfth century. Its urban fabric reflects its long history, from Roman times onwards. The town hall in High Street occupies the same site as the medieval Moot Hall, demolished in 1843 after nearly seven hundred years' use, and replaced by a short-lived building which proved inadequate both spatially and structurally. This was, in turn, demolished in 1897, and John Belcher's splendid town hall rose in its place. The consequence is that although it maintains significant historic links, its architect has had to provide the accommodation necessary for running a twentieth century borough on a relatively small area at the junction of the town's chief street, and a small road, West Stockwell Street, that drops steeply to the north.

Considering that the building is jammed onto such a restricted site, it advertises its presence well. The most obvious way in which this is achieved is by the inclusion of a tall clock tower, 49 metres high, rising from the east end of the building, topped by a statue of Helena, mother of the Roman Emperor Constantine, and Colchester's patron saint. Although the tower itself is an excellent design, there was some critical comment when it was new that there was not enough room for it to be expressed – that it struggles up from the surrounding accommodation. This, though, is a harsh judgement. It is a feature that can be seen rising above the rooftops from outside the town centre. It is certainly easy to see from the east, along the length of the rising High Street, where the scale of the building is, in any case, much greater than its surroundings. Nevertheless, even when the body of the building is lost to sight, the tower features in brief views between shops and offices glimpsed from within the tight-knit centre. In addition, it has to compete with the 'jumbo' water tower, a huge and intrinsically interesting structure, the direct and functional design of which, however, is hardly elegant.

Figure 3.9

Colchester Town Hall. The tower acts as an effective landmark, despite competition from the 'jumbo' water tower at the summit of the hill. It can be seen from the tight-packed streets within the town, and from a distance

Figure 3.10

Colchester Town Hall. The High Street façade is a festive *tour de force*. Its rich, sculptural quality marks it out from its neighbours

Belcher's treatment of the High Street façade of the building enables it to be picked out along the length of the street, most obviously by the balcony projecting from the mayor's parlour at first floor level. Three great pediments break through the cornice line at the top of the façade, supported on large columns giving extra plasticity to the wall plane, and helping it to stand out from its neighbours.

Belcher was one of the pioneers of the 'Wrenaissance' style, developing it in conjunction with his young employee, Arthur Beresford Pite, during the 1890s. He also promoted arts and crafts ideas in relation to large, urban buildings. At Colchester, his work is rather festive. Indeed, each year it is the place where the Oyster Feast is held, which marks the opening of the oyster fishery, an ancient and significant event in the local economy. This, and other historical and industrial issues associated, are commemorated both inside and outside the building. Currently it sports no fewer than eight flagpoles, both horizontal and vertical, and four balconies are featured. A contemporary review noted 'a slightly Genoese flavour' to the style chosen, but it is really the 'Wrenaissance' at its most uninhibited.

Because the town hall occupies a very tight site, a decision was taken to suspend the Moot Hall – a replacement of the borough's meeting room which had stood on the site since medieval times – high above the street at second floor level. Immediately below is a suite of committee and civic rooms, such as the mayor's parlour. Various offices occupy the ground floor. This arrangement is expressed in the elevation to High Street, by facing the ground floor in Portland stone, and then letting the courses of red Hedingham bricks read above. Window surrounds, sculpture niches and the balustrade to the roof are all in stone, and the brickwork is further interrupted by giant columns rising through the two upper floors, and sitting on the plinth formed by the ground floor cladding and its projecting cornice. The columns support pediments which break through the cornice and run into the roof balustrade – segmental at either end of the façade, and triangular in the middle. Although, in description, this may sound like an exercise in architectural bombast, it is, in fact, well judged and although it would not do in London or Leeds, is highly appropriate to an old country town.

Around the corner, in West Stockwell Street, the language changes with a façade defined by two three-storey bays to either side of a central section, the line of which, projected up, forms the tower. Abutting, along the steeply falling street, is the block in which the law courts are situated. There is Portland stone to the ground floor, with a lunette and heavily rusticated voussoirs to the entrance; red brick above with alternately blocked quoins to the round-headed windows at first floor level, and rectangular windows to the second floor below the handsome cornice. Instead of a parapet there are stone faced dormers.

The tower itself is of a pattern found in many 'Wrenaissance' buildings, although it may well have been popularized by Belcher. A plain brick shaft rises out of the building's façade, with clocks to each face. Halfway, or so, up its length, stone replaces brick and a version of Wren/Hawksmoor church towers takes over, most closely related to the west towers of St Paul's. There are two main top stages, the lower of which has pedimented and balustraded openings to each face, with seated figure sculptures at the chamfered angles. The tower is topped by a bronze sculpture of St Helena.

On the whole, Belcher's building communicates itself very well, giving messages about civic function and history. At the same time, although it has dignity, it seems to imply that its civic role is to be enjoyed and celebrated. The ability to make a building communicate these complicated messages, as Belcher has done, through the nuances with which its languages are employed has long been neglected and lost.

Figure 3.11

Bradford Town Hall Extension. Richard Norman Shaw's witty design for the extension to the gothic revival town hall. Shaw employs a variety of stylistic details to produce a stimulating whole

Before leaving this section mention must be made of at least one scheme which is an extension to an existing building. Perhaps the most interesting and accomplished example is the work done at Bradford Town Hall by Richard Norman Shaw, in conjunction with the City Architect, F.E.P. Edwards. Mention has already been made of the need to dispose the accommodation on a tight, triangular, urban site, but much of the scheme's interest lies in its use of architectural language. Many significant buildings in central Bradford were built in a heavy gothic revival style. The existing town hall, designed by local architects Lockwood and Mawson, was no exception. Shaw was concerned that his extension should complement the original and not 'jar' visually, but not only was he designing in a different period, but he had all the resources of a leading practitioner whose great gift lay in the manipulation of architectural language. Commentators have found a certain amount of humour in Shaw's response to the existing building. Derek Linstrum notes, for instance, 'Shaw's addition is a brilliantly witty design, maybe slightly mocking the earnest Gothic style of the sixties ...'.[8] Despite these specific references, however, the architect wove in a variety of different architectural elements, and the whole is synthesized from quotations from many different periods. Direct quotations to the existing building occur in the first floor windows with their pointed arches. Below are heavy, round-headed openings, almost romanesque in character. Elsewhere, there are 'Tudor-bethan' details, particularly in the extensive use of mullioned windows and oriels with leaded lights and stained glass. Gargoyles and a tourelle reintroduce a gothic note. However, a substantial part of the building is in the 'Queen Anne' style, made popular by Shaw. Here it is a melange of French eighteenth century and sixteenth century elements and English seventeenth century influences. Shaw's genius is evinced in the fact that the whole forms an overall unity, whilst being diverse and interesting in details. Internally, in contrast, the council chamber is typically 'Wrenaissance'.

Fringes

Stockport and Deptford Town Halls – designed in competitions in 1903 and 1902 respectively – continued the baroque and 'Wrenaissance' theme, but within the context of undistinguished sites.

Stockport Town Hall is, in some respects, similar to a celebrated Victorian forerunner, Leeds Town Hall. The

Figure 3.12
Stockport Town Hall. The town hall has an elaborate façade to mark its presence along one side of a dreary traffic route. Away from the main road, Portland stone quickly gives way to more modest brickwork

site lies to one side of a major road, and the length of the building and its main façade are parallel to the road. Although, in the case of Stockport, there was sufficient room to create a grand composition it feels as though it needs a large square or 'place' in front to complement the façade. Instead, busy Wellington Road South runs fairly steeply down to the centre of the town. The building is, in fact, some distance away from the commercial centre, but as the borough was made up of a number of districts, the town hall was probably seen as its focus. Indeed, it is noted as an 'improvement' which would, no doubt, engender local pride amongst the residents of an area which grew willy-nilly with a rapid increase in low quality building stock as the effects of industrialization occurred.

Although located in a bleak and characterless out of town area, the town hall does make its presence felt by virtue of the fact that it is set in an elevated position, and that the tower is 40 metres high. It is, like the rest of the main façade, somewhat over-wrought, rising through three major stages – the clock being at the lowest stage. There is no pretence that the rest of the tower is of any use at all, except as an advertisement for the building's presence. It is a mere superstructure through which the wind may whistle. The second stage of the tower is very similar in form to the corner towers of Thomas's Belfast City hall, designed well before Stockport. The whole structure in white Portland stone may remind the local inhabitants of a wedding cake, but it can be seen from the main line railway which runs through the town on its way south from Manchester, and this serves its purpose well.

The tower sits on the centre line of a very grand Portland stone façade. The main entrance, beneath the tower, is approached up flights of steps, and is flanked on each side by a pavilion in rusticated stone. These pavilions have triangular pediments supported on ionic columns rising through first and second floors. The columns are paired at either end of the pavilions, but the entablature breaks back towards the centre where single columns support each side, which is interrupted by an arch thrusting its way up into the pediment. Five bays of fenestration then run to more subdued corner pavilions. Beyond the main façade, the building is more humbly, though rather more sympathetically treated in red brick with stone dressings. It may be observed that Thomas's composition is somewhat overwrought, particularly the showy tower and the pavilion compositions that squeeze its base. The treatment of the same architect's work at Belfast City Hall seems to indicate that restraint was not one of his virtues.

Deptford Town Hall in south-east London suffered, from the point of view of siting, in a similar way to Stockport. At present, in fact, and possibly even when built, it has probably the worst site of any of the examples discussed. This is a pity, because in many respects it is one of the most interesting buildings included. It is located at the side of the busy A2 Dover road, here called

Figure 3.13

Deptford Town Hall. Lanchester and Rickard's handsome façade confronts the banality of the building's surroundings

New Cross Road, with only a few metres of pavement separating it from the pounding traffic which throws up dirt and dust at the façade of the building. The surrounding buildings are of little consequence. Those on the same side of the road are humble and domestic; facing the building were more pretentious structures, but these were of poor quality and have now descended into squalor.

The town hall is fortunately located on the outward extremity of a bend in the road, which means that it can advertise its presence, particularly to those approaching the site from the western (i.e. London) direction. One feels that the main elevation – for this is a building difficult to see in the round – is doing its best to project forward and announce itself without relying too much on a single feature to shout out. In fact Deptford Town Hall does have a clock tower, but this is not really a separate structure, rather a 'top hat' to the building. It straddles the ridge of the roof above the big gable that forms a pseudo pediment on the centreline of the façade.

The eaves of the gable project outwards for some considerable distance, but this is matched by the centre section of the building on ground and first floor, which breaks forward. The forward thrust is further enhanced by a curved oriel and balcony at first floor level, emphasizing the main central entrance below. A heavy cornice follows the line of the façade and oriel at the top of the first floor.

The appearance of the building is rather nautical, in some ways reminiscent of the stern of a great sailing ship, in others referring to customs houses. It has also been suggested that it takes its cue from seventeenth century country town buildings, such as the Guildhall at Guildford, Surrey, where the hall forms part of a busy street scape with other properties tight up to either side. Like Deptford, this is a site where there is no chance of a square in front.

The character and expression of this memorable building are mainly due to the symmetrical façade, behind which the rest of the accommodation is contained within an unremarkable structure of stock bricks. It seems, however, that Lanchester, Stewart and Rickards chose a forceful means of emphasizing a significant structure on a site which only has linear qualities. In other words, this is an instance where the street is a corridor, not a place to pause and reflect, and it has been impossible to create an open space which would complement the dignity of the building and the importance of its function.

Creating an appropriate setting

At Lancaster, things were completely different. This ancient borough originally had a town hall located in the Market Square. The need for a larger building was recognized in the 1890s and the Corporation acquired land in Dalton Square, well to the south-east of the city centre. Although the new building was to occupy a 'footprint' area of approximately 40 metres by 67 metres and was built hard up against public roads on its south and west sides, the scheme for its development involved the

Figure 3.14

Deptford Town Hall. The clock tower and its weather vane sail proudly above the roofs of humdrum domestic buildings, but the rear of the town hall, itself, is built in ordinary London brick

Figure 3.15

Lancaster Town Hall. The scale of the building sets it apart from its surrounding. The tower is visible above the rooftops and the portico projects forwards from the line of the street

creation of public open space. To the east, Robert Street was moved outwards, enabling the provision of gardens on that side of the building and a private road with wrought iron gates at either end. More importantly, Dalton Square, itself, was altered. The main entrance to the town hall stands on the south side, the other sides are lined with bland but pleasant late Georgian houses. Although the roads around the square slope away to the north its centre was made into a flat platform curved at the ends, surrounded by a substantial stone balustrade and accessed by steps down at the town hall end, and up at the north side. In the centre of the square, on the same axis as the town hall portico, is an elaborate memorial to Queen Victoria, the statue of the Queen by Herbert Hampton, standing on a substantial plinth upon each side of which are relief panels illustrating Victorian worthies in the fields of statesmanship, science and engineering, the arts and exploration. She faces her son, Edward VII, whose seated figure, in a depiction by F.W. Pomeroy, is located in the pediment of the town hall's portico.

Thus, within a rather cramped and small scale urban context an attempt was made to provide a grand building and complement it with external spaces that would enable the building to be seen. This is, in part, successful, but Lancaster has a fairly tight-knit fabric, and the town hall makes its presence felt in three ways. First, by bulk. Its scale is much greater than its surroundings and both George Street and Thurnam Street are dominated by the building's great mass of Longridge stone rising direct from the pavement. This is at least 17.6 metres high, and on the Thurnam Street side, 67 metres long.

Next, there is the portico. This has six ionic columns, each 9.75 metres high set on a stepped podium, above which is located a bold pediment. The whole, on the centreline of the façade, projects 3.6 metres forward of the building's face. Not only is it a prominent feature when seen from the north approach, but the way in which it projects enables it to advertise the building's main entrance when seen from the east and west.

Finally, and inevitably, there is a clock tower. This rises from within the building, attaining a height of 44.5 metres, the cupola, a handsome termination rising above the big pale faces of the clock, looking out across the little city. Conversely, of course, it can be seen from many points round about, even at night, for the 3 metre diameter faces are designed to be illuminated. Attention was further drawn by the provision of bells to strike the hours and chime the quarters.

Lancaster's town hall, therefore, provided another focal point within the city, and the whole composition of building and external space added a new and important area outside the bustle of the existing market place. The

Figure 3.16
Lancaster Town Hall. King Edward gazes from the pediment of the town hall portico, towards the statue of his mother in the centre of the newly created square. (Photo: Lancaster City Council Museums Service)

Figure 3.17
Cardiff City Hall. Lanchester and Rickard's elegant baroque clock tower proclaims its presence across Cathays Park. (Photo: T Lewis. Reproduced courtesy of *Architectural Review*)

citizens were lucky that generous benefactors were available in order to help bring this about.

Before leaving this section, mention must be made of a scheme designed and constructed in the grand manner. This is the development of Cathays Park, near the centre of Cardiff, almost a collection of palaces in a great sweep of parkland. The town hall was complemented by law courts to one side, and, later, the national Museum of Wales to the other, in addition to which Glamorgan County Hall and buildings for the University College were included in the development. It is instructive to study the buildings, as they show a progression in the manner of design during the Edwardian period. However, it is the first major building, the town hall, that concerns us here. Resplendent in faultless Portland stone with gilded detail, it is, nevertheless, well away from the rather haphazard centre which had grown very rapidly during the nineteenth century. To some extent, the beautiful dome over the council chamber, with H.C. Fehr's Welsh dragon at the summit belching (metaphorically) flames at the city centre, is eye-catching, yet separated by great open spaces and roadways from the rest of Cardiff. In keeping with the scale of the development and, one would imagine, the necessity of marking it out from a distance, the architects added a clock tower some 59 metres high, rising from the mid-point of the west range of the building. For a substantial part of its height, the tower is an elegantly restrained shaft, square on plan, which breaks out to greater detail at the level of clock and bells. Sculptures sit at the angles, whilst the openings are flanked by columns with a Borromini-like cornice above. Over this, the tower diminishes in size, becoming curved, until it finally terminates in a decorative flourish. The gilded clock face itself sits on the surface of the tower, contrasting its metallic precision with the heavy modelling of the stone behind. Lanchester, writing of the project, noted that 'this dial has been constructed in skeleton form, as it was felt that an illuminated face at this elevation would too severely cut up the architectural lines of this [sic] ornament'.[9] The whole therefore reads better at a distance.

It has been difficult to isolate some of the elements discussed in this section, and it may be that the architects, artists and craftsmen association with the buildings described acted intuitively rather that analytically. Nevertheless, there is plenty of evidence that the position of the building within the urban hierarchy and the location of the building within the urban fabric – the extent to which it should agree with its surroundings, and the extent to which it should advertise itself – were all components of the design process.

Edwardian architecture also exhibits a great deal of external enrichment, so far only described in broad terms. Intrinsically interesting, it is also symptomatic of the close relationship between the architect and other artists and craftsmen, which is such a significant feature of the Edwardian scene.

CHAPTER FOUR

Integration of the arts – external enrichment

Edwardian buildings do not speak an abstract architectural language that appeals only to a small number of initiates. They strive to communicate on several levels and for a variety of different reasons. In broad terms, most of the messages they carry are very direct indeed. Although a large proportion of them may be related to specifically architectural subjects – form, the disposition and variation of spaces; the building's dialogue with its context – the means by which others are conveyed is through the fundamentally non-architectural medium of enrichment, designed and executed by non-architects. Of course, the line between what the architect designs and what the artist–craftsman executes can be blurred, but the original intent lies with the architect as a rule. At one end of the scale, the execution could be the literal translation of an architect's demand in a standardized way for a frieze or moulding, for instance. On the other hand, the request for sculptural detail could be left in all but outline to the artist.

Externally, Edwardian civic buildings can sometimes be read almost as a book. The contribution of sculptors in the execution of allegorical figures and groups helps to establish the building within its context. It is tempting to imagine that at the time of construction the building's importance varied in direct ratio to the number of sculptural works included in its design.

Aside from this, however, sculpture groups and relief panels also inform the passer-by about the purpose of the building. On one occasion, at least, the sculptural work has been appropriated as a national icon. F.W. Pomeroy's figure 'Justice' which stands on the lantern high above the dome over Mountford's 'Old Bailey' is a symbol for the legal process. Many civic buildings go further than this, however, and seek to epitomize the place where they are, to reinforce a county's or city's identity. County halls have stained glass panels in windows containing the coats of arms of the noble families who have been important in its history; relief panels illustrate local industries and commercial activities; carved shields represent boroughs within the county. The City Hall in Cardiff, for instance, speaks not only of the city itself, but also of Wales. The building may look like the offspring of an alliance between Viennese and Parisian palaces, but there can be no mistaking the meaning of the huge dragon poised over the dome above the council chamber on the centreline of the main elevation.

Heavy direct symbolism is therefore incorporated, but there is another level where enrichment and elaboration works. This is in the way in which the various points of the building are treated to provide the observer with a clue as to their relative importance. Both the arts and crafts movement and then the modern movement made it reprehensible to give a building a highly designed main façade with less elaborate and cheaper work making 'poor relations' of the other elevations. The building is a three-dimensional whole, integrating space, form and material; a stigma attaches to a showy public front with a mean private area behind. Indeed, examples such as Henry Hare's Wolverhampton Central Library with its 'Queen Anne front and Mary Anne back' are still difficult to swallow but one wonders whether this resulted from a desperate cost-cutting measure by Hare, leaving part of the building unfinished like the façades of so many Italian churches. Nevertheless, several Edwardian civic buildings discriminate between external treatment not only to allow money to be spent to greater effect to enhance the main façade, but so that, from the point of view of propriety and readability, the grand entrance is stone clad with sculptural adornment, whilst the workaday offices are in wholesome red brick walling relieved with stone banding, door and window surrounds.

Much of the enrichment is the product of artist–craftsmen working in stone carving and the modelling of brick, or other ceramic materials such as terracotta. In addition, though, wrought iron work is significant in the production of balustrades, gates, railings, clock and lantern brackets that enhance so many Edwardian civic buildings.

Interior treatment is similar in its delineation of areas. Town halls, for instance, may have a grand ceremonial public entrance lined with marble, the walls split horizontally by cornices, architraves and dados, and vertically by pilasters. Flights of polished-stone steps rise to the suites of civic function rooms and the council chamber above. There, rooms often have panelled walls and elaborate ceilings defined with heavily modelled plasterwork; the public hall itself, usually over-elaborate. The corridors in these areas would have been respectable in the palaces of English dukes. Moving away, though, it quickly becomes apparent where the threshold is crossed from ceremonial space to the functional space of offices for the department of education, the borough surveyor or the medical officer. Even though these may be spacious and well-proportioned by modern standards, the plainness of the plastered walls and stark ceilings is, to modern eyes, in shocking and violent contrast to the luxury elsewhere, which would form an appropriate context for Alma Tadema's sybaritic maidens.

Sculptural works were often an important embellishment to Edwardian civic buildings, and were regarded as 'the noblest form of architectural ornament'.[1] Town halls, in particular, were keen to display statues of local worthies or historical characters associated with the borough. Public libraries and art galleries would include busts or figures of famous literary figures or painters. In addition, allegorical groups or sculptures were popular, especially those linked with local economic activity or topographical features.

Although the nature of civic buildings at this time may have demanded this kind of iconography, those of a similar purpose built before or since have been notably lacking in sculpture which is integrated into the architectural scheme. There are exceptions, of course, but prior to the late nineteenth century it was mainly confined to standardized classical subjects, and following the Edwardian period was seen, if at all, during the 1930s in the work of artists like Epstein, terminating in the 1950s. The reason for the presence of this integrated sculptural effort is to be found in the increased amount of public art in the late nineteenth century and the development of what is known as the 'new sculpture'. In conjunction with this was the growth of a relationship between the architect and the artist. This development manifested itself not only in the production of statues and groups, but also in the development of the superior carving of architectural detail and non-figurative subjects.

The origins were twofold. First, there was an upsurge in interest in public and commercial decorative arts in the aftermath of the Great Exhibition, which included the growth of art education and the establishment of the South Kensington museums. Second, and some decades later, the arts and crafts movement encouraged the breakdown of barriers between the arts, whilst acknowledging, at least as far as architects were concerned, that architecture was 'the mistress art', an all-encompassing discipline in which the work of many other artists and craftsmen was brought together. It is generally recognized that the most significant building in setting the scene for the use of sculpture and relief over the Edwardian period was the Hall of the Institute of Chartered Accountants, in the City of London, designed by John Belcher, and completed in 1893. The sculptural detail for the Institute was undertaken by Hamo Thornycroft (1850–1925) and Harry Bates (1850–99), and much of the character of the façades is due to the way in which their work is integrated into Belcher's external design. During the following decade and more, public buildings and often commercial ones, were not considered complete without figures, relief panels or modelling specially designed for the architect's commission, not to mention railings, door furniture, weather vanes and other detail. Although it may be difficult to think of Belcher, the builder of large urban structures, as a protagonist of what may appear to be homespun arts and crafts philosophies, he was, in fact, a member of the Art Workers' Guild and a staunch supporter of its aims in practical terms. He believed that the architect must take the lead in the design process, but should produce suitable context for the sculpture, 'a jewel whose beauty is to be enhanced by an appropriate setting'.

The efforts of the sculptors should also be recognized in the development of 'the new sculpture' and its relationship to architecture. According to Susan Beattie, 'the transformation of architectural carving and modelling from anonymous, scarcely noticed craft, to dynamic, seductive art was the greatest collective achievement of the New Sculptors and one of the most rational expressions of Arts and Crafts ideals in nineteenth century history'.[2]

It is not surprising, then, in this review of buildings produced in the great period of architectural sculpture, that the names of these 'new sculptors' should occur in conjunction with some of the most prominent buildings of the time, and that there should be a strong link between some architects and sculptors. It is clear that once a working relationship was established and the artistic intent was clear between both parties, these links occur again and again. Of the architects whose work is described in this book, several such liaisons are represented. Mountford, designer of Lancaster Town Hall, employed Frederick W. Pomeroy (1856–1924), a gold medallist of the Royal Academy School, from his early civic works such as Sheffield Town Hall, begun 1890, through his most famous achievement, the Central Criminal Court, or 'Old Bailey', and then Lancaster Town Hall at the end of his life. Henry Hare used the versatile Frederick E.E. Schenck at the Stafford County Buildings and Oxford Town Hall at the beginning of his career, and later in the public libraries which made up the bulk of his output in the first years of the new century. Lanchester and Rickards required a broader representation in their major buildings than could be provided by a single individual, but were consistent in their choice over a variety of important public commissions. No doubt, Edwin Rickards relied upon those kindred spirits who could translate his fluent sculptural drawings into the reality of stone. There was certainly a fruitful association and friendship with the architectural sculptor Henry Poole (1873–1928). Others who enjoyed a rewarding relationship with Lanchester and Rickards were the decorative sculptor H.C. Fehr (1867–1940), Paul Montford (1868–1938) and Donald McGill.

There is little question that the integration of sculpture into the spirit of the design is most pronounced in Lanchester and Rickard's work, thanks mainly to the enthusiasm and facility of the latter in harnessing his facility for baroque invention. In most cases, however, figurative sculpture with contextual and historical significance is treated rather in the manner of saints in medieval cathedrals, with niches which form part of the architectural scheme but which, from a visual point of view, could house any statues of an appropriate size. At West Riding County Hall at Wakefield, for instance, the niches were in the piers separating the arcading at first floor level on the main elevation to Bond Street. Allegorical figures represented the industries of the West Riding – mining, iron founding, textiles, glassblowing, agriculture, engineering and pottery – and were executed by W. Birnie Rhind (1855–1933) who was also notable for architectural and memorial work in Scotland and Canada. These have been removed, and although regrettable, their loss is damaging

(a)

(b)

Figure 4.1

(a) *Colchester Town Hall*. Sculptural detail abounds on the High Street façades at Colchester. (Photo: Colchester Museums.) (b) In addition, entrance to the law courts, West Stockwell Street, is guarded by the head of Justice on the keystone of the arch

to local pride rather than to the overall scheme of architecture. At Colchester Town Hall, historic figures take their place in baroque niches, at top floor level, two of which face West Stockwell Street, in the expanse of wall running down from the base of the towers. The remaining four face High Street and are set in the brick panels between the porticoed bays. Colchester, as has been noted, is an ancient borough, and the statues, carved by a local firm of stonemasons, represent individuals as diverse as Queen Boudicca and Lord Audley. None is more recent than Jacobean times, but all are in period costumes, like petrified participants in a local pageant. There is further local symbolism in the statues at either corner of the tower, which peer down at the bystander or out across the roofs of the town from the second stage of the structure where the construction changes from brick to stone and becomes more elaborate in a manner deriving from English baroque church towers. Here, the work is again by the local sculptor L.J. Watts, who executed the niche figures. Colchester's military role is represented by a seated Roman soldier, spear in hand; agriculture by a female figure carrying a wheatsheaf; fishing by a contemporary representation in oilskins, sou'wester and sea boots, and engineering, strangely, by what could be a rather severe Greek philosopher of the stoic school grasping a cogwheel. Perhaps a more modern appearance would have invited comparison with Alderman James Paxman, the local engineering magnate who gave £3000 for the construction of the tower. Over all is a large bronze figure of St Helena, at the pinnacle of the composition, and just below her at the corner of the tower's top stage stand ominous looking ravens, apparently guarding the saint.

Deptford Town Hall, too, has 'local pageant' statues. The theme is 'British Admirals'. They stand along the main façade of the building between the first floor windows, facing out across the obscenities of the trunk road and the conglomeration of hideous run-down commercial buildings, looking towards the River Thames, the site of Drake's knighting by Queen Elizabeth I, and the location of the chief naval depot in Samuel Pepys's time. Each admiral stands on a projecting bracket, and over him is a cornice at the same height as the window heads from which swags descend to frame the upper half of his body. At the east end is Drake himself, then Admiral Blake, Cromwell's naval commander. To the west of the segmental bay are Nelson and an idealized British Admiral, circa 1905. Thus, a new civic body was given historical respectability and was related to the wretched urban sprawl which it governed and which was desperately in need of identity. The town hall was the symbol of this new entity, not simply a place which permitted the operation of municipal functions.

Public libraries did not need to be so overtly local in this way, and they usually included representations of

Figure 4.2

Deptford Town Hall. To the right, Nelson looks down from his first floor bracket, whilst, in the foreground, winged tritons support the segmental bay over the entrance

literary figures and those associated with learning and scholarship. At Hare's Islington Central Library, Francis Bacon and Edmund Spenser occupy the niches at either end of the grand, main façade looking on to Holloway Road. This is a baroque *tour de force*, and it is odd to see the figures, clad in Elizabethan costume, set in pedimented niches, located in rusticated stone 'pavilions' high above the pavement. Hare's unstinting attempt to create a splendidly sculptural baroque screen gives these figures an unsettling air of incongruity. Holden's contemporary library design at Bristol is, typically, an exercise in formal manipulation, and plasticity of detail is not part of the overall theme. Sculpture is present, however, in the form of no fewer than twenty-one representative figures located on the main front to Deanery Road but strictly subjugated to the architectural scheme. The figures are sheltered by arches that span the three recesses in the centre section of the façade. These recesses frame the ground floor windows and oriels over, and the figures are located immediately above the oriels, thereby

Figure 4.3
Islington Central Library. Spenser and Bacon gaze over the urban chaos on Holloway Road from their pedimented niches in Hare's extravagant baroque screen

Figure 4.4
Bristol Central Library. Charles Pibworth's sculpture groups are neatly kept in place in Holden's design, and are not allowed to disrupt his exercise in architectonic form. (Photo: T Lewis. Reproduced courtesy of *Architectural Review*)

fulfilling their didactic role whilst not interfering with the architecture. This is in complete contrast with mainstream Edwardian baroque where sculpture enhances outline. The work is by a local man, Charles Pibworth, and is best described as being in panels, but it is not relief work even though the figures are not completely in the round. Pibworth's three groups are life-sized and the themes are 'Religious Development', in the centre, with representations of St Augustine and the Venerable Bede amongst others. To the west, 'Chroniclers' include William of Malmesbury and Cynewulf; whilst to the east the theme is Chaucerian. Although Holden continued to use sculptural work to decorate his later buildings, the way in which the Bristol work is subjugated to the formal, architechtonic development points to the path ahead. Exuberant use of figures to add to the architecture, as an integral part of the expression, as typified by the work of Lanchester, Stewart and Rickards, had largely disappeared by the end of the Edwardian period.

Allegorical figures and those with an architectural purpose but no specific title are also common in Edwardian civic architecture. Examples of these have been noted in the case of Colchester Town Hall and West Riding County Hall, where they represent local trades and industries. Cardiff City Hall has figures that are more relevant to the principality of Wales in general. Perhaps there was a premonition of the possibility of a greater regional significance for the building. Certainly this is enhanced by the most striking example of its sculpture, the great lead dragon, designed by H.C. Fehr, sitting on the centreline of the main façade. At the end pavilions are groups representing 'Welsh Unity and Patriotism', and 'Poetry and Music', by Henry Poole and Paul Muntford. Flanking the drum to the dome of the council chamber are further groups by Montford and Poole, based on the theme of rivers associated with the city. Although these works constitute the major sculptural items, there is sculpture elsewhere, most notably on the clock tower, where Fehr's figures of the Four Winds crouch at the tower angles at the base of the second stage.

This sculptural work has its own integrity. The groups, dynamic in their own right, with swirling draperies and lines of force running in counter directions, nevertheless resolve themselves into sufficiently static forms to help define the form and massing of the building. Seen from a distance, they assist the transition from one plane to another, place textural emphasis at key points in the overall design, and increase the amount and density of shadow over significant areas of the façade. They also add to the silhouette of the building, or help to attract the eye, the Four Winds on the clock tower being a particularly good example of this.

Deptford Town Hall, by the same architects, is, of course, not nearly so lavish, and the silhouette is much more restrained. However, the winged tritons supporting the segmental bay over the main entrance are marvellous architectural features. Whether they fulfil any physical support function is immaterial. They are a visual necessity and add charm, exuberance and a sense of occasion to the act of entering. The mermaids at the formally similar Hull School of Art by the same architects perform a similar function, though supporting a second floor balcony. In the pediment at Hull is a glass mosaic designed by A.G. Jones and made by the Bromsgrove Guild, whereas at Deptford there is a stone relief carving of a naval battle.

The segmental bay motif also appears on the main (Storey Street) front of Lanchester and Rickard's Wesleyan Central Hall, Westminster. Here, the female figures do not provide physical support, but hold swags across the top of the great staircase window, almost as though they are holding a curtain up, to reveal the window beneath. Fittingly, they are more modest in attire and demeanour than in the examples described above.

Figure 4.5

Cardiff City Hall. A profusion of allegorical sculptural elements are used in this building, and contribute to its overall outline. H.C. Fehr's lead dragon soars above the dome of the council chamber. (Photo: T Lewis. Reproduced courtesy of *Architectural Review*)

Figure 4.6
Wesleyan Central Hall. Female figures holding swags across the window lighting the great staircase give an almost theatrical feeling to the building. Elsewhere, eagles and helmets add a militaristic note. (Reproduced courtesy of *Architectural Review*)

The bay has a character that, in other circumstances, may serve as the entrance to a theatre or opera house, or at least a grand palace in which one expects ceremonial of some sort. This expectation is further enhanced, inside, by the great sweep of the staircase. It was, one suspects, designed without any sense of irony by the architect, and is exactly opposed to what is normally regarded as the Methodist view of life.

The other sculptural decorations which enhance the building also seem, at first sight, inappropriate. They mainly derive from Roman precedent and are warlike and triumphalist in their symbolism. They can be rationalized in specific terms of their relationship to Methodism and the Christian faith, though attempts seem tentative. More generally, symbols of fighting and triumph are not inappropriate to a religious movement which began in competition to the established church, and set out to bring spiritual enlightenment amongst the 'dark satanic mills' and teaming urban sprawls of the Industrial Revolution. However, Rickards was an intuitive artist who would have chosen sculptural detail to enhance the line of the building and its form and the play of light and shade over its surface. The nature of the decoration was, no doubt, what he felt was appropriate to the building as a work of art, rather than a reflection of its purpose. The urns, trophies, shells and swags that he used in Central Hall can be found in his designs elsewhere.

As in all Rickard's work, the sculptural detail decorates and enhances plane and form, often sumptuously, but without smothering it. The dome of the building, in itself a huge urban ornament without any utilitarian function, is enriched with cast lead shells and other features, executed by H.C. Fehr from Rickard's original sketches. Along the base of the dome, at its chamfered angles, are lead trophy groups – urns, helmets, crowns, flags, spears, swords and standards beautifully cast by Singer of Frome to the designs of Henry Poole. Architecturally, these help in the transition between the vertical stone wall plane and the curved lead surface of the dome. In addition, they are at the chamfered corners

Figure 4.7
Wesleyan Central Hall. The dome with its cast lead enrichment is, itself, a huge urban ornament, and like that of St Paul's Cathedral, is not seen from the interior

of the central block of the building, exposed where the surrounding masses are terminated vertically.

Most of the wall surfaces are rusticated, with heavily incised joints between courses, with occasional smooth bands and panels of stone. Beneath the corner trophies, for instance, are tablets, without inscription, flanked by swags and draped with flags or cloth hung from spears. This excellent carving, and much other work on the building, was by Poole. On the main façade, tablets are set between columns in the space above the arched window heads and below the attic storey. Helmets or eagles impinge on the cills of the windows above, and lamps on the arch mouldings below. The triglyphs to the frieze have eagles, lion, human and ox heads. The pavilions facing Tothill Street have shields on their rusticated end bays, with a fine display of musical instruments above.

Despite the lavish use of carved ornament, the overwhelming feeling of this building is one of austerity. Certainly, carving is judiciously handled, and specific architectural detail enhances the nature of the building. Cornices and entablatures, for instance, help outline the blocks which mass up to compose the overall form. Columns define the plane of the wall surface, contrasting with the horizontality of the rustication, but not stepping forward to produce strong shadows, or to introduce a rhythm which detracts from the composition.

John Belcher's creative use of specifically architectural detail in Colchester Town Hall is especially interesting, as he was one of the main originators of the Edwardian baroque style. The manner he adopted in this building, built midway through the period, is worthy of further discussion. Belcher used and adapted architectural components for sculptural effect. The striking way in which the columns and pediments on the main façade are used, both inherently in the building design and to emphasize the building's position within its context and the urban hierarchy, is an example. The heavily modelled cornice helps to tie these elements, and forms a strong line to terminate the building's façades. Above, there is a balustraded parapet, the receding plane of the roof and, seen from the High Street, the coat of arms and tower beyond. The building has a stone façade at ground floor level, with heavily incised joints. The keystones to the windows that penetrate this stone work break forwards and are decorated with masks and volutes, effecting the planar transition to the projecting string course above, which marks the termination of the stone cladding. In the storeys over this, the wall is brick with stone used as dressing around windows and for niches and balconies. Each niche is a small theatrical presentation of its sculpted character, on the High Street front, bracketed out from the wall, surrounded with a flounce of stone with a smooth, creamy recess behind. The niches and window surrounds to West Stockwell Street are linked by a string which sweeps out to take in the stone blocks supporting the figures.

The balconies in the bays with segmental pediments are supported on richly carved scrolled brackets, but their balusters are chunky and heavy. Projecting back from the balconies themselves are the strange pedimented aedicules that project through the glazed screens lighting the Moot Hall, to the building's interior.

This exuberant building, however, possesses a clarity in its expression, which some may feel is absent from the buildings at the beginning of the period. C.H. Reilly famously noted, in the 1930s when regard for the bric-à-brac period was at its nadir,

The entanglements of detail, how well we know them even today! But in what was called the 'free classic' of a quarter of a century ago the building was never free from them. Oxford Town Hall ... occurs to me as an example of the kind of works, effective enough on paper ... and attractive to the amateur, which was sweeping the country ...'[3]

The irony is, of course, that Hare was the least amateur of architects. His work at Oxford is in the style of the time, and one that was felt to be appropriate to the city. Nevertheless, it must be admitted that there is a lack of clarity in the hierarchy of detail, say compared to Colchester, which is, in part, a characteristic of the late Elizabethan and Jacobean architecture from which Hare took his inspiration. He also had to expand the detail to the scale of a large civic building. Having said this, its intricacies are excellently executed with style and panache. The simpler, more rustic style to Blue Boar Street is more to modern tastes.

The 'Kirby Hall' gables tend to lose their drama because their surface is covered with detailed carving interspersed between small columns with projecting entablatures – the plane of the major elements is thus broken up, reducing this architectural statement. In addition, the skyline is broken by small obelisks, fussily treated and by mythical and heraldic beasts. The curve of the gable against the sky or roof behind cannot be picked out easily by the eyes. Further confusion reigns in the elaboration of the balustraded parapet with its winged beasts, and the punctuation of the cornice line by the central gable with its carved coat of arms, and the domed semi-turrets which flank the central section of the St Aldate's façade. Admirable though any of these elements may be in isolation, read together they create an effect that is over-busy.

Further down on the façade, the oriel windows belly out from the division between the paved arched ground floor windows. Pilasters on the division sweep outwards to bracket the oriel bases. Above, a strong line of moulding runs right across the front creating a major horizontal shadow line, breaking in and out as it encounters various features. Even so, there is a tendency to weaken the effect by the use of carving to the oriel bellies which detracts from the strength of the horizontal feature. Virtually any opportunities to create strong architectural rhythms are lost by the weakening effect of excessive detail. This is not to say that Hare is incompetent, although the building is, of course, an early work. The elaboration of ornament is of its time, and interacts with the choice of style, from a period of English architecture when originality, qualities of detail and overall ambience are more important than formal quality.

In the near-contemporary Staffordshire County Buildings, where contextual issues dictated the use of a late seventeenth century style, the control of detail seems much more acceptable, and the form less compromised. The carving at both Oxford and Stafford was executed by William Aumonier. This artist–craftsman was one of the most frequently employed of his generation, and his work is found in distinguished buildings by the best of Edwardian architects. However, the design pre-dates the true Edwardian 'Wrenaissance' period by some years. It demonstrates the acceptance by the architect of an appropriate style without the underpinning of historical literature on the period by, for instance, Blomfield and Belcher and Macartney, from which a basis of architectural theory was later derived. In other words, the Staffordshire County Buildings are still bric-à-brac.

County Hall at Wakefield, also designed in the first half of the 1890s, is, like Hare's early work, bric-à-brac in its stylistic eclecticism. Indeed, the architects noted the use of 'English details exemplified in such buildings as Kirby and Wollaton Halls'. However, the decoration is more sparse, and it is easier to read the line of the building. This may have something to do with the nature of the grainy sandstone used, which is not so susceptible to carving as the limestone used at Oxford Town Hall. There are carved relief figures representing Science and Art in the stepped gables facing Bond Street and Cliff Parade, and just below the upper stage of the corner

Figure 4.8
Oxford Town Hall. A 'Kirby Hall' gable at Oxford. The outline of its shape is further elaborated by obelisks and sculptural detail. Geometric patterns, masks and grotesque heads decorate the oriel window

Figure 4.9

County Buildings, Stafford. Despite the use of mullioned windows, and the picturesque oriel to the Chairman's lavatory, Hare confines his detail to places where it enhances the overall scheme of the building

Figure 4.10

County Hall, Northallerton. The central bay of Brierley's building is restrained in its use of carving, and there are no allegorical figures. The overall effect is restrained and elegant

tower. Other decoration is largely confined to the oriels, and the solid balustrade which runs between the pavilions, along the main Bond Street and Cliff Parade façades at second floor level. Apart from this, there is a good deal of plain, undecorated wall area, except in the region of the main entrance. The first floor balcony, forming a corner canopy over the entrance arch, has intricately carved coats of arms between its balusters. Figures in bas-relief sculpture stand to either side of the arch, and seated, occupy its tympanum. They represent Justice, Health, Progress and Education. This building, though, reserves its greatest display of decorative arts for the interior.

Moving a decade on, to the County Hall at Northallerton, the changes in style, and the development of an underlying design philosophy can be clearly seen. The building is a 'Wrenaissance' palace, clearly defined, and disposed around axes. There is no allegorical or figurative sculpture, and the carved decoration is used to enhance and emphasize certain key formal elements. The carving, itself – swags, coats of arms and ornamented capitals – is very much in the Grinling Gibbons-like tradition of late seventeenth century England. All in all, the building is a model of the kind of design that was promoted through the writings of historians and commentators such as Sir Reginald Blomfield, and exemplified in their own works. Brierley's own preference, in any case, appears to have been towards a certain austerity, but the quality of the materials and detailing mitigate against this.

A little later, Lancaster Town Hall illustrates a move away from the 'Wrenaissance' style, and signals the beginning of the end of exuberant Edwardian baroque. It was Mountford's final work, and it is instructive to look back across his distinguished career – first to the eclectic Sheffield Town Hall, built in the early 1890s, through the

Central Criminal Court (Old Bailey) of a decade later, a prime example of high Edwardian baroque, then the dignity and stateliness of Lancaster, with its restrained, mainly architectural detail. Apart from the sculpture in the tympanum of the main portico, Mountford confines himself to decorative swags around openings, executed by Gilbert Seale and Son, a family concern, not unlike that of William Aumonier, specializing in carving and architectural sculpture. In the portico, Seale worked in the medium of 'Stonuvelle', an artificial composition.

The portico contains sculpture by F.W. Pomeroy, who, as has been noted, had a long association with Mountford. Here, he represented Kind Edward VII, seated in his coronation robes, flanked by female figures, 'one holding a mirror and scales representing Truth and Justice; one the sword and the crown representing Freedom and Loyalty'. Then there are two boys holding the arms of Lancaster and Lord Ashton.

This figurative work is constrained within the pediment's triangular tympanum and thus does not interrupt the profile of the architectural elements. The other sculptural work is completely detached – in the form of the Victoria Memorial, facing the Town Hall, set in the square built to complement Mountford's building. The tympanum sculpture is safely contained, and nowhere acts as a foil to the architectural massing, or a transitional mass in its own right, contributing shadows on the façade, and helping the stepping back of the façade, as may be seen in earlier work. From about the date of Lancaster Town Hall, indeed, civic buildings become more severe. Leading architects were influenced by American *beaux-arts* examples, and the emphasis switched from decoration and enhancement to playing a game of proportion, light and mass with purely architectural elements.

Of the two later examples mentioned in this book, the trend is discernible. The Birmingham Council House

Figure 4.11

Lancaster Town Hall. Built towards the end of the period, Lancaster Town Hall eschews sculptural baroque extravagance and takes its character from the work of James Gibbs and his contemporaries

Figure 4.12

Birmingham Council House. The massive baroque detail of the entrance relieves a fairly austere building. The elements are common to *beaux-arts* practice. (Reproduced courtesy of *Architectural Review*)

Figure 4.13
Glamorgan County Hall. This building represents *beaux-arts* design from a young architect. Sculptural detail on the building is all but abolished

extension by Ashley and Newman – much bigger than some other town halls in their own rights, is a severe looking building, despite the continued use of high baroque elements, such as the sculptural treatment of the main entrances. Most detail is rectilinear in nature and the swirling lines and wilful breaking of cornices seen in buildings from a decade earlier has disappeared. Sculptural groups no longer dominate. Although transitional between the baroque and *beaux-arts* phases of pre First World War design, there is a general sternness of appearance which presages what is to come.

Vincent Harris's Glamorgan County Hall has a main façade that could be straight from an American journal of the period. It depends for its relief upon purely architectural detail. There is sculpture, but it is detached, and the groups are kept to either side of the entrance elevation. On the other three sides, the building is treated in a palazzo style, with bare walls relieved by the strong horizontals generated by a heavy cornice with attic above and balcony to the rear.

The buildings signal the virtual end of the arts and crafts tradition of incorporating the works of artists into the exteriors of buildings. One or two examples occur fitfully later in the century, but by and large after about 1910 sculpture, if used at all, was not considered as part of the architecture.

CHAPTER FIVE

Space and organization

The spatial disposition of a building depends upon the variety of spaces enclosed and their relationships. There is no doubt that Edwardian architects employed a great deal of ingenuity in dealing with this aspect of building design and a number of the buildings described in this book were, furthermore, located on complicated and severely constrained urban sites which sometimes encompassed the integration of existing buildings or building fragments.

Despite the problems of location upon a site having irregular boundaries with buildings crowding in on either side, these are, at least, parameters which help the architect to create a responsive design. Where a site is open, then the form of the building responds to a theoretical rationale devised or adopted by the designer.

In creating civic buildings, particularly those associated with local government, the spatial requirements were diverse. The provision of a council chamber, for instance, and a suite of rooms for committees and entertainment on civic occasions, contrasted with the need to create ranges of space for council officers — both individual offices for chiefs and shared offices for clerks and lower grade professional personnel. In addition there was a need for storage space, rest rooms, kitchens, WCs and facilities needed for the operation of the building itself, such as boiler houses and fan rooms. If the building were to be a town hall, then in addition to these, a public hall was usually required with its attendant staircases, lobbies, platform, retiring rooms and so on. In many cases other civic functions were incorporated: police and fire stations, museums and libraries. The task of rationally and successfully organizing these spaces to create a workable solution was no mean feat. In their control of and response to the functional 'programme' of these complex buildings, Edwardian architects produced schemes which function as well as those produced by a later generation for whom 'function' was virtually the be-all and end-all of design.

Of course, the town hall, is at one end of the scale of complexity; library buildings, fire stations and other types are less complicated. Even so, the development of public library design during Edwardian times was an important subject upon which much was written. The degree to which public access was allowed, the way in which control was exercised over the increasingly greater numbers using the facilities, and the balancing of public against private space were all factors that needed to be taken into account.

Town and county halls

Whatever the distribution on plan, the vertical organization of these buildings was very similar. The number of storeys varied, naturally, with the amount of accommodation required and the dimensions of the site, but even so, few buildings were more than three or four storeys high, perhaps with some extra space in the roof. Typically, the ground floors were raised some distance above the surrounding streets or squares. This was so that the most important public reception spaces were located above the jostle, noise and smell of the city outside; in addition, it gave a sense of importance to the contained activities, they literally looked down upon what surrounded them. Finally, of course, the *piano nobile* – as this elevation of the ground floor was termed in classical design – had to be approached by a flight of steps, giving a chance to visitors to reflect, whilst climbing them, on the important and formal activities awaiting. Upward movement is, self-evidently, elevating. In Edwardian times, few would have considered it appropriate to enter direct from the pavement. No one would have considered walking down steps to enter somewhere of social or political importance.

Raising the main entrance floor meant that there was normally a lower ground floor below, partially sunken beneath street level and surrounded by an 'area', so that full height windows could be provided. This enabled the provision of reasonable quality office space, perhaps even a police station. Any further basements provided would normally be for storage, boiler rooms or air handling plant.

In many cases, the *piano nobile* was more than one normal storey in height, giving impressive proportions to the grand spaces contained. Entrance halls often rose through more than one storey and as such may have been surrounded by subsidiary spaces such as cloakrooms, WCs and rest rooms at mezzanine level. Grand stairwells linked the important reception spaces. The first floor in town hall buildings would continue the theme of grandeur, being richly decorated. Above, at second floor level, would probably be standard office accommodation with less lavish floor to ceiling heights. In some buildings, extra floors were accommodated in the roof space and lit by dormer windows. This was one of the features allowed by the London building regulations, so that more office space could be provided, given the severe constraints on total building height. However, it was a useful expedient that was also employed outside London, helping the building's overall bulk to be minimized.

The following examples show both the ingenuity of architects in solving spatial problems and the way in which, in less restricted circumstances, generic solutions were arrived at which would be difficult to improve without the agency of complicated technology.

Green field solutions

The city and county halls at Cardiff and Northallerton represent instances where 'green field' sites enabled planning and layout untrammelled by contextual constraints. Astonishingly, in the case of Cardiff, Lanchester and Rickards complained about conditions imposed by cost limits on what, today, seems one of the most lavish of Edwardian municipal palaces:

> *The site itself gave an opportunity seldom offered in this country, the complete isolation from any other buildings, and the almost ideal setting furnished by the park surroundings naturally suggesting a monument, in the abstract, of the symmetry and proportions commensurate with other public buildings of the Continent and America, where expense has apparently been no obstacle and space has been unlimited.*

However, here, 'the space was adequate, but the reduction to simple terms and anything like monumental simplicity ... was hardly possible, especially as in this case, as usually, the amount to be expended was definitely stated'.[1]

The building was formed as a giant rectangle of two-storey office ranges surrounding a huge courtyard. This was divided by a block containing the assembly hall – with the rates office below – the financial engine which propelled the municipal machine. The space to the south was subdivided by the entrance hall, grand staircases and ante hall. All of the main rooms and offices face outwards from the ranges, a corridor running the full length of the internal perimeter, with corner staircases on the north side.

The south front has the greatest architectural emphasis. Its length is divided by the entrance vestibule and council chamber, and at each end is a pavilion. Behind this richly treated façade at first floor level are the main committee rooms and mayor's parlour, as well as the council chamber. These are reached by ascending either of the twin staircases leading up from the entrance hall to the ante hall – now known as 'the marble hall' – above, a most impressive space, demarcated from the stairs by paired marble columns which run around its perimeter. Light comes in from the sides and streams across the stairwells into its centre. At one end, across its marble floor, doors lead through to the hall, at the other, to the council chamber.

Away from this splendour, however, the building comprises a series of spacious and well-lighted offices, where the finishes employed are much more spartan than in the ceremonial parts of the building. The long distances imposed by running the rooms in sequence to one side of the corridor only, could, no doubt, have been lessened by double-banking the accommodation, yet the corridor would have been a gloomy affair. What is more, there is little doubt that the architects wished to create the impression of long palace-like forms amidst the grass and trees of Cathays Park.

Although Cardiff City Hall was designed in 1897, and was the first building of substance on its fine Cathays Park site; it was not opened until 1906, and within two years a competition was held for the Glamorgan County Hall nearby. The new building, designed by E. Vincent Harris, a rising star in the architectural firmament, is in stylistic contrast to Lanchester and Rickards' exuberant baroque, and also introduces a spatial disposition of clarity and resolution. This is not to say that the plan of City Hall is muddled in its execution. Lanchester was a skilled planner and had a clear and effective brain. Harris's building, however, is typical of the *beaux-arts* movement that was popular amongst young architects. Earlier work is pragmatic, placing an emphasis on pictorial composition and architectural language; *beaux-arts* work is systematic, ruthless in its rationale and aspires to grand classical statements. This is clearly demonstrated by Glamorgan County Hall. Harris achieved an almost

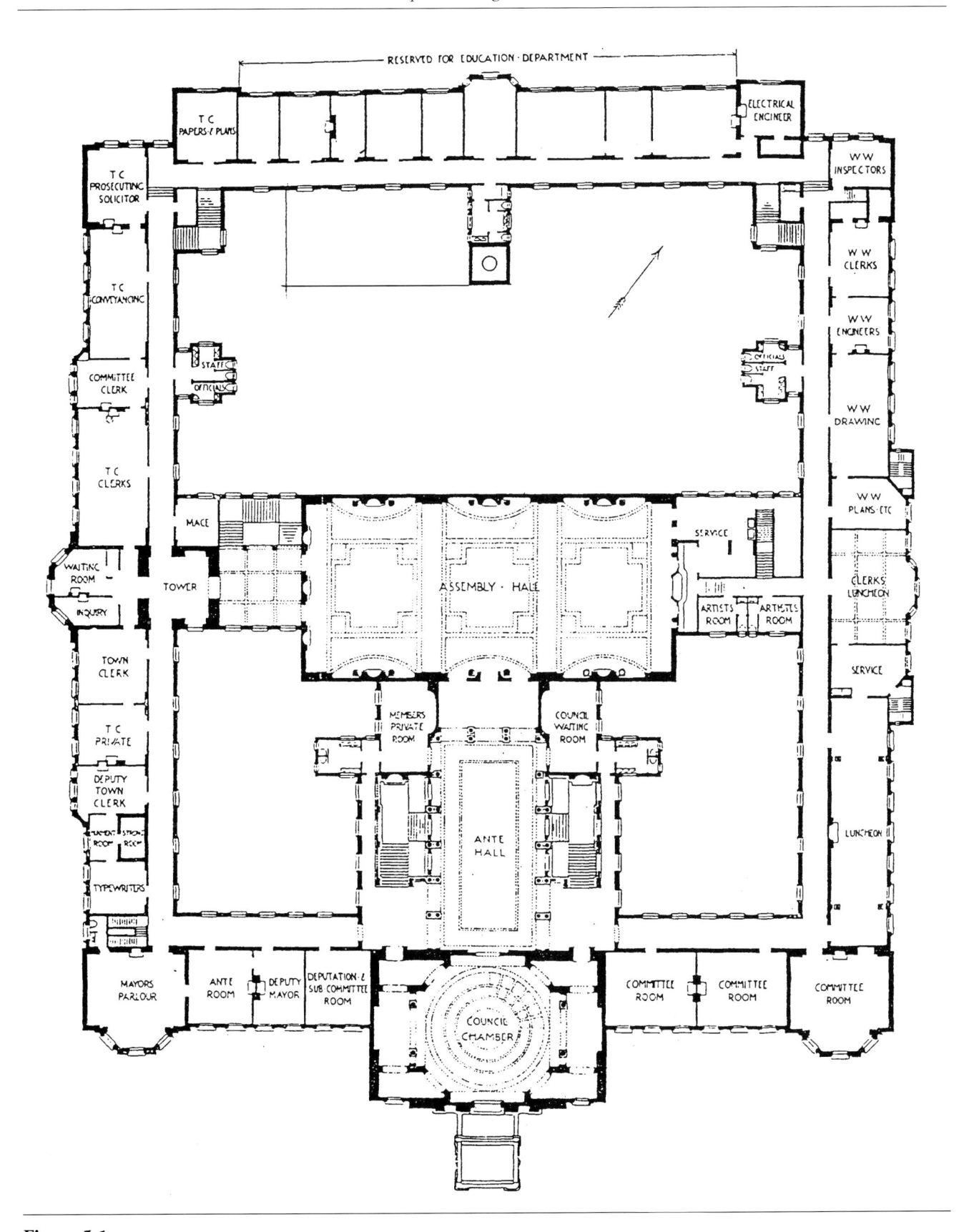

Figure 5.1
Cardiff City Hall. First floor plan. Long ranges of offices are served by a corridor looking onto internal courts. Prestigious accommodation is located on the south façade, with the assembly hall behind

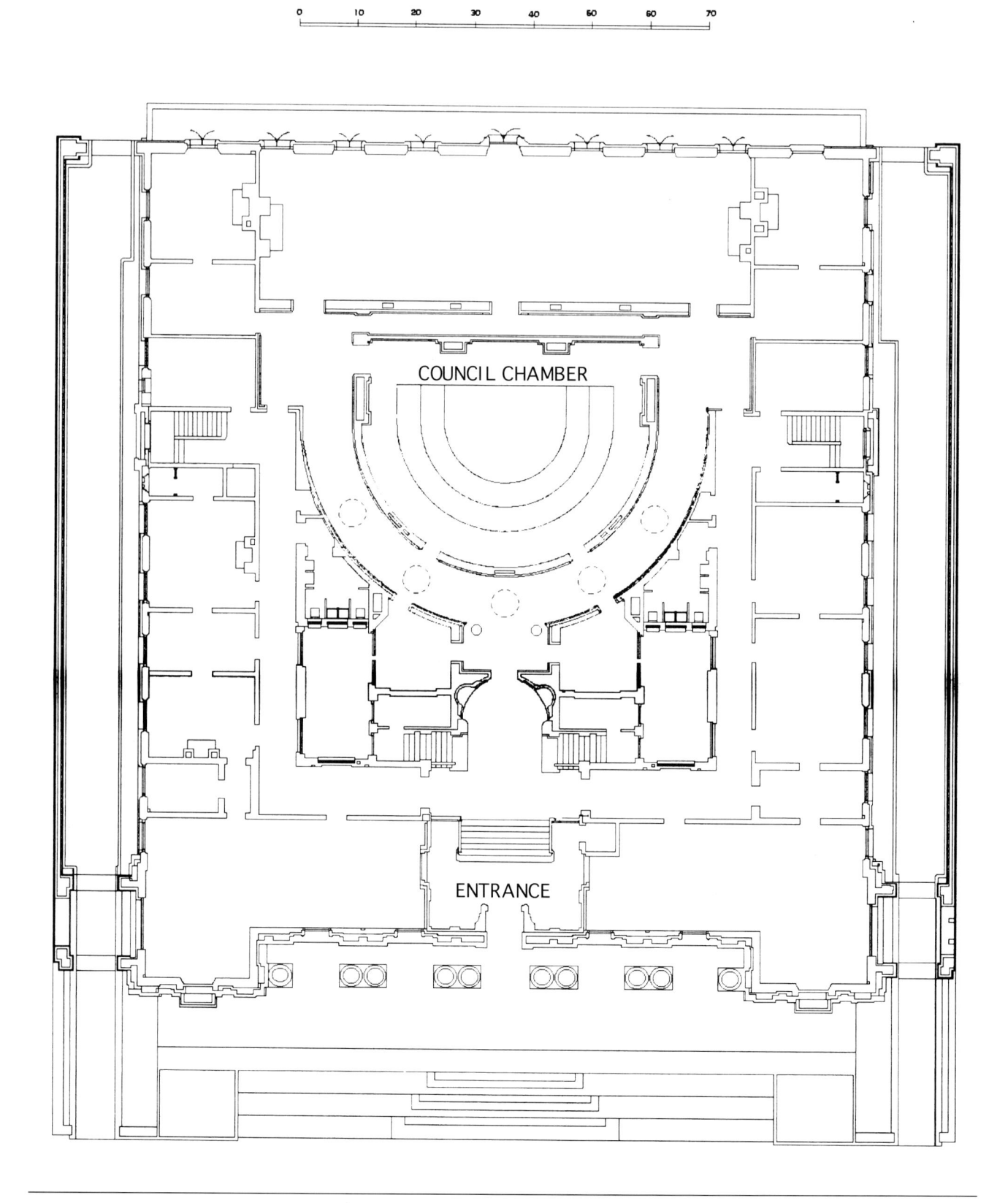

54 Edwardian Civic Buildings and their Details

Figure 5.2
Glamorgan County Hall. Ground floor plan. Monumental, *beaux-arts* planning, showing the change in form later in the period

Roman grandeur and austerity. The council chamber and committee rooms are located at entrance level, with a strong central axis running through the building about which the major rooms are disposed. Subsidiary spaces are segregated vertically, located at first or second floor level. Much use is made of top lighting, which enhances the monumental nature of the spaces. Overall, the plan is a rectangle, into which all internal spaces are fitted in a resolved manner. Whereas irregularity may have been valued at one time, it was now eschewed.

At Northallerton, North Riding County Hall was located in a less elegant but equally free site. A field, 'a stone's throw' from the railway station, if almost a mile from the town centre, was thought to be suitable. The field was 9.75 acres in area and the Souvenir Brochure of the hall's opening in 1906 states that '[the] Site allows ample room ... for the extensions which form part of the scheme now partly executed'. Expansion was always expected, therefore, and the building completed in 1906 was the first phase of a series of developments that went on into the latter half of the century. A north wing was added in 1914, and a south wing in 1929, with other extensions in 1928 and 1937. In 1940, an east wing was built, completing a rectangle with the developments so far undertaken. From this, a new north wing sprouted, projecting towards the police headquarters of 1910. All of this work was undertaken by Brierley's firm to harmonize with the original block, even though the architect of the building had, himself, died in 1926. It was not until 1955 that other hands took over the continuing expansion.

The 1906 building is still the hub of formal council activities with its committee rooms and council chamber. It is composed around a strong central axis, and is a 'dumbbell' plan on two main floors with a long range of rooms facing out to the gardens and site entrance served by vaulted corridors to the rear. The corridors terminate in staircases at either end, where the short north and south wings of the dumbbell return at right-angles to the rear, and are pulled forwards from the main façade to form end pavilions.

The council chamber is a separate rectangular block on the centreline of the main range and to its rear. The staircase from the entrance hall rises half a level to the chamber which is approached through an ante room, in the form of a wide vaulted corridor. The stairs return from this level and terminate on a landing adjacent to the corridor serving the suite of committee rooms. The grand committee room projects out from the range as the centre pavilion over the entrance. Altogether, it is a rational classical plan, well handled, so that the maximum effect is achieved to enhance important and ceremonial spaces.

This main block is generally devoid of standard offices for clerks, but it does contain rooms for the heads of services, the education secretary and the clerk to the council, being located on the ground floor to the left and right of the entrance, and the county surveyor next to the Grand Committee Room on the first floor. This, and the three other committee rooms, are en suite.

Despite the pretensions of this luxurious building, there is a touch of the utilitarian in the inclusion of a muniment room and the technical instruction stores half a level down from the entrance hall below the council chamber! This clearly demonstrates the priorities of the time, but it seems strange that on such a large site, boxes of chalk, piles of textbooks and laboratory flasks should occupy space within the envelope of a building devoted to the enshrinement of the democratic process and the highest levels of operation of a large and important organization.

CONSTRICTED SITES

Unlike the buildings discussed above, those on tight urban sites, such as Colchester and Deptford town halls, still celebrate the importance of public occasion and ceremonial activities by the inclusion of a grand staircase, where carefully considered and often dramatic changes of level lead up from town streets to the great rooms above.

Deptford and its smaller sibling, the contemporary Hull School of Art, both designed by Lanchester, Stewart and Rickards at about the same time, had sites which enabled the development of a squarish plan form. A lighted central staircase hall with associated landings and ante rooms could thus be positioned at the heart of the building, giving direct access to logically arranged rooms around, avoiding long corridors. This arrangement meant that principal rooms could be positioned along external walls and benefit from outward views and light. It was, of course, only feasible with buildings of this modest size. Anything much bigger would have required wings, or long ranges grouped around large open internal courts.

The central hall has the disadvantage of requiring a deep access lobby to the hub of the building through the outer ring of rooms. At Hull this is achieved by pulling the entrance out under the projecting segmental bay above, and positioning the supporting columns on the platform at the top of the steps leading from street level. The doors to the interior are then set back well behind the outer skin of the building, reducing the depth of the entrance vestibule. Thus, those entering pass through an external porch, and then a square vestibule. A passage with access to side rooms draws the visitor on to the hall with its higher levels of illumination. At Deptford the process is similar, with progression through three zones before the entrance hall itself is reached.

Figure 5.3

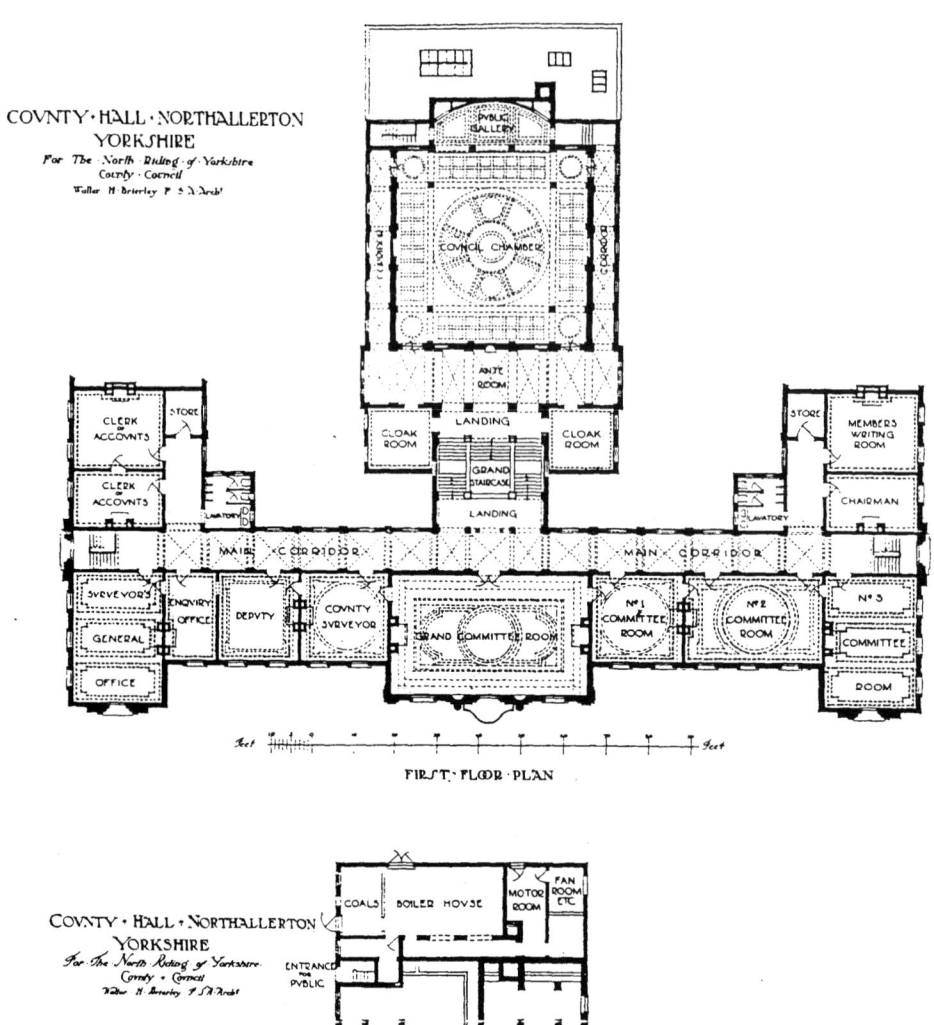

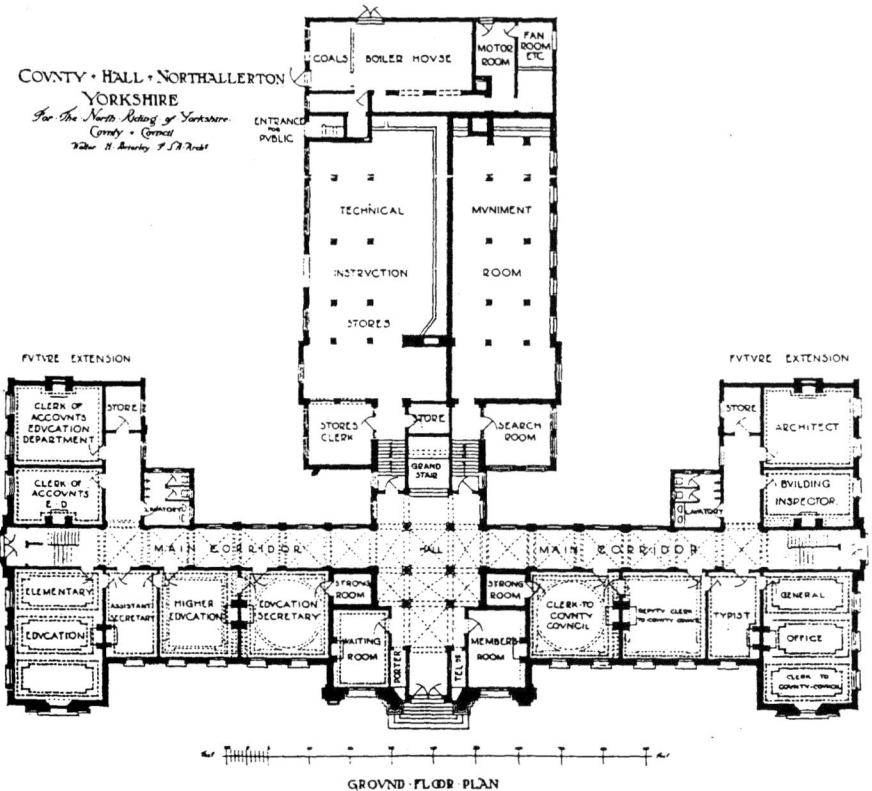

County Hall, Northallerton. Ground and first floor plans. The building was designed for expansion from the outset. The green field site allowed for a palatial main façade and approach

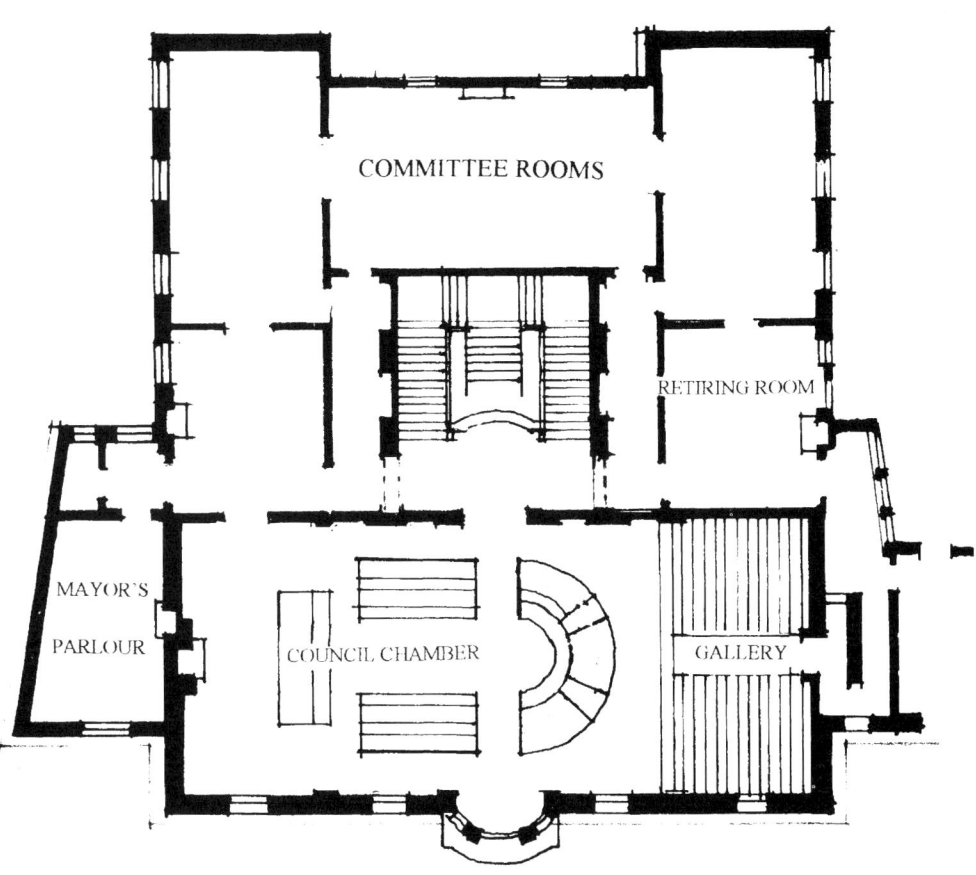

Figure 5.4

Deptford Town Hall. First floor plan. The plan is disposed around the fine central stairhall

At ground floor level, in the town hall, the rooms of the chief borough officers and their staffs are reached through a series of carefully designed ante spaces, peripheral to the hall. On ascending the main staircase centrally to a mezzanine landing and then back up on either side of the hall a gallery is reached which fronts the council chamber, running full width across the building at first floor level. The doors to the chamber are on the axis of the staircase, and the architects have pulled out a little segmental balcony here, opposite the doors and projecting over the stairwell.

As in other respects, these relatively small civic buildings by Lanchester, Stewart and Rickards are excellent and inspired examples of the fusion of planning logic, spatial control, detail design and artistic integration.

Belcher's Town Hall at Colchester is, similarly, a first rate work of architecture. Unfortunately, the shape of its site does not allow for the centralized planning described above. However, the architect continues to make the staircase the element that holds the design together from the point of view of the building user. The shaft is situated at the rear of the main range of the building, its window looking into a small irregular vertical space between blocks. Certainly, the level of illumination afforded by the landing windows and toplight help it to act as a visual focus, and its central position along the length of the main range cuts down the length of horizontal circulation along corridors which serve accommodation on either side. The line of the corridors is offset on plan from the first floor where committee rooms and the council chamber are entered, to the top floor where the width of the moot hall pushes it back towards the stairs.

Big, important spaces are, of necessity, stacked one above the other in this design, with the public hall right at the top, yet the spatial control exercised by the architect makes what is a difficult problem seem simple. Vertical progress is pleasant and stately, with broad, shallow stairs, despite the limited plan spaces which make it possible.

On a much smaller scale, Hare's Henley Town Hall, is a compactly designed building. It occupies a rectangular block, its main façade being on a short side, facing downhill. The gated entrance porch is located at the top of a flight of steps, beneath an elaborate pediment, overlooked by the clock tower. The main staircase, public vestibule and entrance spaces are at this end of the building. On the principal entrance floor, the building is divided into four compartments, latitudinally: the main circulation spaces; two committee rooms with a central, vaulted ante chamber giving access to either side; a council chamber, also doubling as a court room; and, beyond, a stairwell giving public access to the hall on the top floor, a kitchen, WC and service stair. On the floor

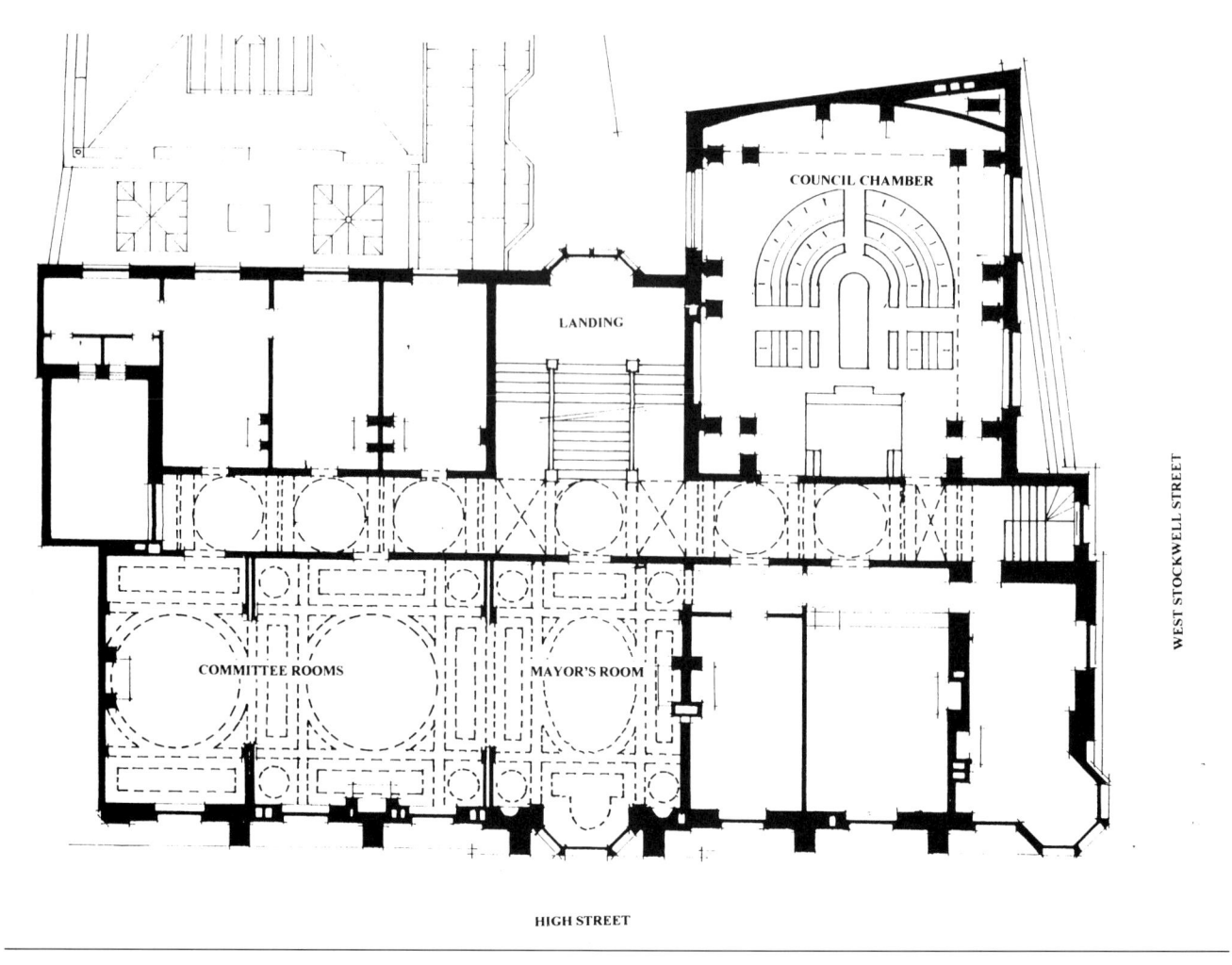

Figure 5.5
Colchester Town Hall. First floor plan. This is the plan as originally conceived, and though slightly altered in execution, shows the way in which lavish accommodation was positioned on a tight, historically significant site

below is office accommodation for the borough surveyor and his clerks, other offices and a drill hall. The top floor is occupied by the public hall, with a platform and retiring room at one end. A service room at one side indicates potential for banquets and other civic occasions.

In common with many buildings of this type, given the floor to ceiling height, Hare has taken the opportunity to introduce a mezzanine floor between the entrance level and the hall. In this he has located the caretaker's flat, though the bedrooms are in the roof space. The whole layout provides dignified accommodation within a comparatively small envelope.

Lining the street

Stockport Town Hall and West Riding County Hall have long ranges of office space and formal rooms like Cardiff and Northallerton, but modified by the nature of the site. At Wakefield, for instance, the Rishworth House Estate, which was purchased for the erection of County Hall, was of ample size for the building but was bounded by a rough parallelogram of streets. The main ranges, therefore, line Bond Street, Cliff Parade and Burton Street, with the most important rooms facing the former. Rishworth House was retained during the building process so that council functions could continue, but what was left after the main ranges were taken into account was a diamond shaped open internal space, broken at its eastern corner. The design of Gibson and Russell splits this into two, with a large-scale block containing the council chamber, its ante rooms and the grand staircase. Regrettably, and in accordance with Edwardian practice in general, there seems to have been no attempt to treat these spaces as anything other than huge light wells.

In compressed plans, as has been seen, spaces are arranged around a central circulation hub. Where the site allows expansion, then, in many cases, the circulation is still kept to the centre. Wakefield, Cardiff and

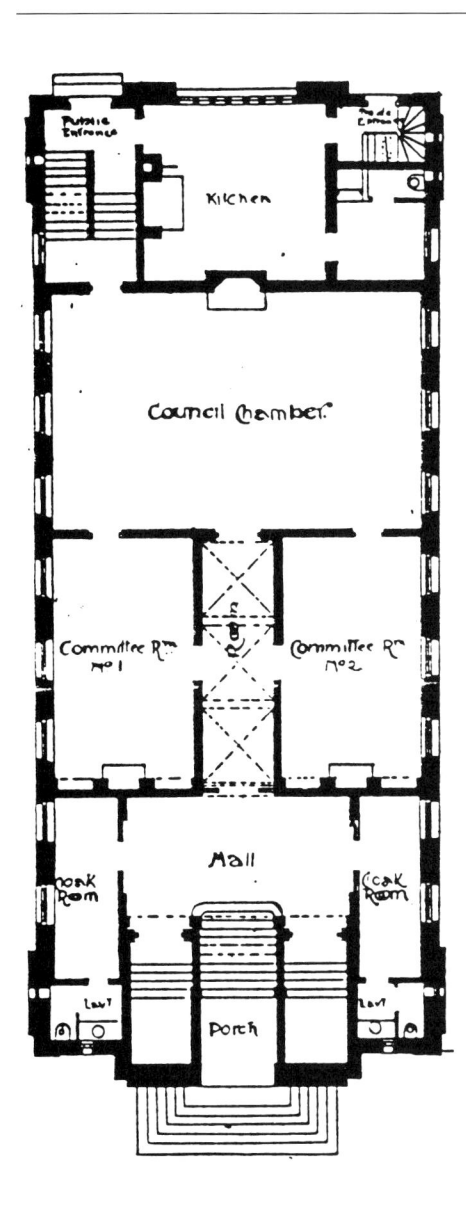

Figure 5.6

Henley Town Hall. Upper ground floor plan. Hare's clear division of space within a simple rectangular form

Stockport all have a planning system with rooms facing outwards along the ranges, and a corridor serving them looking onto the inner courts. This 'race track' approach is hardly compact, but does allow corridors to be well lighted and varied, so that although clerks may have to trudge lengthy distances between departments, at least the journey is a pleasant one, and, in addition, ceremonial and other important spaces can be treated expansively and in a dignified fashion.

At Wakefield, the internal wing, bisecting the courtyard, effectively producing two triangular light wells, is broader than the other ranges. Its angle is such that the axis of the entrance to the building at the junction of Bond Street and Cliff Parade is carried through the main entrance hall and council chamber. Thus it is possible to progress through an enfilade of spaces from a corner entrance, usually something that is inconsequential and difficult to handle in architectural terms. The council chamber is at the heart of the complex.

Stockport Town Hall, is built on a sloping site, and one that has a very definite front and back. Unlike the West Riding County Hall, it has to accommodate a large public hall, as well as the suite of formal council rooms and the council chamber. In the main, though, it follows the pattern adopted by Cardiff and Wakefield, of single aspect accommodation served by a corridor looking onto an internal 'area'. The council chamber, like that at Wakefield, divides

Figure 5.7

County Hall, Wakefield. Ground floor plan. An example of long office ranges served by a corridor facing internal courts. The overall plan is a parallelogram responding to the street pattern

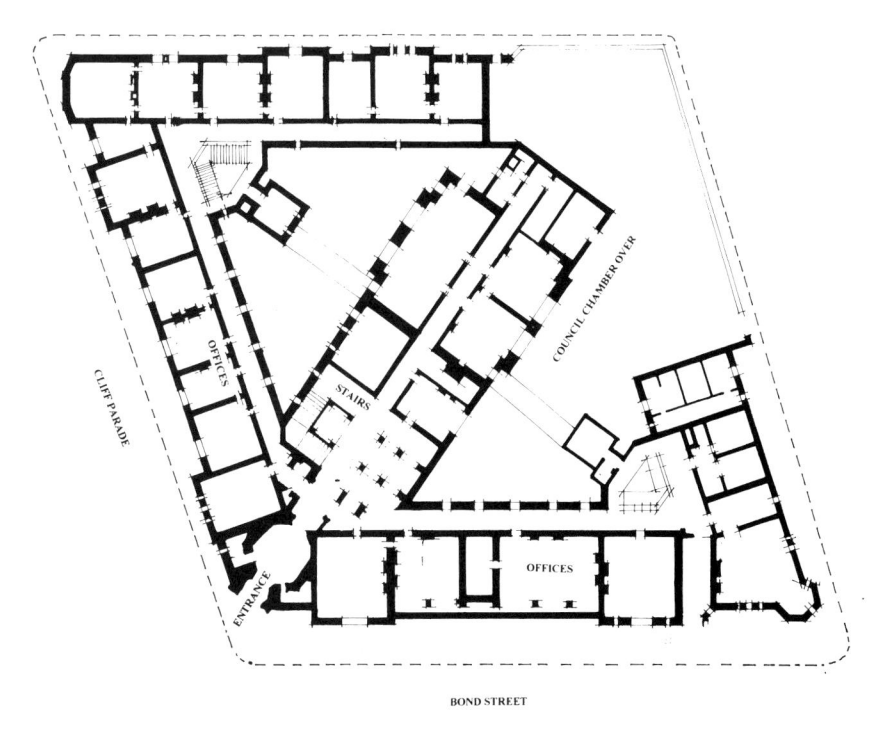

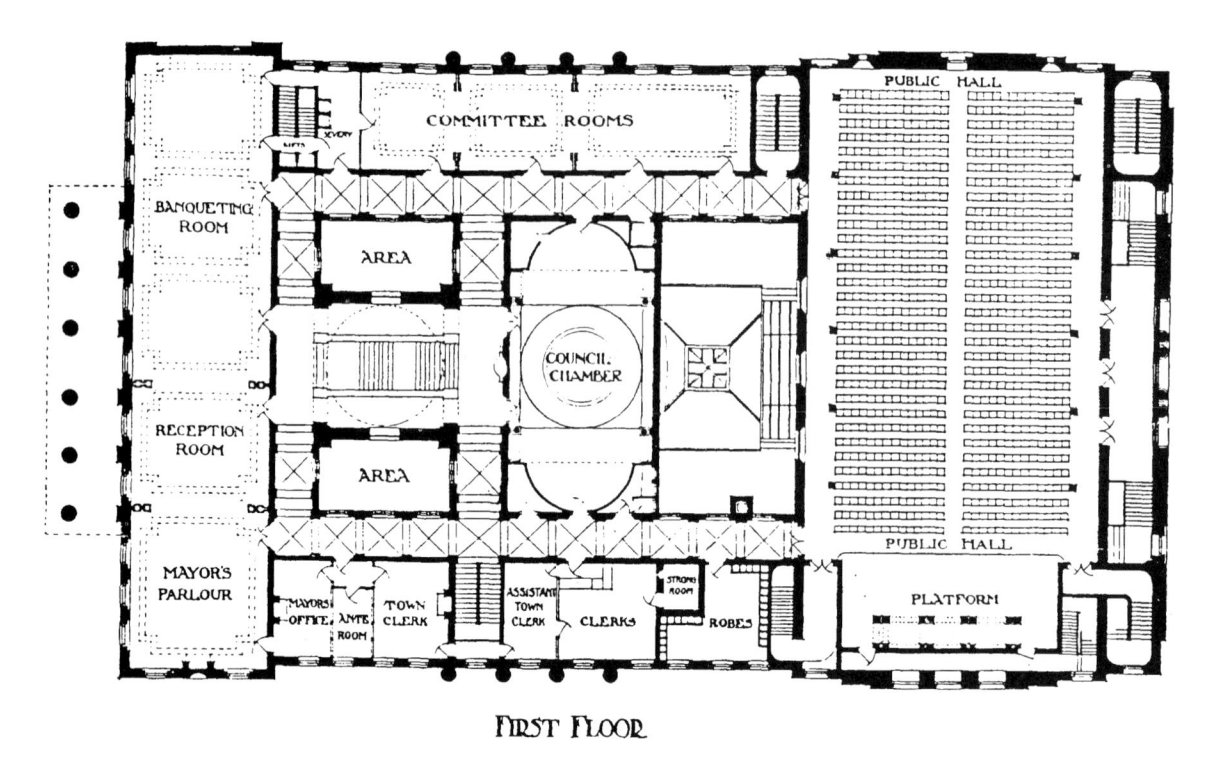

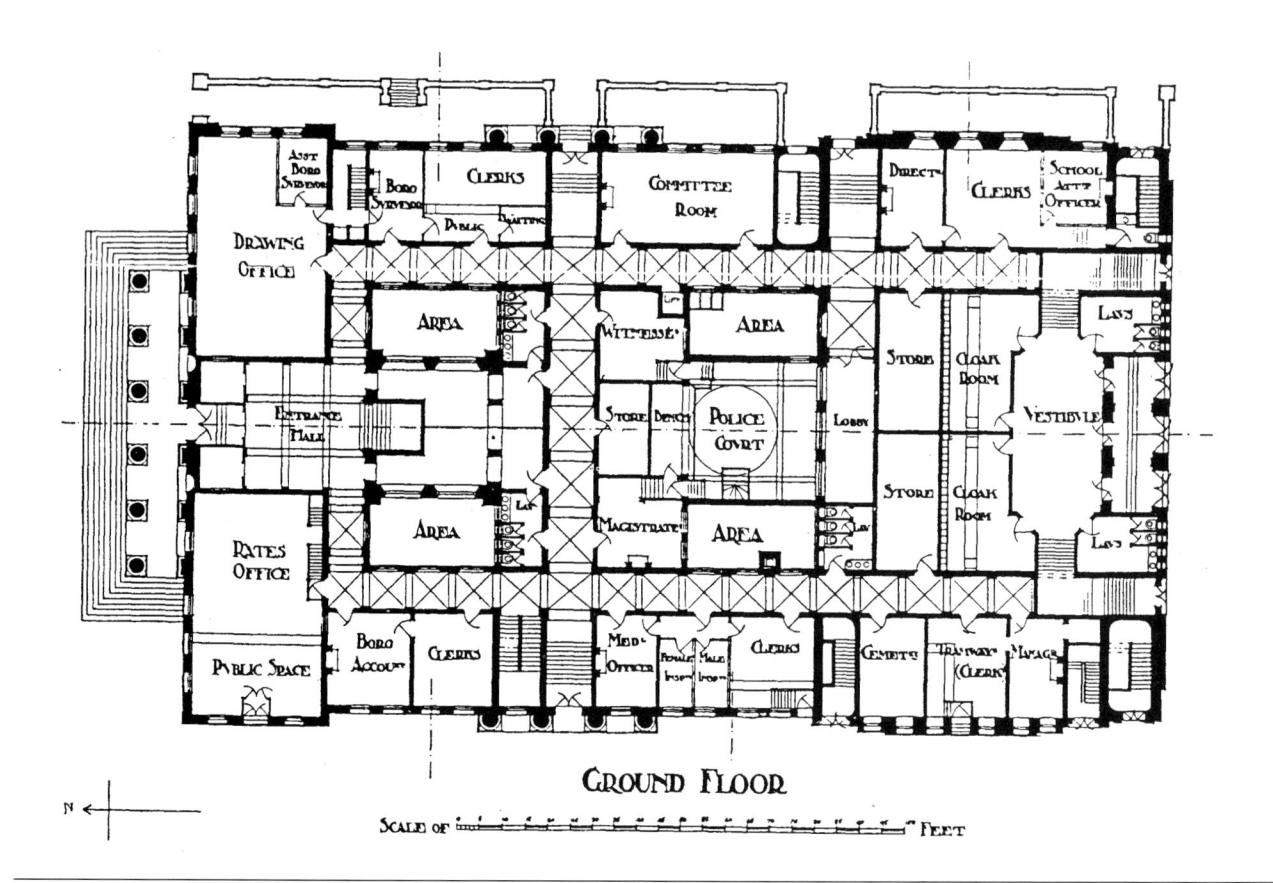

Figure 5.8

Lancaster Town Hall. Ground and first floor plans. A compacted and rationalized plan, though on a large scale

the internal space, except that the site at Stockport allows a conventional orthogonal plan, with right-angled corners. The fourth side of the rectangle, though, comprises the public hall and its associated circulation areas. It is of a very different spatial nature to the rest of the building, but constraints of site size do not allow it to be separately articulated or expressed. Despite the apparent grandeur of the building there is a good deal of diverse accommodation packed into one place. Lanchester's comments at Cardiff are more understandable in this context, however splendid Edwardian civic buildings seem to modern eyes.

Like Stockport, Lancaster Town Hall has a regular rectangular plan; reception rooms, committee rooms and offices are ranged around the perimeter of the site and served by a corridor. Like Stockport, too, Lancaster has a large public hall at what may be described as the 'rear' of the site. This is because although Lancaster can be appreciated in the round, it has a definite front, facing a specially modelled public square. The hall is simply bounded by a narrow street.

There is not adequate room on the site to create a large open internal court, and the centre of the building is occupied at ground floor level by a police court, and at first floor level by the council chamber. Nevertheless, light is admitted to the heart of the building by 'areas' within the overall building envelope. It seems that the architect, Mountford, produced the conventional plan form discussed above and that the council chamber occupies the central void in the same way as at Cardiff, Wakefield and Stockport.

The great extension to Birmingham Council House, located on its island site, and connected to the existing accommodation by a bridge, linking the art galleries, over Edmund Street, is similar in terms of spatial organization, even though it is on a very large scale. Ranges of offices line the streets around the perimeter of the site, and the internal void formed is subdivided and impinged upon by internal spaces. This gives rise to a series of courts which light the adjacent rooms. Here in particular, a huge general office, related to the gas department, projects backwards from the Edmund Street range into the midst of the site, and is linked towards Congreve Street and Margaret Street by further narrow blocks of offices.

As far as civic buildings on open or distinct urban blocks are concerned, the use of perimeter ranges containing central courts broken by large scale accommodation seems typical.

KNITTING IN

Thus, where space permits, a definite planning typology can be seen. There are cases, however, where sites are so complicated or restricted – particularly in city centres, that the architects' desire to organize logically and hierarchically has had to be subjugated to the urban morphology. Hare's early work at both Stafford and Oxford falls into this category. The Stafford building is, perhaps, the most extreme case, knitting into existing buildings in a city centre block, with its main façade facing a narrow, secondary street and its formal entrance through the extension of an existing loggia. There is, of course, no requirement for a public hall here, but there is still a need for a council chamber, associated committee rooms and dignified circulation areas. Hare located the grand spaces at first floor level. Below, a vaulted central corridor leads to a range of offices on either side, approached from an entrance hall, which is at the centre of the Martin Street façade.

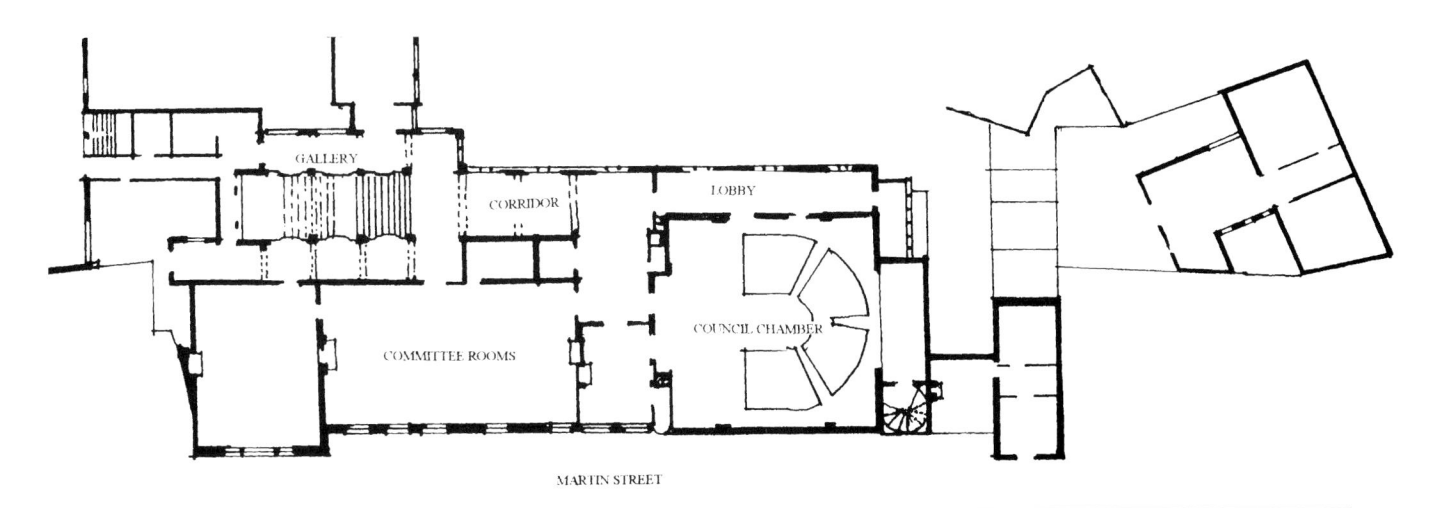

Figure 5.9
County Buildings Stafford. First floor plan. Essentially a linear building but linked to other properties and knitted into the urban fabric

There is no formal connection between the two classes of accommodation, but there is a physical connection – Hare contrives a grand staircase relative to the councillors' entrance from the loggia of the Judge's House rather than the Martin Street entrance (used by officials). The staircase is surrounded by a gallery then a broad corridor leads to the council chamber, its ante room and the members' lobby. There is little spatial correlation between the planning of either floor, although Hare skilfully organizes lines of structure to follow through from one to the other. Nevertheless, the design is a clever and successful scheme, reconciling different functions and spaces, the need to respond to existing fabric, and the requirements of both an administrative and ceremonial building. At Oxford Town Hall, Hare is, again, dextrous. Here, the necessity was to address a major thoroughfare with a grand statement, and then to shoehorn extensive and diverse accommodation – including a public hall – in part of a city block, whilst also composing an elevation to a narrow side street.

As originally conceived, the Oxford Town Hall was really three buildings in one: the public hall, civic suite and administrative offices; the public library and the police station and sessions court. To provide for such diverse functions on a tight yet prestigious site in the centre of a historic city would seem nothing short of alarming to a present-day architect, yet Hare achieved a fine building from what, even for him, must have been a testing problem. With the passage of time, of course, both the library and the court/police station have been moved to new sites to allow for their increased use.

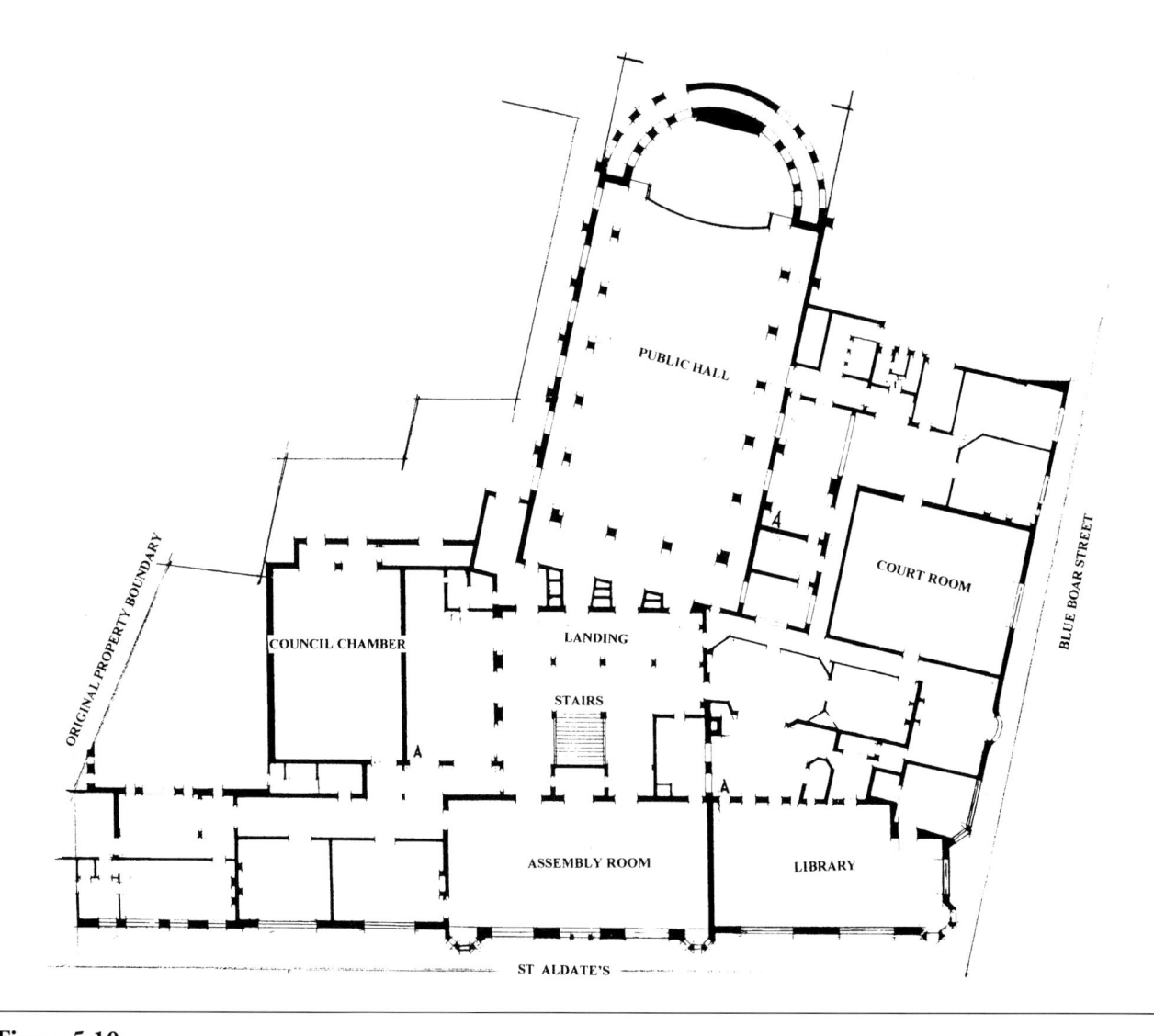

Figure 5.10
Oxford Town Hall. First floor plan. Hare's skill in building a 'portmanteau' town hall on a difficult historical site is illustrated in this plan. 'A' denotes 'area'.

The site, itself, was cobbled together from a number of properties of irregular shapes and disparate areas, and its maximum depth was just over 68 metres. However, although propriety did not allow a tall building, there was the possibility of vertical as well as horizontal diversity, and the competition documents noted that 'cellars will be required under all buildings'.[2] Incidentally, there is the remains of a notable late medieval cellar contained within the later work. Above, is a ground floor, grand first floor and a second or attic floor. The schedule for competitors was most particular about what accommodation should be provided on what floor, and specified the dimensions of even insignificant rooms down to the nearest foot (e.g. solicitors' room 23 ft × 14 ft) whilst noting 'The measurements hereunder are presented as approximate only'.

The council required that the library should be located at the corner of the building. Moving away from this, to the east, along Blue Boar Street, was the police station and court rooms, whilst council offices and civic suites ran up St Aldate's to the north. The large 'single cell' spaces – the public hall and the council chamber – were positioned in the inner angle formed by the 'L' shape of the building served by a grand central hall and staircase, but remote from the streets. In order to provide this deep plan layout, light and ventilation had to be admitted to the building. Hare achieved this by the use of three 'areas' – spaces between chunks of building too small to be internal courtyards, but too large to be described as light wells. One of these – to the south west – takes up the crank in the plan, where the angle of the Blue Boar Street range adapts to the St Aldate's range. This admits light to what was the library. Another 'area' to the east of this allows light and ventilation to the police cells and parade room at ground floor level, and the south side of the public hall above. A third 'area' lights offices and cloakrooms on the ground floor and the council chamber and staircase at first floor level.

Although the minor staircases forming the vertical connections between floors are positioned from the point of view of convenience, that serving the library near to where the west and south ranges meet at the corner oriel turret, is separately expressed and helps to articulate the change of form and style. However, it is the willingness to devote a large amount of space to the grand staircase, entrance hall and first floor galleries at the heart of the building that helps to make the plan work, at least as far as the town hall element is concerned. In addition it helps to resolve the axial change – from that related to St Aldate's to that related to Blue Boar Street.

As far as the allocation of areas is concerned, the usual town hall pattern is followed, with offices allocated to borough business on the ground floor and council chamber and committee rooms over. The library had lending and reading rooms off the street entrance vestibule, whilst the more splendidly treated reference library was at first floor level.

Similarly, the police station and its associated areas occupy a ground floor location, whilst the sessions court is positioned above. The line of the heavy wall forming the western end of assembly hall demarcates police and civic functions at ground floor level, and is followed by a public corridor.

The resolution of so many disparate areas is testament to Hare's skill as an architect, but, this was just part of his task in designing Oxford Town Hall. At a time when buildings have become increasingly specialized, the location of all these public functions on one site and the fact that the architect was not only able to cope with them but to produce a memorable building seems a monumental achievement.

Libraries

Town and county halls had to respond to specific local conditions and requirements, and the need to transmit appropriate symbolism, but although plans were varied, certain types can be discerned. In the case of public libraries, the dictation of functional requirements, and similarities in location and size, lead to the identification of types of planning solutions that were illustrated in books and articles written on library design. Given the number of libraries constructed, some degree of standardization in spatial provision was inevitable. In some cases, however, libraries were seen as institutions simply concerned with the handling of books, in others as the hub of community life, with galleries for the display of art and lecture rooms also provided. The Carnegie Corporation even went so far as to publish a leaflet, *Notes on the Erection of Library Buildings*, which called for the library to act as a community centre with an auditorium and provision for other leisure activities.

Most British central libraries, and the larger branches, contained common provision: a lending library; a reference library and reading and newsrooms. The reading and newsrooms were, at the time, heavily patronized, and it was normal to provide a large area with easy access from the street. Although librarians may have been in favour of single-storey accommodation, it was rarely possible to provide this, because of the size of urban sites. Reference libraries were frequently located at first floor level; one had to make an effort to get there, but there was something satisfying in the act of rising up and ascending to the higher planes of knowledge. Lending libraries could be located at ground or first floor. Many were of the 'closed' rather than 'open access' type. Books were chosen from a catalogue and their availability noted from an indicator board, located in a public vestibule, and orders were given over a counter to a library clerk who retrieved the desired volume from a stack behind.

The provision of these facilities, therefore, generally required three substantial spaces located convenient to a public circulation area, large enough to enable people to collect their thoughts, organize their load of books, meet one another and read public notices. In some cases this circulation area was located centrally, in others, perhaps the majority, it was at one side of the building. There were, of course, other non-public rooms to be provided: staff accommodation, storage and handling facilities, rooms for binding and cataloguing, and sometimes a caretaker's flat. These were usually relegated by architects to basements, mezzanines and roof spaces.

Within the designs of major rooms some, like reference libraries, seem to follow a standard pattern. Open and closed access lending libraries, however, operated very differently. In the 'closed' system control was absolute, and the designs for these are similar to banking halls – a large volume divided by a counter and screen, in front of which the public congregate, behind which the clerks perform their functions, safeguarding the store of knowledge. The 'open' system allowed for free browsing, and planning layouts were devised in order to ensure surveillance down the rows of shelving, with control over the entrance and exit. This was so that books would not be stolen and so that behaviour could be monitored.

Holden's Central Library at Bristol, on its steeply sloping site, must have caused problems to the library staff because there was no alternative but to segregate accommodation vertically. A small lift was provided but one supposes this was hardly adequate given the scale of operations. The basement to Deanery Road is, in fact, set at a higher level than the accommodation to its south, which is level with Lower College Green. This zone contained inspection and storage space for books and newspapers, with a patents room on the Deanery Road

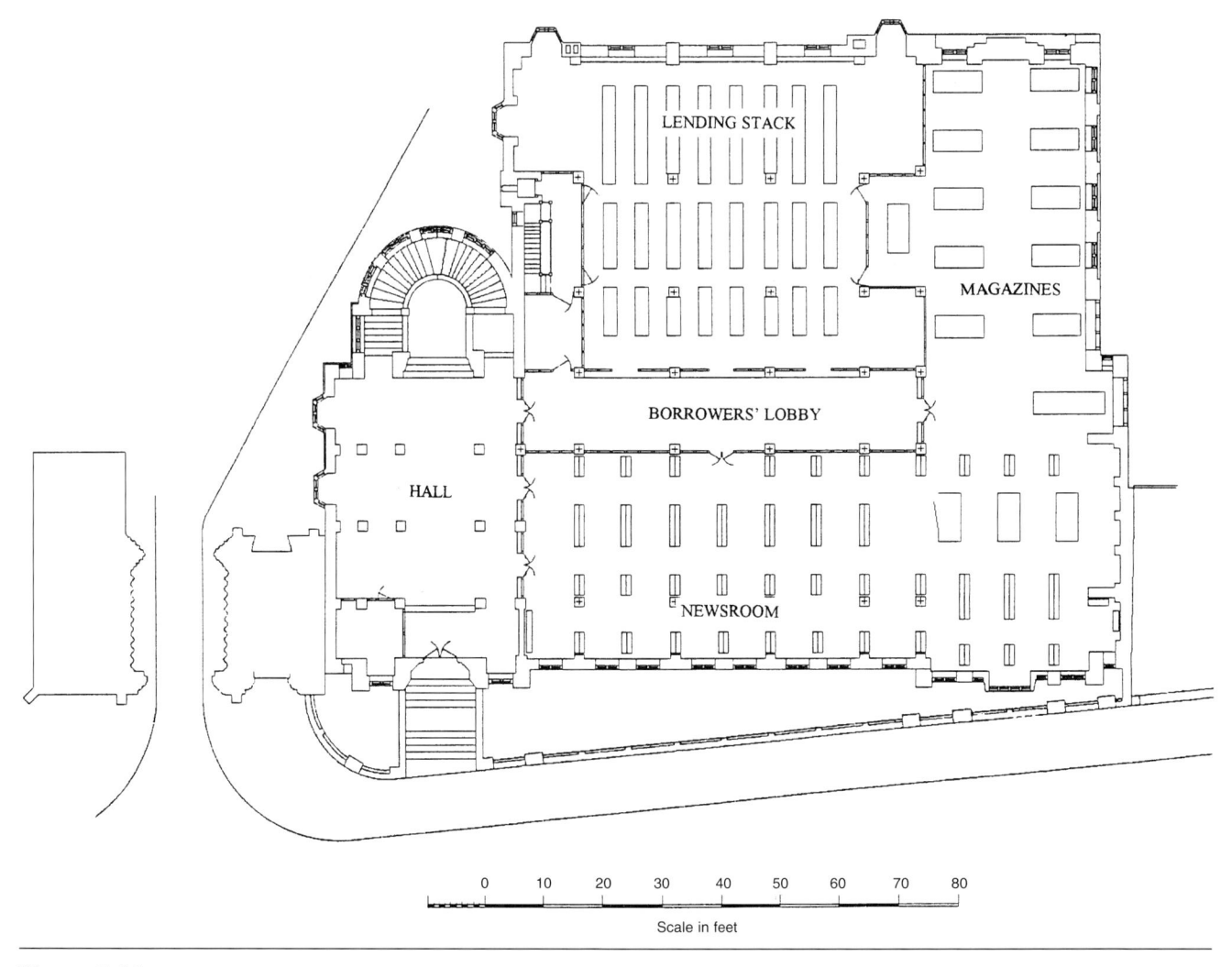

Figure 5.11

Bristol Central Library. Entrance level plan. A large library with a deep plan and side access and circulation on a steeply falling site

side. To the south, a horizontal division was made by a mezzanine below which was provision for the lower floor of the caretaker's residence, male staff mess and cloakroom and a boiler room. Above, the women could eat, unmolested by men.

At public entrance level – ground floor to Deanery Road – were the hall and staircase, the news and magazine rooms and the lending library. Over this, stretching the full length of the north frontage, was the reference library. To the south, the administrative offices, 'Bristol Room' and a broad vaulted corridor leading to the reference library, surrounded an open light well, which also illuminated the lending library book store below through roof lights.

As far as public spaces are concerned, the library falls into a conventional side entrance pattern, with the hall and stairs to the east and the main areas leading off. The building has a deep plan, though, and despite the provision of glazed screens, the north facing ground floor news room must have been dark, and the borrowers' vestibule behind (a 'closed' system was used originally) positively stygian. At first floor level, the plan becomes two interlocking rectangular 'doughnuts' with the open lightwell to the south and a glazed covered atrium to the reference library, which has two gallery levels.

Henry Hare was much involved in library design after the turn of the century, and his scheme for Islington Central has a fine large scale Portland stone baroque façade providing a public face to Holloway Road, with an entrance to one side. This gave access to the accommodation immediately behind the façade, and also to the spaces deeper into the site which run at right-angles to it. It is a two-storey building with the reference library at first floor level, where provision was also made for lecture rooms, administration and a committee room.

The lending library, reading room and 'juvenile room' were all accessible from Holloway Road, although a newsroom was omitted from this scheme. The lending

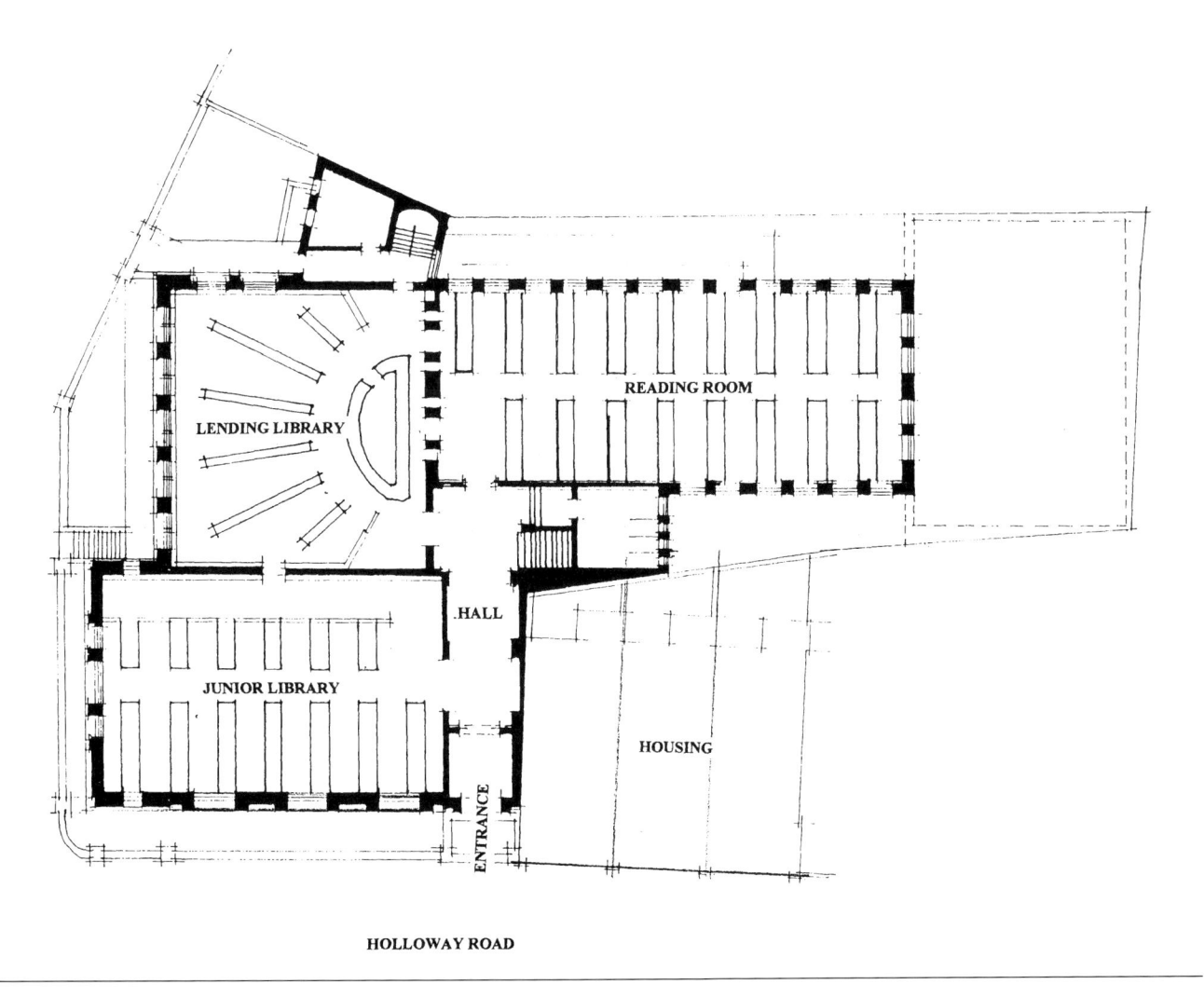

Figure 5.12
Islington Central Library. Ground floor plan. Hare's clear plan features an open access lending library

library plan is square, being designed for the use of an open access system with shelving arranged in a fan shape, radiating from a central desk at the entrance/exit. The principle is rather like a scaled down, part-panopticon.

Hare's earlier library at Wolverhampton (1898–1902) is very different, not only in the choice of style, which is a sort of free-Tudorbethan/baroque mix in contrast to Islington's high baroque. A central entrance hall, entered from an arcaded porch on a corner site, leads to wings to either side, which are parallel to the defining roads. One of these wings forms a square plan occupied at ground level by the newsroom. To the other side of the hall is the longer, six bay newsroom. In the early years of the century, these would have been the most heavily utilized part of the building. Upstairs, after ascending the handsome stone stairs, were the reference and lending libraries. The Wolverhampton librarian was the originator of an indicator system, and the lending facility was therefore of the 'closed' variety, with a public vestibule adjacent to the first floor landing. The reference collection occupied the short, square plan wing. The librarian's room, and the book repairing room were located in the 'web' between the wings, looking out across the road junction from above the entrance hall. A simple but effective plan, this was one of the many variations on the theme of public library design. Although the emphasis on specific provision has now changed – open access lending rooms having taken over from news and journal rooms as the major element in most libraries – it is gratifying to see that Edwardian designs have proved adaptable. They will probably continue to be so as electronic information technology gains importance.

The Wesleyan Central Hall

The Wesleyan Central Hall is, of course, not a civic building in a specific sense, yet it displays so many of the features of Edwardian public buildings, that for the sake of this survey it may well be considered so. It contains public spaces, administrative accommodation and a large hall, in common with many of the town halls already examined. Here, of course, the hall itself predominates to a great extent, and the building is organized in a way that is almost archetypal, with a large single cell space surrounded by lesser halls and rooms.

When conceived, the project was properly called the 'New Wesleyan Central Hall and Connexional Buildings'. Its aim was to mark the beginning of a new century of Methodist activity, but also to provide 'a visible and monumental memorial of the past'. More practically, it was to 'provide ... for the needs of the various departments of the church ...'.[3] To this end, a library, small conference hall and refreshment room were included in the schedule of accommodation, together with suites of committee rooms and offices. The assembly hall was to provide seating for approximately 2,700 people, roughly split between the main floor and gallery.

The main floor of the hall is suspended above the ground floor library and the adjacent small hall, at first floor level. It rises up through the remaining two floors of the building to be crowned by a shallow, saucer-like dome. The great cupola, seen from outside, is independent of this – rather like St Paul's – though having no formal similarity. To the eastern side of the hall, behind the main façade facing Storey's Gate, are a series of crush halls and circulation spaces. These lead up via the grand staircase from entrance level. On the opposite, western, side of the building are banks of offices, though with committee rooms at ground floor, and mezzanine with offices above. The basement has a similar layout, but the large tea-room is interrupted by the column grid carrying the huge weight above.

Essentially, the plan form is square, with symmetry about the east–west axis, and near symmetry about the north–south axis. The main hall is expressed as it rises high above the surrounding spaces, but its walls are exposed on the north and south façades and carried down to ground level in between end pavilions. The internal organization is thus reflected in the massing of the building. It bears no stylistic resemblance to its surroundings, nor does it reflect the shape of the great buildings nearby. Instead, it makes its own statement, a powerful, self-contained form. No doubt, it could have been successfully located in any one of a number of places. One of its objects was to announce Methodism in the capital, and this it succeeds in doing by providing a distinctive element, within sight of the political hub of the Empire.

In summary then, Edwardian civic buildings seem to have resolved themselves into plan forms or spatial organizations that are typological. This is particularly the case in terms of public libraries, where many were constructed during the period and efforts were made by architects, such as Hare, to identify or standardize ways of planning. In town and county halls, the greater complexity and need to respond to differing contexts, leads to greater variety, but essentially the elements comprise ranges of offices, committee rooms, formal or processional circulation spaces, and large single-cells, such as council chambers or halls. Having noted this, one could easily have made a point about diversity. The fad for standardization and the negation of the personal element introduced by the architect was something that would become fashionable as the century wore on.

Despite the diversity of Edwardian civic buildings, there are spatial elements which seem to have become popular if not standardized during the period. Two of the most notable are the council chamber and the reference/lending library, which are discussed in Chapter 7.

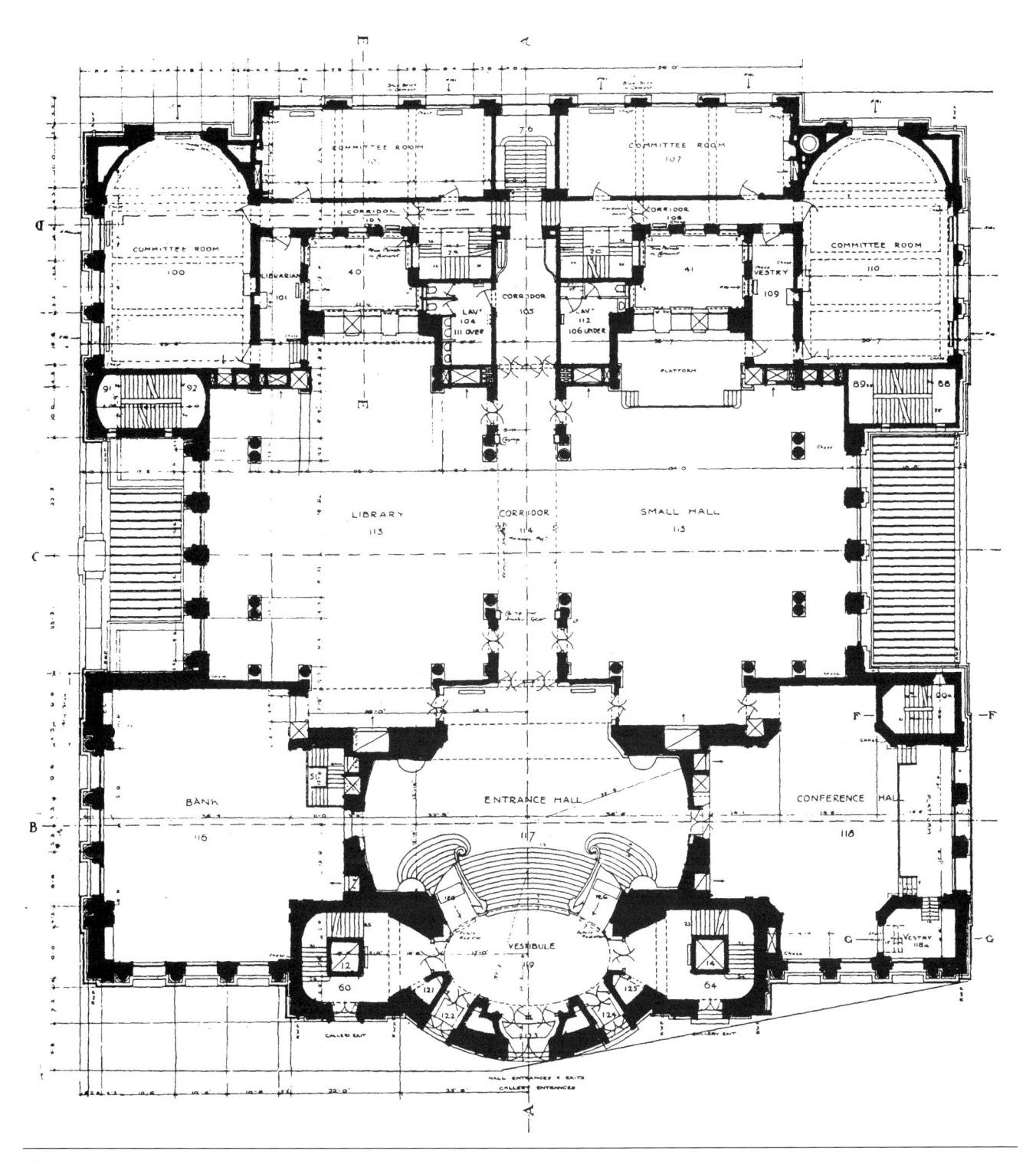

Figure 5.13

Wesleyan Central Hall. Ground floor plan. Accommodation surrounds and is massed up against the great central hall located on the level above. This is similar, in many ways, to theatre planning

CHAPTER SIX

The art of entering

The regard for context displayed by Edwardian civic buildings has been discussed. The building does not exist as a discrete object, but care and consideration is given to how it impinges upon public thoroughfares and open spaces. Important messages are given through the building's language about issues relating both to its functioning and its importance within the city fabric. Manipulation of scale, richness of detailing, changes in texture and colour and the relationship of solid to void are all techniques used in order to achieve this. Linked with this issue, is the question of how the building should be entered. In Edwardian architecture, this is closely associated with the issue of propriety: who should enter, where and how? At a time when etiquette was all important, when class divisions were minutely observed and when people dressed in a relatively narrow range of clothing appropriate to status and occasion, it was inconceivable that all comers should enter an important building in the same place or way.

In addition to this, many Edwardian architects expected the experience of entering a civic building to be a special event, and used their creativity and ingenuity to enhance the process. There is, invariably, careful consideration of the transition from public space (outside) to private space (inside) or from the exterior where a certain type of behaviour is allowed, to the interior, which although still public space, has a more restricted set of criteria applicable to what one might or might not do. The entrance sequence was of paramount importance in conveying these messages.

The main entrance to Bristol Central Library is in Deanery Road. One is kept from approaching the building itself by the 'area' – a slot-like space between the wall and the pavement to enable light to reach the basement windows. For most of the length of the façade, therefore, one walks along railings, designed to prevent hapless pedestrians from falling into the 'area'. The railings are simple in form, but clearly designed to match the gridded rectilinearity of the building. Access to the public entrance is via steps and a landing which act as a bridge across the void, at the east end of the building. Given the symmetrical nature of the Deanery Road façade, the entrance may be supposed to be in the middle, but this is a library with a plan type based on a side corridor circulation space, allowing entry to major ground floor areas, with a staircase at the end for vertical circulation.

A first flight of steps, with five shallow risers, takes the visitor past a pair of lanterns guarding the entrance, onto the landing, which is protected by wrought iron gates, folded back against the railings when the building is open. A further five risers bring the visitor up to the ground floor level of the building, but by the third riser permeation of the building envelope is begun, as the highest point of the arched entrance is passed. At the

Figure 6.1

Bristol Central Library. A model of the entrance sequence, which involves movement outside to inside up a flight of steps, across a 'bridge' and a sequential penetration of the building's stone skin. (Computer generated image: Vasilieos Balampanos)

Figure 6.2
Bristol Central Library. The entrance hall with its mosaic clad vaulting and marble piers is the culmination of the entrance sequence. (Photo: T Lewis. Reproduced courtesy of *Architectural Review*)

position where the keystone is located is an escutcheon, which runs into the corbelling of the oriel above. The opening then narrows and the arch diminishes in height as the stone skin is penetrated. In the tympanum of the arch is the building's name, and a handsome rectangular moulding with rose and foliage carving surrounds the door opening. The doors themselves – two pairs, though with the outer bolted back during normal opening – are plain but well proportioned with a glazed upper half above handsome brass plates. When they are pushed open there is a surprise. Although a few more steps have to be climbed, one is immediately transported into a different and highly atmospheric world. The hall is vaulted, and has big, square piers supporting semicircular arches which delineate the vaults. The main vaults are square on plan, with narrower, rectangular vaults either side; they lead to a short flight of steps and a landing at the end at the bottom of the main stairs. Electroliers hang from the centre of each vault, and the eye is drawn to the increase in light at the end of the hall, where the great curved stair tower rises. What makes the experience of entering more remarkable is colour and texture. The piers are clad in marble up to the springing point of the arches (cipollino dado, Grande Antique plinth and Irish green capping). Beyond this, covering the surface of the vaults, is mosaic – small rectangles of blue glass. There are marble slabs to the floors. All in all, there is almost a feeling of submarine caves about the space. Thus, the citizens of Bristol have been welcomed to their main library for more then ninety years: first by a carefully controlled series of engagements between the public and the building during the entrance process, then a surprising and stimulating experience within.

Edwardian architects were careful to control the entrance process to all public buildings, often in a variety of interesting ways. However, the time-honoured method of approaching an important building, a portico with steps up, was not neglected. Of the examples described in this book, Lancaster Town Hall is most typical of this approach. The great portico, with ionic columns 9.75 metres high, projecting 3 metres from the face of the building, sits upon a podium surrounded by steps. The portico is on the centreline of the façade and of the remodelled Dalton Square with Queen Victoria's memorial in the middle. To advertise the entrance even further, a pediment containing sculpted figures, including the king, rises above, and overall is the clock tower and cupola.

An arched entrance, with niches to either side, gives access to the entrance hall inside, though a few more steps between narrow walls have to be surmounted before the building is finally entered. Once inside, marble clad surfaces predominate, and the grand staircase, 3 metres wide, rises at the end of the 8.5 metres square hall, carrying the symmetry one stage further. Although this somewhat unsubtle progression may be intimidating to the general public, ceremonial and processional sequences were important in the Edwardian view of civic life, and still have a place today. Town halls, after all, are not merely functional buildings, but help to symbolize the image and spirit of a place.

When it comes to making a grand impression, however, Stockport Town Hall is foremost. The problem is that the roadside site does not enable a great axial approach equal to the building, and so some effort is made by locating dogleg steps about a wall and parapet feature on the centreline of the composition. This breaks through balustrading which separates the pavement from the town hall grounds. By mounting the steps, the visitor is orientated onto the entrance axis, and once through the heavy portico is presented with a marble-lined hall and a grand staircase which divides and runs up between fine bronze balustrades to a galleried hall above.

Walter Brierley had no such constraints when he designed County Hall in Northallerton. The green field site enabled him to dispose the building such that a palatial approach was easily obtained. Despite this, the building has a rather private appearance, not forbidding, but very reserved. This is emphasized particularly by Brierley's restrained architectural language, and is less welcoming than its urban cousins.

Before approaching the building, however, the visitor is met by railings marking the boundary between the public highway, which is rather suburban at this point, and the grounds. These railings curve inwards to form a bay, with handsome stone gateposts and wrought iron gates, which open onto an axial drive, lined by shrubs. The drive focuses on the main entrance, on the centreline of the main façade. Although the building is low key with red Leicester stock brick walls relieved by Hollington stone dressings to window surrounds and other architectural detail, most elaboration is reserved for the three-bay central pavilion. The middle of the

Figure 6.3

Stockport Town Hall. The axiality of the façade clearly indicates the entrance, yet the approach has to be made via dog-leg stairs which lead from the pavement running parallel to the building

three bays is stone faced with a broken pediment in the best Vanbrugh manner, and balconied French windows to the first floor, flanked by engaged Corinthian columns rising through two storeys. The entrance itself is an arched opening in the face of the wall, recessed, and sealed by two heavy panelled doors which are approached up a short flight of steps. These are cut back as they rise between the column pedestals, and then through the skin of the building. Beyond the doors is a fairly narrow and rather dark vestibule, illuminated by windows in the door and the fanlight over, yet the eye is drawn forward by the higher lever of light from the windows to either side of the grand staircase ahead. Progress across the hall is demarcated by rows of columns to either side, supporting the vaulted ceiling over; these indicate movement to the staircase, but the main corridor, at right-angles, intersects before the stairs are reached. Increased illumination on the stairs and its landing draws the visitor onwards.

The grand staircase rises first as a single axial element, continuing the dead straight line followed all the way from the public highway. At the top of the flight is a landing and a vaulted ante room to the council chamber. Here the staircase splits and runs back on itself to the landing and corridor in front of the main committee room, which with its balcony occupies the centre position of the façade.

The use of light, the spacing of the columns and the way in which the stairs are used all aid dignified progress through the hall and up the changing levels: from the chequered marble floor below to the council chamber ante room; from the landing up to the suite of committee rooms which forms the main range of the building front. Brierley's restrained use of architectural effects provides an appropriate setting for the gathering of worthies come to debate and legislate on local issues. It is very well judged and a fine architectural experience.

In contrast to the axial approach, corner entrances are usually the most difficult to contrive in architecture. At County Hall in Wakefield, however, although the main entrance is at the corner of Bond Street and Cliff Parade,

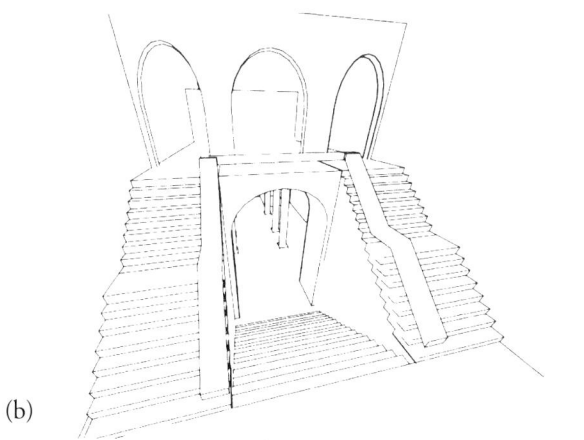

Figure 6.4

County Hall, Northallerton. (a) In a continuation of axiality that leads along the drive and between the columns of the vaulted entrance hall, a staircase rises to the council chamber. A pair of return stairs doubles back to the landing and committee rooms above. (Photo: T Lewis. Reproduced courtesy of *Architectural Review.*) (b) Computer generated image (Vasilieos Balampanos)

in terms of the building's plan form it is at the obtuse angle of a diamond or lozenge shape, and therefore a natural point at which to bring in visitors. There is no public space in which to congregate, and the pavement is comparatively narrow. However, the balcony to the chairman's room projects out, forming a canopy, and the arched opening, protected by wrought iron gates, is carried inwards as a vaulted space, which forms a porch, neither inside nor outside. It is a mixture of public and private space, giving the opportunity for those using County Hall to prepare themselves to enter: to shake off the rain, fold umbrellas, chat briefly to colleagues; to adjust thoughts away from the busy traffic-laden streets to the business that is to go on within.

From the porch, a pair of half-glazed doors leads through into a vestibule, a domed octagonal room with marble floor and walls, the marble panelling being carefully designed around radiator recesses. It is clearly a transitional space, however, and more doors lead into the entrance hall. From the confines of this sequence, space opens out into a large hall, where corridors feeding the main ranges of the building converge, and where a great staircase rises to the upper floor.

The hall is somewhat gloomy, but it is rich and full of incident. Octagonal columns and vaulting give a somewhat 'churchy' feel, but this is dispelled by the 'Wrenaissance' treatment of joinery – particularly a carved door and screen to the main axial corridor. To the walls of the staircase are gesso murals (see Chapter 7) of historical and allegorical subjects – a foretaste of the extensive work of artists and craftsmen to be found on the first floor of the building. The large windows lighting the staircase and landings are filled with stained glass.

The whole effect is somewhat overwhelming and a little confusing. The sandstone vault ribs and piers, and the stained glass contribute to a certain ecclesiastical gloom, but are countered by the polished Hopton wood stone of the staircase and the marble balusters, if not the mystical quality of the arts and crafts murals and decoration. All of this is encountered after a fairly straightforward entrance experience, and only a few metres from the prosaic streets outside.

(a)

(b)

Figure 6.5

County Hall, Wakefield. (a) The entrance is at the angle of the building, and the visitor passes through various stages: first under the balcony, then up steps and through gates into the porch, then into the octagonal vestibule and finally into the entrance hall, from which a great staircase ascends to the level of the council chamber and committee rooms. (b) Detail of the entrance gates. (Photo: Albert Booth)

Figure 6.6
County Buildings, Stafford. The grand staircase rising from the entrance hall to the 'long gallery' above, leading to the council chamber and committee rooms (from a contemporary illustration)

Henry Hare sometimes favoured a different entrance device. It appears in at least three of his civic buildings, though in one case by force of circumstance. This is the loggia. In the case of the County Buildings, Stafford, the tightness of the site and the need to fit into an existing fabric pressed the solution upon him. At Oxford Town Hall and Wolverhampton Public Library three arched openings are employed, and perhaps loggia is too grand a word. In the case of Wolverhampton, this arcading allows the skin of the building to be carried above, whilst at pavement level a sheltered external space is formed for people to wait or compose themselves before being sucked into a maelstrom of traffic at a busy road junction.

A similar feature used at Oxford Town Hall some years before is on the picturesque Blue Boar Street façade, facing a narrow lane rather than a busy junction. But here, too, although providing a way into the banalities of public toilets and a corridor giving access to the police station, it allows one to step back under the protection of the building out of the way of the narrow thoroughfare.

At Stafford the story is different, and more complex. The context of the building has already been described – a town centre block hemmed in by other buildings, and with the main façade facing an inconsequential street. The west side of County Buildings, however, abuts historic buildings facing the Market Place. These are the Shire Hall (1798) and Judge's House (1802), which were 'inherited' by the County Council. Although a fairly modest public entrance to the county offices was provided midway along the new façade, the facilities were intended for the transaction of council business rather than public ceremonial entertainment, and it was desired that the county councillors should enter the building from the Market Place on the adjacent St Martin's Place, near to the ancient seat of county authority. Hare achieved this by extending the arcaded loggia to the Judge's House and placing a discreet entrance within. Although the councillors were required to turn through two right-angles from one vestibule to another before gaining the entrance hall proper, progress would have been quite stately. Moreover, the top-lit, domed hall is spacious, with adjacent cloak rooms, and, at the end, an arched opening leads directly up a grand flight of stairs, giving access to a 'long gallery', above, linking with the council chamber and other principal rooms.

Figure 6.7

Deptford Town Hall. A flight of stairs begins the entrance sequence, before the visitor is brought under the balcony above, and then into a porch. Passing through the doors, there is a vestibule and short corridor, before the domed entrance hall proper with its staircase (see Figure 8.16) is reached

In many Edwardian civic buildings, the use of a balcony is a favourite device – particularly in the case of the town hall, where it might be expected that a local throng would be addressed, perhaps upon election night or a ceremonial occasion. Lanchester and Rickards hit upon the notion when designing Deptford Town Hall. Oddly, though, there is no public space within which an audience can be addressed, only the mayhem of the busy Dover Road – probably a death trap even when the building was built in the early years of the century. What is more, the balcony is attached to a curved oriel window leading out of the council chamber, not the mayor's parlour as may be expected. Nevertheless, the oriel and balcony at Deptford form one of the most elegant features to be found in any building of the period, and, of course, it fulfils the dual function of advertising the entrance and bringing the visitor under the shelter of the building. Here, a relatively steep but short flight of steps is ascended, bringing one first under the balcony and then within the porch, with its wrought iron screen and lantern to the spandrel of the actual opening. The balcony and oriel is supported by a pair of winged tritons. These together with the curving cornice above and the wrought-iron balcony are evidence of the creative fluency and sumptuousness of Rickards' detailing. They are an invitation which it is difficult to resist.

The architects repeated this theme at Hull School of Art, built at about the same time as Deptford Town Hall. It is difficult to imagine that the headmaster would have anything of relevance to say to the fish-filleters bustling by in Anlaby Road, but he has a balcony to the projecting curved bay of his first floor office, supported this time by plain columns. Here, there is a much larger balcony to the second floor, where the bay terminates and a railing curves around its cornice, charmingly supported by a pair of mermaids. Access to the building from the public thoroughfare is between a pair of low piers surmounted by lanterns, up a flights of steps and into the building, between the columns and under the bay.

Lanchester's ability at planning is most spectacularly coupled with Rickard's baroque fancy at the Wesleyan Central Hall, but before considering this example, one further case of entrance below a balcony is worthy of examination.

Although Colchester Town Hall stands on a corner site, and its elevated position and tower make it visible from some distance, the building signs itself very particularly to the approaching pedestrian. The entrance is not beneath the tower, but is half way along the main elevation to High Street. The richness of the façade attracts the eye, even if drawn initially by the tower, and the position of entrance is advertised by a balcony leading from the mayor's parlour, and projecting out over the pavement by almost 2 metres. To provide further emphasis, two freestanding stone columns are located towards the edge of

Figure 6.8

Colchester Town Hall. The entrance is marked externally by the pair of columns standing at the pavement edge. Again, the visitor passes beneath a balcony before entering the building and rising up a flight of steps into the vaulted hall. (Photo: S.B. Bolas and Company. Reproduced courtesy of *Architectural Review*)

the existing pavement, in front of the building. They display bronze coats of arms and have ornate lanterns on top. This is not quite the Piazzetta at the edge of the Grand Canal, leading to St Mark's Square, but a similar idea, providing a festive 'gateway' to the entrance.

The process of entering the building itself begins between these columns and the façade, first passing under the projection of the balcony, then moving up two steps, between the piers to either side, and under the arch of the entrance opening itself. The spandrels of the arch are enriched by sculpture and a coat of arms. Although there are wrought iron gates to close off the building, these are folded back within the depth of the lobby, so that the doors are located in a glazed timber screen. The scale, here, is large, even though space is at a premium.

Figure 6.9

Wesleyan Central Hall. (a) The sequence begins modestly, but soon becomes an impressive and stately experience, rising up staircases that flow from level to level. This is grand enough for a national opera house. (Reproduced courtesy of *Architectural Review*.) (b) From ground floor level; (c) from mezzanine on first floor staircase; (d) and (e) views from above (computer generated images: Vasilieos Balampanos)

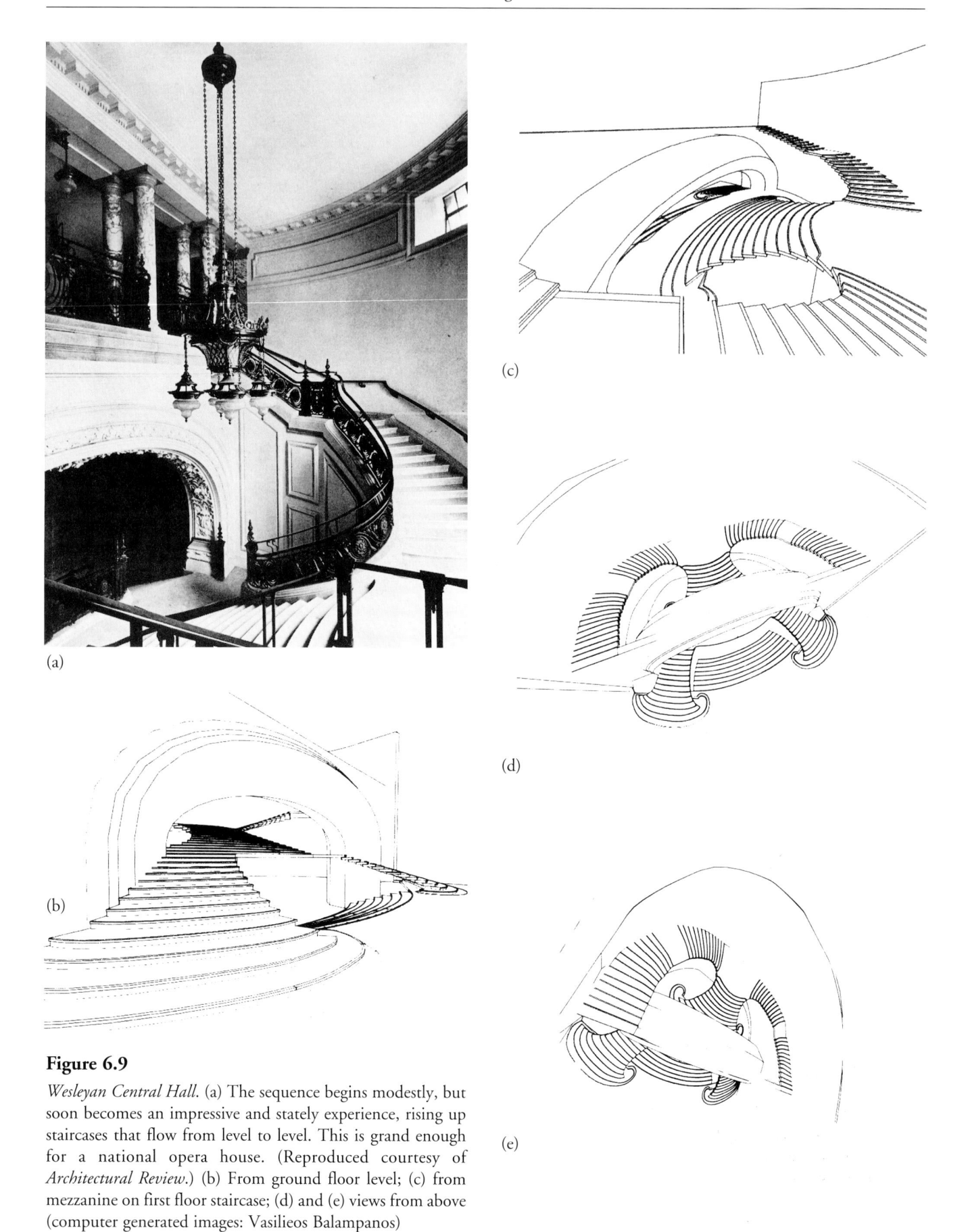

There is a flight of steps leading to the floor level of the main entrance hall. These are set back inside the building, and are in a 'well' surrounded by stone balusters. The entrance hall itself has a shallow vaulted ceiling supported by plain Doric columns, paired at the head of the stairs, and the bottom of the grand flight leading up and out of the ground floor. This sequence is very well controlled. An impressive effect is achieved within a restricted space. The columns demarcate the main 'processional' route into the buildings, with subsidiary spaces to either side. Movement through and up is emphasized by the window to the mezzanine landing, the brightness of which leads one forward together with the polished brass hand rails. A statue of Queen Victoria sits imperiously on the landing facing incoming visitors.

All of this is achieved within a comparatively narrow block of building, without being overbearing or fussy, yet the scale is grand and the experience dignified without being pompous. Movement through the building is encouraged. It is a very well judged piece of work.

The encouragement of movement is a theme which is explored in most Edwardian baroque buildings. None more so than Lanchester and Rickard's Wesleyan Central Hall in Westminster. Whilst it may not have the charm of its smaller cousins at Deptford and Hull, it has a grandeur and, in the staircase, a plasticity of form and control that singles it out as perhaps the most accomplished example of its kind within the period. It shares the projecting segmental bay feature with the town hall and art college, located on the central axis of the main façade. Despite this, however, the visitor must be, at first, a little disappointed. There are three square shaped openings located in the bay – one at either side and one in the middle – over which is the great window that

Figure 6.10

Headquarters of Bovril Limited. A commercial project designed by Lanchester, Stewart and Rickards, and a reminder that sometimes as much design effort could be expended on mundane premises as on civic buildings. (Photo: E. Dockray. Reproduced courtesy of *Architectural Review*)

lights the stairs, yet apart from a few steps, there is little to prepare one for the huge building into which one is entering. Once through the deeply set doors there is a vestibule of elliptical plan, which is rather austere and somewhat unwelcoming. From one side rises a curving flight of stairs, increasing in radius as one ascends, and enclosed by other staircases, sweeping up on each side. At the top, the entrance hall proper is reached.

Light comes from behind, and although one is faced by a great arch with doors to ground floor accommodation, the temptation is to swing round and follow the light which comes from the huge window illuminating the staircase. Turning, stairs curve back up out of the entrance hall and on to a landing beneath a large depressed arch which divides the entrance hall from the segmental bay in which the rest of the staircase is accommodated. Here, a central single flight runs up to a mezzanine and then splits, with stairs following the line of the wall up to the first floor. In a sense, this is all part of the entrance sequence, for the assembly hall itself is located at this level, suspended high above its surroundings. The staircase is a *tour de force*, flowing down from the upper to lower levels, the curving edge of each tread adding to the feeling of liquid movement. The effect is enhanced by Rickards' beautiful handrails and balusters.

There can be little doubt of the importance of the entrance sequence to Edwardian architects. Perhaps generated by an overemphasized sense of propriety, or the need for civic pomp and ceremony, the experiences achieved are nevertheless much more poetic than aluminium door frames in glazed screens which for later generations glibly separate public and private space; inner and outer activities.

CHAPTER SEVEN

Space and character

Edwardian civic buildings, by their very nature, have spaces where people can meet and converse. Corridors, lobbies and staircases assume an importance in these building types, which may be lacking in others, and this is a fact that was recognized with delight by their architects. The dimensions and proportions of such spaces vary from building to building, and of the examples chosen there are differences, also, in architectural, stylistic and detailed treatment. Having said this, nearly all town and county halls have broad corridors or ante rooms linking the most important committee rooms with the council chamber. They are all elaborately treated and finished in expensive materials. More examples of such commonality can be found and, on closer inspection, an almost generic way of designing some rooms was adopted.

Hare's County Buildings at Stafford and his Oxford Town Hall, built at the beginning of the period, are somewhat diverse. They are stylistically different and have different functions, but even in their common spaces, such as the council chamber, there is no agreement.

Oxford's formal circulation zone is not a broad corridor, but 'a landing', a spacious area surrounding the head of the main stairs. It is delineated by columns and is covered by a series of square bay vaults with stone ribs between. There is ample space, adjacent to the council chamber for councillors to gather and talk, and the whole landing has the feeling not of a functional circulation area, but a place where debate and dealing takes place. Overall, its character is late gothic or 'Tudor', a fact enhanced by the mullioned windows with their leaded lights and coats of arms.

At Stafford the layout of County Buildings did not permit the same circulation system as at Oxford. As has been seen, the councillors' entrance was through a loggia to the Judge's lodgings off Market Place, but the council chamber itself was at the opposite end of the building – in urban terms, a good walk down Martin Street. Hare therefore used a spacious lobby with glazed dome at ground floor level, a fine stone staircase, rising from it in a straight flight, and what was described as a 'Tudor long gallery' – a broad, vaulted corridor – linking the stairhead to the council chamber. This whole spatial zone was intended for councillors and not for officers or clerks who had to use another stair. Perhaps, from the point of view of local democracy, it was as significant a space in terms of decision making as the council chamber itself. In the matter of style there is a strange mixture of 'Jacobethan' and 'Wrenaissance'. In the lobby and the gallery there is panelling with timber casing to beams and to the ribs of the vaulting. Around the stairwell, the balusters seem Jacobean, and the effect is enhanced by the leaded windows through which light is admitted to the area. On the other hand, the curved nature of the vaulted ceiling and some of its plasterwork seem reminiscent of the late seventeenth century. Purists may be offended, but the ambience which Hare created is highly appropriate.

Elsewhere in the first phase of County Buildings the same stylistic ambiguity applies. The committee rooms – the large one, the Oak Room, and the smaller, the White Room – are both panelled. The Oak Room has a coved ceiling and the White Room, vaults. Most of the detail is 'Wrenaissance', yet the mullioned and leaded-light windows introduce a different note. The library, however, is thoroughly 'Wrenaissance'. In form, it follows some of Wren's church interiors, and has a shallow central dome modelled in plaster by F.E.E. Schenck. This is divided radially with figures in each section and is not unlike the painted ceiling in the council chamber at Colchester Town Hall, designed at about the same time. The library was a later addition to the Stafford buildings.

The major spaces at Oxford Town Hall, by contrast, are unremittingly 'Jacobethan'. The Assembly Room, for instance, one of the suite of civic spaces on the first floor,

Figure 7.1

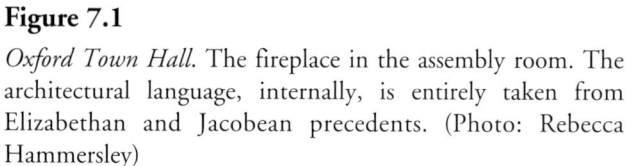

Oxford Town Hall. The fireplace in the assembly room. The architectural language, internally, is entirely taken from Elizabethan and Jacobean precedents. (Photo: Rebecca Hammersley)

has a coved ceiling, with a raised centre section, timber ribs and pendants. There is a fine fireplace with arcaded gallery over, supported on marble columns. The vaulted mayor's parlour with its excellent panelling and plasterwork is also a successful essay in the style.

In contrast, Colchester Town Hall is one of the best examples of high Edwardian baroque civic buildings. The main staircase, rising from the entrance to first floor level leads to the mid-point of a vaulted and domed corridor running the full length of the building. It gives access to the committee rooms and mayor's reception room which front the building and the robing rooms and council chamber to the rear. Above is the moot hall. Belcher succeeds in achieving spaciousness, even though the site is cramped, and in consequence the building rises higher than most of the others described here.

Figure 7.2

County Hall, Northallerton. (a) The mezzanine lobby space fronting the council chamber. (b) View on the stairs leading back up from the mezzanine level to the first floor landing and corridor. The detail and architectural features throughout are taken from the English baroque

County Hall, Northallerton, although on a green field site, also has a broad vaulted first floor corridor, which is lighted from one side, serving only rooms to the front for most of its length. The grand committee room is on the central axis, with three further committee rooms to one side, and originally, accommodation for the county surveyor on the other. The entrance to the council chamber, however, is half a level down, across the stairwell. It is fronted by an 'outer-room', a wide vaulted space running the full width of the chamber and open to the mezzanine landing of the staircase. It is entered between columns supporting the vault above.

Such grand, vaulted corridors, as has been seen, are usually reserved for special areas, but are the norm at Lancaster Town Hall. The entrance, staircase and landing area are very lavishly treated, and from them the corridors penetrate the building, forming a grid across both ground and first floor plans. Although, in the main, accommodation is grouped to either side, large light wells, or 'areas' allow sequences of windows to be inserted to illuminate the corridors. Most of the ceremonial spaces are at first floor level. The mayor's parlour, banqueting room and reception room form an impressive enfiladed suite of accommodation across the main façade; committee rooms are located at right-angles to this along the garden front, and the council chamber is at right angles again, forming three sides of a square around the stairwell.

Lancaster, is, of course, an expensive example and more showy, internally, than most. However, it again

Figure 7.3
Lancaster Town Hall. A first floor corridor, lavishly treated with marble panelling, but lacking the profusion of detail to be found in the earlier work of the period. (Photo: Lancaster City Council Museums Services)

emphasizes the importance of the 'corridors of power' in these building types. At the beginning of the period they may be likened to sixteenth century examples, with chamfered columns and quadripartite vaulting. Towards the end, they could be mistaken for the interiors of Wren's palatial buildings. However, Vincent Harris's Glamorgan County Hall, designed in 1908, illustrates a new severity of approach. Its stark *beaux-arts* character gives grandeur to the setting by studiously ignoring the 'entanglements of detail', so popular fifteen years before, at the beginning of the period. These details, though fussy, brought warmth and humanity to the scene. Harris's fine, curving council chamber corridor, top-lit by small domes has a geometrical severity in its detailing and a restraint in the use of materials, finishes and applied art that seems to reflect the scholar's view of the great buildings of classical antiquity. Indeed it is perhaps, more appropriate to the wielding of autocratic power than the 'gentleman's club' atmosphere of, for instance, Hare's early work.

The provision of public assembly rooms for meetings, oratory and musical performance is the preserve of the town hall, emphasizing its role at the hub of civic life, as a centre for political and cultural, as well as administrative activities. The assembly room tended to follow a similar pattern: a rectangular space approximately one and a half times as long as wide with a platform at one end, to the rear of which an organ is located. There is usually a gallery or galleries to accommodate large audiences. At Oxford and Lancaster the galleries run round three sides and are supported on columns or piers which then run up to take the edge of the roof vault ribs. The hall at Colchester is an exception in that there are no galleries, and it was, no doubt, primarily intended for civic receptions, banquets and dances. In other examples there was the ability to fulfil these functions as well, and

Figure 7.4
Oxford: a galleried hall with an unusual apsidal end. Despite this and the extravagant bric-à-brac detail, the form is not dissimilar to later examples. (Photo: Oxfordshire County Council)

Figure 7.5

Colchester: the Moot Hall, a resplendent 'Wrenaissance' example, which followed its predecessors by being intended for banquets or meetings, rather than concerts. (Photo: Colchester Museums)

Figure 7.6

Lancaster: a galleried concert hall which like many spaces of this type has a ceiling reminiscent of those in Wren's churches. (Photo: Bedford Lemere & Co. Reproduced courtesy of *Architectural Review*)

Lancaster is equipped with a sprung floor for dancing. It is clear, however, that they are also intended for talks, rallies and, not least, concerts. The earliest, at Oxford, had seating for 800, Stockport 1,250, although optimistically shown as 2,000 in Thomas's original competition entry, and 1,700 at Lancaster. Stylistically, they vary from an overworked bric-à-brac at Oxford, which, incidentally has a curved, or apsidal end behind the platform, to 'Wrenaissance' in the other examples. These have barrel vaulted ceilings, not unlike those in some of Wren's churches, discussed below.

Essentially, these spaces have a life of their own, often being used outside the hours when the rest of the building is in operation. To facilitate this they usually have separate entrances and exits and can be sealed off from the remainder of the accommodation. Spatially, also, they may be at odds with the council chambers, committee rooms and offices comprising the bulk of the building. At Lancaster and Stockport, they seem to be relegated to the rear of the building; at Oxford they are subsumed into the interior of the city block of which the town hall forms part. Cardiff also hides its assembly hall within the boundaries formed by long palace-like ranges, which delineate the exterior of the building.

The progenitors of these spaces for public gatherings, are, perhaps, the assembly rooms of the eighteenth century, and before this, historically, the Roman basilica. However, it is the earlier Victorian examples which must have provided the most potent images. St George's Hall at Liverpool, and the later building of the same name at Bradford would, no doubt, be well known to Edwardian architects. Leeds Town Hall is, in terms of volume, largely a public hall, as are some later examples, such as Huddersfield. By the last decade of the century, however, it seems that the type had become somewhat standardized, and although lavishly treated by architects, in the style appropriate to the overall design, architectural creativity was diverted elsewhere.

The 'Wrenaissance' style was used freely by Edwardian architects, and informed the design approach rather than being slavishly copied, but more literal translations of Wren's work can be found in the council chambers of town and county halls and in the reference rooms of public libraries.

The council chamber

Two of the earliest examples used in this book, the County Buildings at Stafford and Wakefield, adopted designs for their council chambers that are to be seen in various guises throughout the Edwardian period. They differ greatly from the chamber of the House of Commons, which one may have expected to have furnished the archetype for local authorities. This was not the case. In the Commons, the main body of the space is devoted to the seating of members, facing each other across a narrow space. The design enshrines the adversarial tradition of British politics, reflecting it through the plan and thereby encouraging it in daily practice. To start with, the Metropolitan Board of Works, which preceded the London County Council in many of its functions, provided a similar plan for the chamber to accommodate early meetings of the LCC, when it convened at its Spring Gardens premises in 1889, but although the face-to-face layout of Westminster was evident at the outset, it was soon replaced with a horseshoe shaped seating plan which was to become familiar in town and county halls over the next two decades.

Perhaps in response to the fact that councils were not split necessarily on party political lines, and there were a large number of independent members – many original county councillors were local bigwigs who had been the magistrates responsible for administration, prior to the formation of county authorities – a centralized plan form was preferred, often with a dome or dished ceiling, helping to create a sense of unity and equality amongst members. In common with most of the architecture of the late nineteenth century and Edwardian periods, some kind of formal and aesthetic precedent was sought for this kind of space, once it was identified.

In the case of council chambers, where the need for a centralized unobstructed space for debate was essential, it seems likely that some of Wren's City churches were an important model. In his *A History of Renaissance Architecture in England, 1500–1800* (1897), Reginald Blomfield pointed out that Wren had built anew for Protestant worship – most other English churches had been built before the Reformation, those in the City of London being destroyed in the Great Fire: 'He [Wren] insisted that, if possible, everyone must both see and hear the preacher'.[1] Even so, the seating layout of churches was not the same as that of council chambers, where any of the council members could rise and speak. Several of Wren's churches do not provide suitable models, therefore, and of the three basic types identified by Blomfield, the second seems to have been a source of inspiration. This was baldly described as having 'domes with arched recesses, with or without detached columns',[2] although the architectural concept behind this description is more complex than it would suggest.

Other commentators later discerned different categories. Writing in 1911, Arthur Keen[3] listed no less than five, pointing out that some of Wren's churches were actually combinations or variations of those he catalogued. There was, therefore, no shortage of examples for Edwardian architects to examine.

Wren faced the challenge of building on tight and irregularly shaped urban sites, previously occupied by the churches destroyed in the Fire. In the case of the domed, centralized plan forms, he resolved the problems presented by the need to accommodate the Anglican liturgy in suitably dignified spaces within these sites with a great deal of ingenuity. What is more, even though the plans appear to be simple and the exteriors often little more than brick boxes, Wren managed to infuse architectural character and spatial articulation by the design of the ceiling and its supports. Central domes are featured, sometimes associated with supporting columns which further demarcate the internal spaces of the church; some plans are out of square, and irregularities in the plan of the building envelope are resolved by judicious use of the columnar grid.

Of Wren's domed churches, St Swithin and St Mary, Abchurch are relatively simple, with octagon supports for the dome. St Mary has pendentives corbelled from the wall and St Swithin has a column-supported entablature. St Stephen, Walbrook is more complex, and was greatly admired in the Edwardian period. It was described by Blomfield in 1897 as 'a church which has been extravagantly praised, but which is undoubtedly one of the most original of all Wren's interiors'.[4] David Watkin describes it as a 'spatially ambiguous combination of the aisled nave plan and the centralized plan'.[5] This is achieved by the positioning of eight columns grouped in a circle around the central point of the rectangular envelope. The columns support an entablature

Figure 7.7

Drawing by Sir Reginald Blomfield of the interior of Wren's St Stephen's, Walbrook

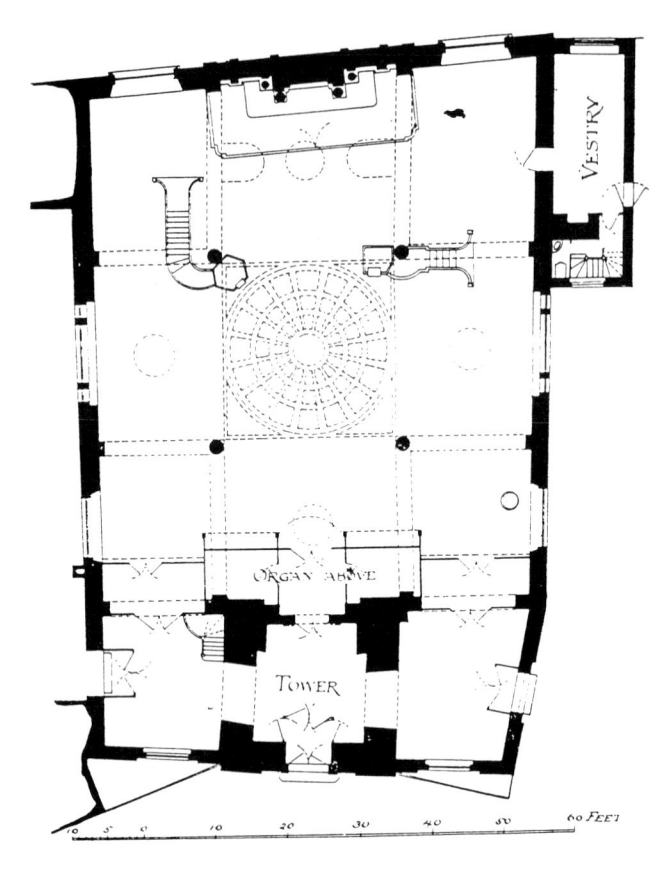

Figure 7.8
Plan of Wren's St Mary-at-Hill

from which pendentives rise to carry the dome. Further columns are set back, carrying the entablature, and a cross shape is delineated. The 'arms' of the cross are vaulted back towards the outside walls of the building from the pendentive arches.

Also influential was the type represented by St Mary-at-Hill, Billingsgate, which combines both vaulted and domed forms. In plan, this is a 'cross inside a square'. Intersecting vaults are held on four columns at the centre, where a dome rises from pendentives. The edges of the vaults run back to the walls on entablatures, which continue around the interior of the building. The square corner bays have flat ceilings, similar to St Martin's, Ludgate Hill, where two segmental barrel vaults intersect at right-angles. The central square where the vaults meet is supported on four columns, and the corner bays are fitted with flat ceilings surrounded by entablatures, which rest on the columns, and pilasters attached to the wall surface. This detail or a variant often appears in Edwardian council chambers.

Although these examples are somewhat larger in plan dimensions than most council chambers, they seem to have had an influence on many. Of course, Wren's aim was to achieve different zones within the unified body of the church by such spatial manipulation. The architects of council chambers were seeking unity, as a primary aim. This was achieved even where galleries were positioned in vaulted recesses off the chamber.

The chamber at County Hall, Wakefield is one of the largest considered here – 50 feet (15.25 m) square and

Figure 7.9
County Hall, Wakefield. View of the council chamber looking towards the chair and press gallery. The dome pendentives are carried on steel beams clad in sequoia, rather than on columns. (Photo: Albert Booth)

40 feet (12.2 m) high, seating about 120 council members, with room for seventy in the public gallery. It is, essentially, the St Mary-at-Hill design, but instead of columns, huge orthogonal crossbeams intersect at what would be the columnar positions to support the pendentives. The dome is central to the chamber, but the arms covered by the vault at each side are not treated separately – the semi-circular seating plan below is independent of them.

At Stafford, the horseshoe seating plan is accommodated in a room 42 feet (12.8 m) square and 35 feet (10.6 m) high to the top of the dome. In this case, the dome is not carried on pendentives, but sits in the central position of a ceiling within a square formed by ribs. The ceiling of this 'Wrenaissance' chamber is coved, similar to that provided for Hare's contemporary 'Jacobethan' design at Oxford Town Hall. The ribs curve down to pilasters, which demarcate different areas of wall. Apart

Figure 7.10

County Buildings, Stafford. A detail of the council chamber from the coving, there is little similarity to Oxford, which is rectangular in plan, with a face-to-face seating layout. The coved type is one of Keen's categories, usually associated with a flat roof in Wren's work but here it is combined with a dome.

Even though in its essentials, this chamber is more simple than most of its Wren precedents, by cutting back into the ceiling coving to locate *oeuil-de-boeuf* windows high up to two opposite sides and by placing venetian windows in the other two walls, an effect of pendentives is achieved. Furthermore, the arched recesses, although no higher than the cornice linking the pilasters which frame them, remind one of the spatial organization of Wren's centralized churches.

Over a decade later, Brierley's council chamber in the North Yorkshire County Council headquarters at Northallerton bears a resemblance both to those at Stafford and Wakefield. It is, perhaps, the most satisfactory of the three architecturally – particularly in terms of scale, extent and appropriateness of detail, lighting and unity. Like its earlier cousins, it is square (13.7 m) but relatively low (7.6 m to the top of the dome). It most closely follows the St Mary-at-Hill pattern, and is provided with both circular lights in the dome and large windows all round in the arched recesses. Tiered horseshoe pattern seating for sixty councillors focuses on the chairman's dais under the arched recess at one end. Opposite, the wall to the recess is omitted, the cornice

Figure 7.11

County Buildings, Northallerton. The council chamber is, perhaps, the most consistent of those shown in following the pattern of Wren's domed churches. This is James Fulton's fine perspective drawing of 1905

being supported on a pair of columns, and the public gallery built out beyond the chamber.

It is worth noting here that the main hall at the Wesleyan Central Hall buildings is very similar, though 'writ large' – with its domed space and recesses, even though it lacks the subtlety of the smaller examples.

The other examples discussed in this book have simpler council chambers, yet there is a desire to provide a central dome and a curving seating pattern. Mountford's Lancaster Town Hall has a pendentive dome supported on columns with very shallow arched recesses to each of the long sides, and rather deeper ones at the ends. There is access through the recesses to apse-like spaces. Beneath the dome is an elliptical seating layout. The room reads as an enlarged square, and the apses, although adding to the length of the plan, are only as high as the cornice from which the pendentives spring. Thus they read as separate spaces.

Stockport is similar to Lancaster, in using a pendentive dome, with deep, vaulted recesses on the short sides. The chamber is lighted by lunettes in the pendentive arches – as at Northallerton – and the horseshoe seating faces the chairman's dais in the centre of the long wall. Entrances into the chamber are positioned under the end recesses – here again, despite the unequal length and width, the square plan centred under the dome dominates.

Deptford and Colchester have rectangular plans, though both with curved elements to the seating. In Belcher's original design the chamber at Colchester is located in a part of the building with an angled external wall at one end. A curving internal wall was intended, so that the room was symmetrical, though with a high level public gallery to two (adjacent) sides only. Deptford has a long chamber running right across the projecting main front of the building at first floor level, giving a difficult

Figure 7.12

Lancaster Town Hall. The council chamber – an elegant development of the type discussed, depending on lighting from above. (Photo: Bedford Lemere & Co. Reproduced courtesy of *Architectural Review*)

length to width ratio. However, a large public gallery was located at one end, producing a more satisfactory overall proportion. It seems that Lanchester and Rickards favoured a square seating layout at one stage, with the dais forming the fourth side, whilst there was also a plan with a curved end. In any case, the centre three bays of the room had a raised ceiling with clerestory window above the projecting segmental balcony window, which lies on the centre line of the façade.

Cardiff City Hall has a circular seating layout plan, but the council chamber is contained within the rectangular centre block of the building's main front. The dome, raised on a 'drum' – really a square structure with chamfered corners – sits over the circle, and the chairman's dais and a gallery opposite are situated in recessed, columned bays. The plan form provides an ideal dignified setting for the chamber of an important assembly.

The grandest of all Edwardian civic buildings, and one of the latest, the County Hall of the LCC, like Cardiff had a centralized council chamber plan. An octagonal form was used, with voting lobbies off to opposite sides. However, instead of a circular seating layout, a horseshoe shape, reminiscent of the old LCC building at Spring Gardens, was chosen. The siting of public and press galleries at a high level in columned recesses outside the envelope of the chamber itself, looking in, is a feature present in several of the examples discussed here, particularly Cardiff, but at London County Hall galleries are located on four sides rather than two. Despite the circularity of the plan, there is no dome over the chamber; instead a circular flat ceiling sits at the centre, with coffered coving and ribs leading up to it from the cornice which runs around the room above the openings. The architect, Ralph Knott, had originally designed a domed chamber, but such examples of Edwardian exuberance were beginning to look distinctly dated by the latter part of the period, and the space as completed is more typical of the straight faced official architecture of George V's reign.

Reference and lending libraries

It is tempting to look for the inspiration of the architects of Edwardian libraries in analogous works of Wren – for instance the library at Trinity College, Cambridge. However, it seems that the features in the most elaborate rooms of public libraries derive from the third category of Blomfield's analysis of Wren's church designs – those having 'naves covered with wagon ceilings with flat or groined ceilings to aisles'. By 'wagon ceilings',[6] one assumes that Blomfield is describing the vaulted naves that were employed in churches with non-centralized plans. This coincides with Keen's category of 'segmental, elliptical or circular barrel vaults'. Protestant churches were preaching houses, and there were often upper level galleries included in these designs, located to either side of the nave over the aisles, between the outer walls of the church and the columns supporting the nave arcade. Such features were to be found in St James's, Piccadilly, St Bride, Fleet Street and St Clement Dane's. The admission of light from the sides is either through 'clerestory' windows cut back into the vault of the roof – for instance in St Bride, Fleet Street and St Magnus-the-Martyr – or through gallery windows, with the nave arches projected back as vaults, perpendicular to the main vault, and terminating in round-headed windows. St James's, Piccadilly, is an example. St Bride's and St James's, in fact, are representative of the two subdivisions of this type: where the aisle vaults spring from the same level as the nave vaults (St James's) and where the aisle vaults 'are entirely below it, and there are both a cornice and a plinth above the nave arcade before the curve of the main vault begins' (St Bride's).[7]

These arrangements were appropriated for use in the reference and lending areas of public libraries. As one might imagine, they are typical of Henry Hare's designs, particularly because of his enthusiasm for the 'Wrenaissance' style in his post 1900 buildings. Variants can be found in the work of others, though, even in Holden's Central Library at Bristol, which shuns Wrenaissance features externally, but which has a splendid reference library in the style. Reginald Blomfield's library at Lady Margaret Hall, University of Oxford, is a smaller-scale version, which ignores the detailed trimmings, but is an elegant and appropriate room for study.

The Hare style can be seen in public libraries at Islington (Central) and Wolverhampton. Here, the lending room is treated to the complete upper floor of one wing of the building, with lighting from all sides. The rectangular plan is suitable for the restricted access operation using indicator boards, which was favoured by the chief librarian. The lending room is in six bays, with the vaulted ceiling divided by ribs, which rest on columns. A balustrade at cornice level runs between the columns, guarding the high level gallery behind. Arched openings between the columns are cut back into the roof. The system of bays enables the distribution of shelving for the organization of books by location. Interestingly, the original reference library had an internal dome and was a centralized space.

At Islington Central Library, the reference library follows a similar theme. The long, vaulted roof has glazing along its axis, and is divided into four main bays with half bays at the ends. In the end walls, *oeuil-de-boeuf* windows provide extra light. Each bay has a clerestory dormer window with reveals cut back into the vault. The cornice supporting the edge of the vault sits forward of the main piers and is supported by huge, tri-partite

Space and character 91

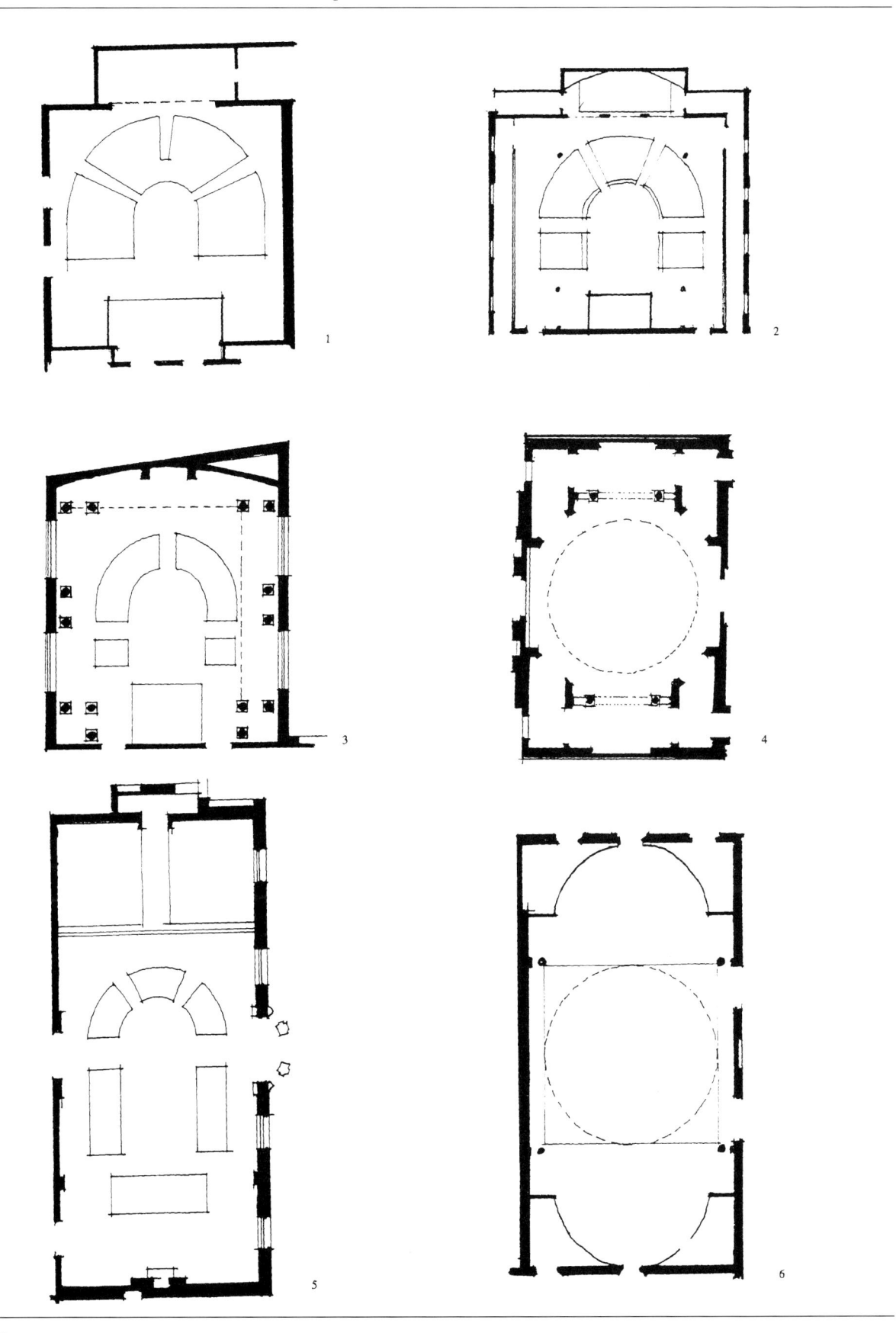

Figure 7.13

Comparative council chambers (plans not to scale): 1 Stafford; 2 Northallerton; 3 Colchester; 4 Cardiff; 5 Deptford; 6 Lancaster

scrolled brackets. There are no side 'aisles', but the wall steps back between the piers to accommodate built-in bookshelves.

Holden's reference room at Bristol could be by the same hand. It is, indeed, more or less contemporary, but it is on a larger scale, approximately 45 m long and 15 m wide, and much taller, with seating for 150 and shelving for 100,000 volumes. It is, in effect, a large atrium with reference tables beneath the roof light, surrounded by galleries on two levels. The entrance is on the long side, at the centre line of the middle of the three major bays, defined by pilastered piers supporting arched ribs. Half bays at either end of this arrangement form screens to helical staircases serving the galleries. At the extremities of the room are transverse groined vaults, with occuli to each side. Internally, these circular windows are expressed as part of the 'Wrenaissance' decorative scheme; externally they are features in Holden's 'Tudor' façades.

On the external wall to the main façade mullioned bay windows rise through from the floor level to the top of the first gallery, at the vaulted end, and the floor of the gallery forms a bridge, looking on one side into the atrium, on the other into the two-storey bay. At the east end, near to the Abbey Gate, the bay forms an oriel over the main entrance to the building.

The detailing of the interior, though creatively approached, seems rather crude. Holden, or perhaps his assistant, were rather ill at ease with the 'Wrenaissance' language. Spatially, however, it is more complex than Hare's work. Like the other examples noted here, its formal origin seems to be St James's, Piccadilly. Perhaps the most interesting feature of the design, though, is the way in which the reference room translates itself into the exterior, the Tudor details of which, however, merely overlay Holden's blocky three-dimensional manipulation of mass.

Figure 7.14
Bristol Central Library. The reference room, following in detail and form the precedent of Wren's churches with naves. There is heavy dependence on top lighting, here, however. (Photo: T Lewis. Reproduced courtesy of *Architectural Review*)

Chapter Eight

Integration of the arts – internal enrichment

In the case of civic buildings constructed between 1890 and 1910, this is a considerable subject. In the first place, there was almost certainly a desire to create rich interiors in buildings to be used by the public which would symbolize the cultural and corporate life of the municipality. Secondly, particularly in the case of county council buildings, the wealthy middle classes, gentry and aristocracy who were involved in the affairs of the council had to be accommodated in the luxurious manner to which they were accustomed. In parallel with this, was the influence of the arts and crafts movement.

As has been discussed, the arts and crafts movement was not confined to country houses, or to a certain sophisticated level of wealthy society, and its influence found its way into civic and even commercial buildings. What would have been designed as splendid interiors in any other period of architectural history, therefore, became, in some instances, galleries of the works of artists, and a showcase for craftsmen. As with external decoration, though, the extravagance waned as the period wore on.

One of the most comprehensive examples of the incorporation of works of artists into civic interiors is to be found in West Riding County Hall, Wakefield. A whole range of artistic endeavour is represented, from large scale mural painting to the design of door furniture. The architects, however, reserved this somewhat overwhelming wealth of decoration and detail for the

Figure 8.1

County Hall, Wakefield. Although tiled corridors were good enough for the clerks, these were enlivened by elegant designs. (Photo: Albert Booth)

most important public and ceremonial spaces. Elsewhere, a hard-wearing, though good quality functionalism takes over, best represented, perhaps, by the corridor serving the first floor rooms of the Cliff Parade range. These are lined with purpose-made tiles in a cheerful sub-arts and crafts style, with the date '1897' worked into the design. In addition, the stairs at the inner angles of the diamond-shaped plan though spatially interesting and elaborate, are not sumptuous.

The 'big splash' is reserved for the entrance and stair hall at ground floor level, the stairwell, and the vaulted space at first floor, leading from the stairs to the chairman's room at the intersection of the corridors serving the main ranges. In the opposite direction, there is the ante room to the council chamber, and the chamber itself, beyond. Of course, there is the usual assemblage of high quality materials that bring a palatial air to the building's interior, but it is the applied art and design that really marks it out and creates an ambience that is very specific to English work of this particular time.

The scene is set by the work of Charles Grange Lowther, who painted the decorations within the staircase and on the vaulted landing. He used oil colours with the addition of various metals and added gesso to give relief effects. The tinted blue-greens, and the warm metallic details produce a character that is somewhat mystical and characteristic of the 1890s both in England and the rest of Europe. His efforts were prodigious, and he obviously made the most of this opportunity to display the range of his personal approach. Indeed, he was at pains to produce 'something as far as I am able to make it, to stimulate that interest in art and higher sentiment that is too much overwhelmed by commercialism'.[1]

Figure 8.2

County Hall, Wakefield. Charles Grange Lowther's 'Viking Ship' paintings on the staircase. Decorative metals and gesso work are used to add incident. (Photo: Albert Booth)

Lowther's work covers much of the entrance sequence of the building. The main entrance hall is vaulted with sandstone columns and arches. To one side, the staircase rises between a pair of columns. Looking up, decorative work can be seen on the walls flanking the rising stairs. Of particular note is the illustration of a Viking ship, ploughing through swirling blue-green waves, whose crests are emphasized by gesso work. The shields along the side of the ship are picked out in copper and bronze. Ascending through this decoration, the landing is reached, where Lowther's paintings, on the wall opposite the stairhead, continue the mood. The landing comprises vaults defined by sandstone columns and arches. Each vault has a mini-dome with a glazed light decorated in stained glass. On the wall surface above panelling, and in the tympana of the arches, Lowther has added allegorical material including winged figures representing 'debate' and 'dictation', implements associated with West Riding industries, and the twin subjects of 'Peace' and 'Plenty', charmingly illustrated by rather sensual 'nineties' girls, the latter maiden made more voluptuous than the former. The entrance to the chairman's room is flanked by another pair of beauties, 'Science' and 'Art'. There is no classical restraint in their depiction.

If this illustrative feast were not enough, those passing along the landing to the council chamber first come into a large square ante room or lobby, with a frieze running around above the panelling. The sides of the room are each approximately 8 metres long, and four different historical subjects are illustrated. These are taken from the Wars of the Roses and are of local interest. The subjects are: the Battle of Wakefield; the crowning of Henry VII on Bosworth Field; the procession of Henry VII and Elizabeth of York through Wakefield; Margaret of Anjou

Figure 8.3

County Hall, Wakefield. The first floor landing, looking from the stairhead. Peace and Plenty occupy the arcading. The door to the chairman's room at the end is flanked by two other maidens: Science and Art. (Photo: Albert Booth)

delivering up her son to the robbers in the wood. Stirring themes, delivered in a stirring manner by H.C. Fehr in modelled and coloured plasterwork. This was becoming a popular medium, based on medieval precedent. The plaster itself was coloured before being painted over, and panels were made from plaster of Paris, cast with fibre.

After contemplating Wakefield's historical connections, councillors would enter their chamber, and find themselves being looked down upon by more decidedly classical figures. Wisdom, Law, Learning and Power survey the decision making that their spirits hopefully inform from the pendentives of the dome which rises over the chamber. Meanwhile, over the entrance doors, figures of Justice, Authority and Industry preside in low relief.

This is by no means an exhaustive description of the applied art within County Hall, and there are striking examples elsewhere in the building. For instance, in one of the large committee rooms on the first floor, modelled plaster forms the overmantle to a large marble fireplace. A mother instructs a child, whilst others look on. The costume is seventeenth century, and the theme is 'Education'. But this room, like many of the others in the building, also contains instances of excellent and unique design effort. The committee rooms have fine fireplaces; the one in the room that was originally a library has a marble surround in an early eighteenth century style, but with arts and crafts tiles within and a splendid brass hood. This room also contains built-in, glass fronted bookcases of American walnut, linked to the panelling. Overhead, the plasterwork of the ceiling is modelled and gilded.

Stained glass is to be found at significant points within County Hall, most notably in the windows lighting

Figure 8.4

County Hall, Wakefield. The ante room to the council chamber with Fehr's splendid Wars of the Roses frieze. (Photo: Albert Booth)

Figure 8.5
County Hall, Wakefield. Handsome identification plates on the doors of the committee rooms, specially designed for the building. (Photos: Albert Booth)

the staircase, and in those to the council chamber. The work, by Smith of London, largely comprises the coats of arms of Yorkshire families. This is, of course, a tradition which one associates with great country houses of the sixteenth century, where the *nouveau riche* of the Tudor period were anxious to establish their pedigree, just as were the new county councils at the end of the nineteenth century.

Much design effort was also put into door furniture and, to a very great extent, electric light fittings. Of particular note in the case of the former are the handsome brass plates attached to the committee room doors, each with a splendidly designed capital letter, 'A', 'B' or 'C'. The finish and weight of the door itself, the nature of the finger plates, locks, escutcheons and handles all add to the feel that the highest quality materials were used, but only after considerable design effort had been expended.

Possibly because the architects were employed on a large and prestigious work in the opening stages of their (successful) careers, their enthusiasm led them to expend so much effort on all aspects of design. Architects today may carefully choose light fittings from a manufacturer's catalogue, and even when Gibson and Russell were working at Wakefield, commercial products were available. Here, however, virtually every important room has its own specifically designed lighting pendant. At the beginning of the use of electric light, architects did not necessarily feel constrained, it appears, by standardized hardware. In this case, at least, it is clear that the thought was of patterns of luminous globes. In the council chamber, for instance, fittings are suspended in groups of three by long chains attached to the arches delineating the edges of the central space. A large lantern is supported by the central chain, and, at a higher level, to either side, the outer chains carry tripartite fittings. The lanterns, themselves, have bulbs above and below at either side. The overall effect, in this lofty space, is of drops of light descending from above. The analogy may be of fruit hanging from a tree, or some kind of shower of incandescence.

Along the vaulted landing at the head of the grand staircase, the intent is similar. The eye is not led along by lighting that emphasizes the structure of the space, or eye-catching fittings, but by globes of light dancing into the distance. This complements the rather mystical quality generated by the wall paintings and the overall decorative scheme.

Elsewhere, in the committee rooms, for instance, the fittings themselves are more prominent. Examples include the 'cartwheel' type and the heavy pendant. In the former, a substantial chain supports a circle of bronze, around the edge of which are scrolled brackets carrying glass shades and curving strips of metal, the spokes of the wheel, run back from the rim to the centre. The cables for each of the six light fittings are made part of the decorative scheme, radiating out from near the top of the central chain and passing down and through to the brackets. The heavy pendant consists of a bulbous, perforated object in brass, with oriental lamp-like connotations hung from above. From each of its upper corners, scrolled brackets protrude through which the electrical flexes are drawn and from which the bulbs and glass shades dangle.

The architects also seem to have designed the switch plates from which the lights are controlled. They are brass rectangles with two or three toggle switches incorporated, and contain relief decoration, with a heavy border surrounding. The larger plates have a design that features a seated naked female figure with swirling drapery forms and marine motifs. One cannot help supposing that much of the internal decoration allowed the architects to give full rein to their desires to express the latest ideas in the decorative arts as opposed to the rather staid exterior. On the one hand, there is almost a hint of Lethaby's *Architecture Mysticism and Myth,* published in 1892, a book containing chapters with titles such as 'The Jewel-Bearing Tree', 'Ceilings Like the Sky' and 'Pavements Like the Sea'. On the others, the swirling decorative nature of continental art nouveau makes a tentative contribution, in the switch plates, for instance.

The extraordinary artistic effort in this building is complemented, of course, by a whole range of high quality finishes. Although contemporary and later examples may not contain so much applied art, a common feature of all civic buildings from the period is the lavishness of

Figure 8.6

County Hall, Wakefield. A pendant electrical light fitting in one of the committee rooms. Nearly all of the rooms were equipped with their own distinctive designs

materials used in the interior. The materials are used where they can make the most effect, and where propriety deems it necessary. It is usual for office corridors to be very plain in their treatment, with plastered or tiled walls, plaster ceilings and a minimum of mouldings. Although the offices themselves are usually well proportioned and well lighted, the comparative austerity of the corridors is repeated within.

In the case of the County Hall at Wakefield, the entrance sequence and staircase, the important circulation areas related to the council chamber and committee rooms, and those rooms themselves are treated to very high quality finishes and fittings. It is often difficult to determine the boundaries of the categorization between craft and art here. Fine hardwood panelling, for instance, may be carved with intricate detailing in the late seventeenth century style, or a marble floor finish break into an intricate pattern.

Figure 8.7

County Hall, Wakefield. Light controls with switch plate probably designed by the architects specially for the building

The octagonal entrance vestibule, a transition space between inside and outside, has marble panelling to the walls up to a height of 9 feet (2.75 m). The main entrance hall, beyond, is panelled with oak, and the floor is of marble. The eye is dominated, however, by the sandstone columns and arches supporting the floor above and delineating the stairwell. Later civic buildings abandoned the gothicism of this approach for the splendour of classical columns in marble. The stairs themselves are in Hopton Wood stone with red marble rails above and below, separated by white marble balusters. These lead to the landing and corridor above, with its marble floor and painted walls, serving the council chamber and leading to the committee rooms. The floors to the council chamber and its ante room are in oak, with Tobasco mahogany wall panelling and gallery fronts. In some of the committee rooms in the building the fine floors are complemented by ceilings in moulded plasterwork.

Although style changed over the fifteen years following the design and construction of West Riding County Hall, the general use of materials for finishes did not, nor did their position within the buildings: beyond a door or a bend in the corridor, sumptuousness gave way to hard-wearing practicality, and although employees had decent spaces in which to work, the 'show' was reserved for the councillors and the areas where the public came to be both awed and impressed.

Nearly all the civic buildings documented here have floors in the entrance sequence – lobby, entrance hall, main corridor – in marble or Bath stone, with patterned black and white paving becoming popular towards the end of the period, and oak boarding or wooden blocks in ante rooms, council chambers and committee rooms. The great entrance staircases are often in Hopton Wood stone, although in Oxford Town Hall Hopton Wood is used for dado panelling on the main first floor gallery, edged by dark Frosterley marble above and below. Both Hopton Wood and Frosterley are, in fact, carboniferous limestones, the former of a creamy colour, the latter dark grey. When polished, they provide excellent high quality finishes – Hopton Wood without the 'flashiness' of marble.

Marbles from Scandinavia and the Mediterranean countries, especially Italy and Greece, were commonly used for floors, wall panelling and columns where the greatest show was required. Cardiff City Hall, for instance, has paired Sienna marble columns in its great first floor ante hall, with bronze bases and capitals. This marble has 'golden-yellow background with light-cream figuring and grey/mauve irregular veining'.[2] At Stockport Town Hall, the grand staircase is in Sicilian marble of a greyish white colour, whilst the hall in which the staircase stands is panelled in Italian marble, with pronounced dark coloured markings. Other popular marbles used in important buildings of the period included, for example, Greek Cipollino which is coloured with light and dark green markings and Vert Antico which had a 'light green background with conglomeration of dark green, dark red and grey patches'.[3] It is easy to see how visual indigestion

Figure 8.8

Oxford Town Hall. (a) View on the stairs with dark Frosterley Marble horizontals (Photo: Rebecca Hammersley.) (b) The landing with its use of Hopton Wood and Frosterley stone, and rich plasterwork to the ceiling vaulting.

could occur if the architect was overenthusiastic with his brief to use this kind of material. By the time that Walter Brierley built the County Hall at Northallerton, Hopton Wood was used for the columns in the entrance hall, with base and capitals of Frosterley and the staircase handrails of the same material.

The treatment of wall surfaces seems to fall into several categories. In some cases, Oxford and Wakefield for instance, good quality stone – Ancaster or Northumberland sandstone – is used in special areas; in others, marble panelling might be employed. Committee rooms and, sometimes, council chambers and their ante rooms have hardwood panelling. Often this is in oak, which tends to predominate, though many buildings use the other popular woods such as mahogany and, on occasion, walnut where joinery work is included.

Moulded or modelled plasterwork, painted, is also common. This is especially so in areas where panels, edged by moulding, and pilasters are raised from the surface in order to divide the wall into visually coherent areas. Offices are plain plaster painted, though the access corridors commonly have a tiled dado.

Much work was put into the creation of ceilings. Modelled and moulded plasterwork predominate. This may be expected, particularly, in buildings such as Oxford Town Hall, with its 'Jacobethan' style. However, 'Wrenaissance' buildings frequently have their major spaces covered by vaulted ceilings divided into bays, perhaps with high level windows cut into the vault. These bays are demarcated by bands of decorative plasterwork of swags, garlands, wreathes and other classical ornament made popular in late seventeenth century England.

Figure 8.9
Cardiff City Hall. The first floor ante hall with its paired Sienna marble columns. (Photo: T Lewis. Reproduced courtesy of *Architectural Review*)

Occasionally, there is a surprise, such as the turquoise mosaic applied to the vaulted bays in the entrance to Bristol Public Library, which perhaps suggests the free-spirit, arts and crafts leaning of its author. However, once in the vaulted reference library, there is a return to stock Edwardian 'Wrenaissance' detail.

Various artist craftsmen were noted for decorative work. Certainly, in the case of plasterwork, the most prolific was George Percy Bankart (1866–1929). Bankart had been trained at Leicester School of Art, had been an articled pupil in an architect's office, was a friend of the celebrated arts and crafts architect Ernest Gimson, and went on to teach plasterwork. However, he was a popular choice by architects contemplating projects involving extensive use of decorative plasterwork, and after working with the Bromsgrove Guild, went on to form his own firm in London. His work encompasses both domestic and public buildings, including Cardiff City Hall and the Victoria and Albert Museum. He worked for Brierley at North Riding County Hall, but also produced a handsome curved ceiling in Brierley's own house, Bishopsbarn, York.

Figure 8.10
Cardiff City Hall. Bankart's elaborate 'Wrenaissance' plasterwork enhances the lines of Lanchester, Stewart and Rickard's fine ceiling in the assembly hall. (Photo: T Lewis. Reproduced courtesy of *Architectural Review*)

Bankart's interest in plasterwork was representative of arts and crafts enthusiasms. The building crafts had suffered a serious decline during the nineteenth century, when novelty, cleverness at the expense of taste and the mechanical production of ornament lead to a legacy of soulless, spiritless and overblown work. Towards the end of the century, of course, the influence of the arts and crafts movement had grown, and by Edwardian times, the general consensus amongst those interested in design was that the terms Victorian and philistine were synonymous. Plasterwork, for example, had been revived through the efforts of a number of artist–craftsmen, some of whom were also architects, and who looked back to a golden age when the creativity of the individual could be directly expressed through his work. Seventeenth century decoration, both Jacobean and Restoration was much admired. The work of the latter half of the eighteenth century was not liked, however, and the output of Robert and James Adam was seen as intricate and flat, but lacking the spirit and directness of the earlier modelled work; it set the pattern for the subsequent decline.

At the heart of the revival was an attempt to get back to the idea of the plasterer as a manipulator of a soft and plastic medium. The Jacobeans worked in situ, modelling heraldry, fruit, flowers and animals. George Bankart described their work as being 'a living vehicle of art'. In contrast, much modern plasterwork was cast in plaster of Paris, and was, in fact, the mechanical reproduction of the work of a modeller who had probably developed his design in a material other than plaster. Thus the inherent nature of the material had not been exploited, and the result lacked the immediacy and charm of seventeenth century work. It was admitted that it was difficult to undertake in situ work in modern circumstances, but it was felt that a plastic quality should be attempted in any design. In situ work involved scratching the lines of a design into a top coat of plaster and then roughening those areas to which the modelling material made contact with special cement – flaked lime and ox hair could

Figure 8.11

County Hall, Northallerton. Plasterwork by Bankart to the staircase 'dome'/gallery. This feature is similar to that in the seventeenth century Ashburnham House, which was a well-known example and was illustrated in Blomfield's *History of Renaissance Architecture*

Figure 8.12

Deptford Town Hall. The shallow ceiling dome over the grand staircase with its 'Wrenaissance' plasterwork. (Photo: Courtesy of Caroline Nicholl, The White House Studios)

be added. This, obviously, presented difficulties in large scale work such as assembly halls, and was only possibly to any extent in domestic situations.

The use of plasterwork to enhance large, plain surfaces was especially pursued by practitioners such as Bankart, who saw it as preferable to paper or panelling. Its use on ceilings was usually to enhance ribs and cornices. In all instances, the effect of the composition as a whole was considered important, as was the readability of detail. The higher the room, for instance, the more exaggerated the detail needed to be when used at ceiling level. Decorative motifs used were often plants, foliage and animals in domestic situations, or those derived from the work of late seventeenth century carvers and modellers, like Grinling Gibbons, in commercial and public buildings.

For all the enthusiasm of artists like Bankart and George Jack, and architects like Ernest Gimson, plaster-

work was used on a very large scale in Edwardian buildings and required the resources of large firms like George Jackson and Sons who had the capacity and skills to supply the growing demand. They did not shy away from new methods, and also had terrific resources in terms of referential material. It was claimed that the firm had a collection of moulds of 'every known period of ornament',[4] numbering over 20,000 as well as thousands of models. Specialist areas within the firm's premises dealt with different classes of work. For large scale ornament, fibrous plaster was particularly useful. It could be easily fixed, and was made from plaster and scrim (canvas) worked into moulds. For more heavily undercut designs, carton pierre was used, a sort of moulded papier mâché, which could be made in large sections.

Jacksons also involved themselves in wood carving, but this duality of output was not limited to commercial practitioners. George Bankart, himself, was well known for lead work, expressing the different nature and process of this material through his designs.

Architectural modellers and carvers, in addition, did not confine themselves to one medium. The firm of Gilbert Seale, for instance, which undertook carving at Lancaster Town Hall, incorporated many skills dedicated to enhancing buildings in different materials, amongst a diverse range of clientele. Perhaps the most celebrated name in this field is that of William

Figure 8.13

A workshop in the premises of George Jackson and Sons, manufacturing 'carton pierre' detail. (Reproduced courtesy of *Architectural Review*)

Aumonier. Three generations of Aumoniers were architectural carvers, all of whom were members of the Art Workers' Guild. The first William Aumonier (1839–1914) worked together with his son for important architects such as Aston Webb, Reginald Blomfield and Charles Holden. Of the buildings discussed in this book, he undertook commissions at Oxford Town Hall and Bristol Central Library. The contribution of craftsmen like the Aumoniers, not quite artists, nor yet tradesmen, who frequently had to work from the designs or directions of others, yet who displayed not only technical skill, but artistic judgement and scholarship, was very considerable in terms of Edwardian buildings. After the First World War their output declined rapidly as styles and architectural theory changed, and it has now disappeared almost entirely from the architectural scene.

Although the quality and type of materials used as finishes is common to most town and county halls, throughout the period the amount of applied art tends to vary, from, on the one hand, the almost overwhelming use of wall painting at Wakefield, to the restraint of Northallerton on the other. In the case of less important buildings, such as public libraries, special efforts were made in entrance halls, on staircases and in reference rooms – in many cases those located on upper floors. Magazine, newspaper and reading rooms, usually near to the main entrance, are often plain, as they attracted casual visitors and large numbers of poor or improvident people who spent time in the shelter and comparative warmth of this public facility. There is in common in all of these buildings, though, an attempt to impress those using the chief public spaces, especially the entrance, and to establish the building's importance within the hierarchy of public spaces in the town or city.

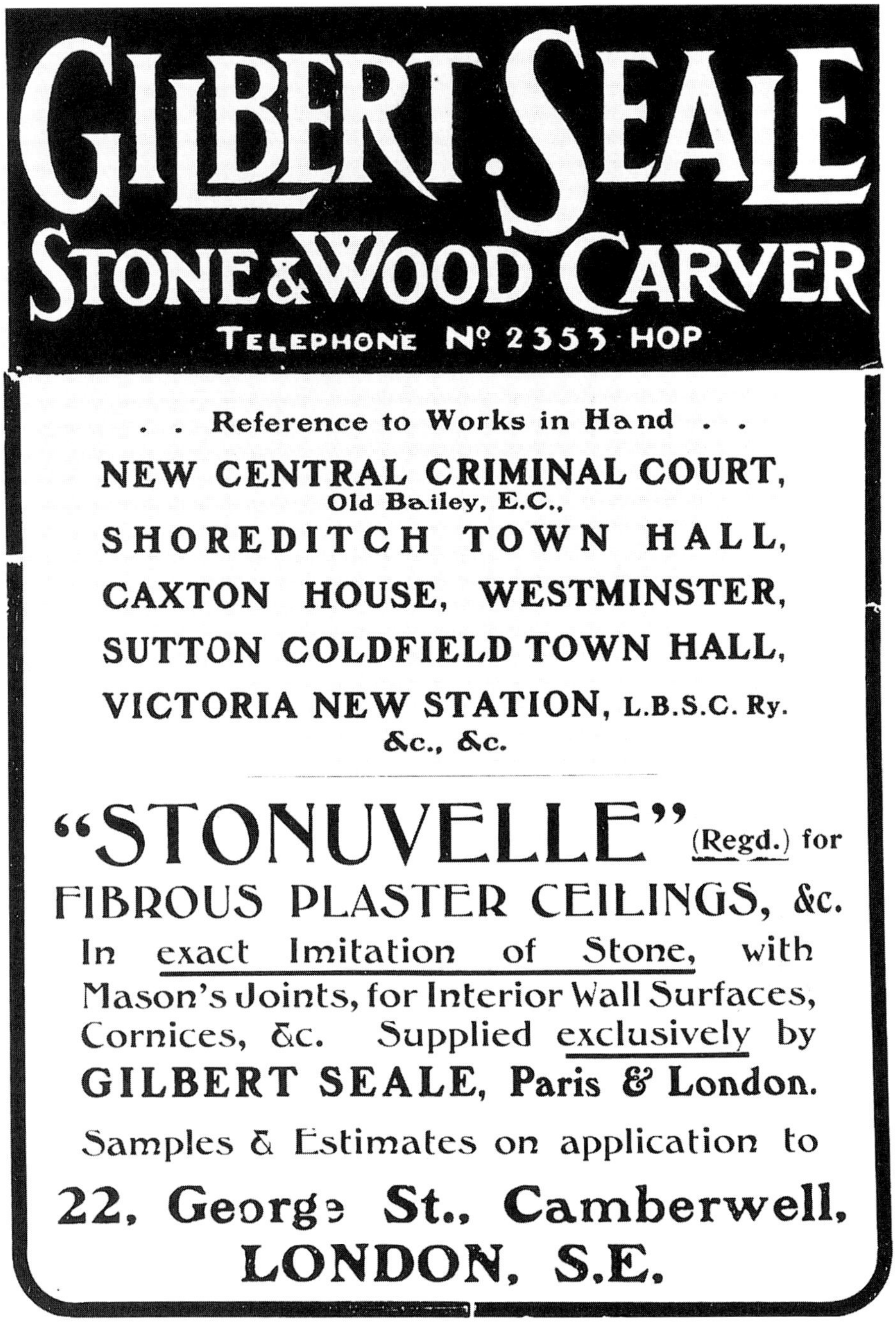

Figure 8.14

An advertisement for Gilbert Seale, who undertook work at Mountford's Central Criminal Court, as well as at Lancaster Town Hall

Decorative and artistic effort was not confined to civic buildings of course, and commercial premises visited by the public, which had to create a feeling of permanence and success, outdid public buildings in some cases. The United Kingdom Provident Institution, for instance, rose in the Strand in the middle of the first decade of the century. Its use of marble and other rich finishes, as with the finest of civic buildings, from the cipollino clad walls and piastraccia staircases of the public areas to the oak panelling and modelled and painted ceilings of the directors' and board rooms. Carving was executed by William Aumonier and other work was undertaken by the craftsmen of the Bromsgrove Guild. In addition to this, there were designs for mosaic by J. Dudley Forsyth and Gerald Moira, who also contributed stained glass. Moira was responsible for the painted ceiling in the board room and F. Lynn Jenkins contributed the design for bronze work which included grilles for fresh air inlets and radiator frames, column capitals and a figure frieze around the circumference of the circular general office.

Strangely, this commercial extravaganza was designed by Henry T. Hare, who specialized in civic buildings – a public competition man through and through. Hare used artists and craftsmen in this building, who had contributed to his work from the earliest days, notably Aumonier and F.E.E. Schenck, although the latter's work at the United Kingdom Provident Institution is confined to the exterior. At Staffordshire County Hall, Aumonier carved the pediments of the doors to the council chamber to designs of H.T. Hare and his adviser, MacVicar Anderson, as well as contributing wood carving in the Oak Room and elsewhere. Schenck, who had worked in the Potteries and taught at a local art school, contributed four relief panels to the council chamber depicting Staffordshire industries. He also contributed moulded plasterwork design at important points within the building. There is no evidence of painting or mosaic, though, and perhaps, generally, the more excessive manifestations of the arts and crafts movement were not considered suitable either for local or county councillors – self-made men or gentry.

Hare's work at Oxford may appear fussy to modern eyes. The fussiness first becomes apparent in the use of decorative plasterwork to decorate the vaults to the main staircase and its first floor landing. It creeps out of the junctions between the arches, but is discontinued before it meets in the centre of the vault ceiling. As excellent as this may be as an example of the plasterer's art and a representation of Elizabethan practice, it tends to unsettle the eye in what is already a busy composition of columns, balustrades, arches, mullioned windows with stained glass panels and a patterned floor. All the same, the landing works well aesthetically, the control of materials and the repetition of columns and arches giving it coherence and a character appropriate to its purpose. There are also some splendid details, which are discussed below.

The style adopted by Hare seems to work well in spaces such as the council chamber and particularly in rooms of a more domestic size such as the Lord Mayor's parlour. However, the main assembly hall is overwrought in its decorative scheme, and one feels that Hare could have shown restraint in an attempt to decorate all surfaces and then elaborate the decoration. Like the rest of the building it is of its time, but reflects mannerisms that appear less acceptable today.

Certain details on the staircase and the landing, however, are those for which one may yearn in contemporary buildings. Of particular note is the venetian window looking down onto the stairwell from a little enclosed space adjacent to the Assembly Room. In its central, arched section, was a clock face, so that the whole window and its surround appeared to form the body of the clock. Below are the arms of the city. These are repeated in a bronze radiator grille on the landing, including the motto 'Fortis est Veritas' in an arts and crafts graphic style, but omitting the elephant and beaver which support the shield, which is set against a background of foliage. At the stairheads, stone griffins holding shields lurk hidden, as one rises, by columns. They are seated on extensions to the balustrades, which act as column pedestals, guarding the stairheads.

(a)

Figure 8.15

Oxford Town Hall. (a) Radiator grille to landing, with the Oxford coat of arms. (Photo: Oxfordshire County Council.) (b) Stone griffin at the stairhead

(b)

Henry Hare used the same artists and craftsmen in many of his buildings. There is little doubt that architects established a rapport with those who were commissioned to develop their own contributions within the overall scheme of the building, or who had to translate the architect's intention into reality. It has already been remarked that the practice of Lanchester, Stewart and Rickards worked regularly with certain sculptors for the exteriors of their buildings. Internally, Rickards' fluency and genius in detail design was often interpreted by craftsmen. However, there were sculptural elements displayed internally in both Cardiff and Deptford Town Halls. Henry Poole, who had contributed external sculpture at Cardiff, added modelled

Figure 8.16
Deptford Town Hall. View on the staircase, showing the plasterwork to the ceiling and the mermaids flanking the council chamber door. Singer's iron and bronze cast balustrades are also in evidence. (Photo: Courtesy of Caroline Nicholl, The White House Studios)

plasterwork scallop shells and mermaids to the sculpture niches over the main staircases, and at the entrance to the council chamber. These charming features recur in Rickard's drawings of Deptford, where the mermaids flank a shell over the council chamber door at the head of the stairs. Nothing could better represent Rickard's free and voluptuous style, at a time when the constraints of the *beaux-arts* were still in the future.

Rickard's perspective drawing, 'view on staircase' of Deptford Town Hall (1903) shows another element which is of significance in his output. This is the design of metalwork, in particular for balustrades. The drawing indicates iron and bronze balustrades running up the stairs on the inside of the well; forming a segmental 'balcony' over the well opposite the entrance to the council chamber; and filling in between the paired marble columns on the landings. Its baroque swirls are supplemented by maritime motifs of ships and anchors. The architect had already designed elaborate balustrades at Cardiff City Hall, and went on to produce those of astonishing elegance at Wesleyan Central Hall, where the sweeping lines of the great staircase are reinforced by the balustrades and hand rail. The motif consists of a series of circular or eliptical panels linked by swirls of metal, divided into bays by stanchions surmounted by spindly finials. The handrail is bracketed up from the balustrade and runs into the finials. It is a sophisticated and interesting piece of design in its own right, but its main purpose is to enhance and elaborate the architectural scheme as a whole.

Lanchester and Rickards were not the only architects to place emphasis on this kind of detail, although in most of the examples explored in this book, the staircase details are in marble. The need for fine casting in metals, especially iron and bronze, however, was common. Without doubt, the leading firm that specialized in this work was J.W. Singer and Sons Ltd, of Frome in Somerset. The founder of the firm was a clock maker, but he diversified into the production of ecclesiastical metalwork, and then statuary. By the time Singer died in 1904, the firm was established as a leading foundry for important sculpture in Britain and the Empire. Detailed, intricate and specialized work to the designs of architects was regularly undertaken. For instance, electroliers or other light fittings were cast by Singers for Stockport Town Hall, North Riding County Hall, Central Hall, Westminster and Cardiff City Hall.

For Cardiff the works produced the three huge multi-tiered bronzed wrought iron electroliers used in the assembly hall. By the architect's own admission, these were 'unusually intricate in design', weighted up to one ton each, but could be raised and lowered by a pulley system (unlike those in the council chamber at Wakefield which are fixed and difficult to maintain). Singer also manufactured the balusters and the iron

Figure 8.17

An advertisement for Singer's foundry. The light pendant illustrated was designed by A. Brumwell Thomas for Belfast City Hall

entrance gates for the hall. In almost all cases, the electroliers used in these buildings were designed specifically by the architect for that particular project. They vary from relatively basic types used in small rooms and those of low status, to enormously elaborate objects suspended high above assembly and concert halls from the centrelines of the vault over. At their simplest, there is normally a metal hoop hung horizontally from the ceiling with a number of shaded bulbs hanging around the perimeter of the hoop. The bell-like shape of the glass shades can create an analogous impression of small flowers dangling overhead. More elaborate examples may be in two tiers with a complex central pendant with scrolled brackets supporting the hoop and guiding the electrical flexes to the fittings below. Mountford's designs for the public (Ashton) hall at Lancaster Town Hall have huge, wreath-like forms encircling the horizontal hoops, and terminating in pendants hanging many feet below. There are, thus, a number of points from which bulbs can be hung, and which give a spread of light below as well as creating a picturesque effect.

Singer cast some of their most impressive light fittings for Wesleyan Central Hall. A pair of enormous octagonal lanterns guards the arched recess in the ground floor entrance hall leading to the small hall and the library. These are echoed by a further pair flanking the great staircase. They are set on stone pedestals, the same height as the door heads, from which rise decorated bronze standards on which the lanterns themselves stand. They help to enhance the grandeur of what is already a scheme conceived with a great architectural flourish. Over the staircase itself is a large pendant fitting supported on chains and comprising a central luminaire with four satellites. In the main hall are four large electroliers, with subsidiary suspended fittings. The list could be extended to many other spaces within the building, but this applies to most other major projects of the time. Advantage was taken of the freedom given by the use of electricity, which was exploited in an imaginative way by architects who regarded the design of fittings as part of their remit.

Architects sometimes also designed furniture specifically for their buildings, not simply fittings. Of course, council chambers were normally provided with fixed seating and integrated writing desks usually in oak or mahogany with leather coverings. However, non-fixed furniture can be found. Charles Holden designed tables for use in the reference room at Bristol Central Library. Constructed from good quality 'twice oiled' teak they are splendidly sturdy and functional and are arranged in rows across the room. Each table can accommodate twelve students and is divided along its length, sloping partitions at right-angles delineating the compartments. At each end of the room is a circular table, with a rotating top. The tops are supported on a central pedestal composed of 'columns' arranged in an octagonal group. Although plain and purposeful, the legs and columns are 'Carolean' in style. The furniture contrasts with the ornate plasterwork of the room, perhaps indicating the meeting place of the 'Wrenaissance' and the arts and crafts tradition.

The most outstanding examples of decorative work in Colchester Town Hall, it may be argued, are related to the provision of coloured glass. Nearly all of the civic buildings described have stained glass windows containing coats of arms related to the towns, cities and counties which they represent, or those of local benefactors and those whose philanthropy made the building possible. Colchester's theme, throughout, is to represent the history of the ancient borough. There is, for instance, a fine large window, executed by Messrs Powell and Sons, the 'Weavers' Memorial' or 'Huguenot' window. This is a pictorial representation of the reception of French, Flemish and Dutch refugees, prior to the estab-

Figure 8.18

Colchester Town Hall. The window on the stair dedicated to Lord Cowdray and made by Clayton and Bell, added in the 1920s

lishment of the weaving industry in the area. Also in the council chamber, St Helena and the Emperor Claudius are represented. On the stairs are windows by Clayton and Bell. Perhaps the most unusual is that dedicated to

Figure 8.19
Lancaster Town Hall. A first floor stained glass window. (Photo: Lancaster City County Council Museums Services)

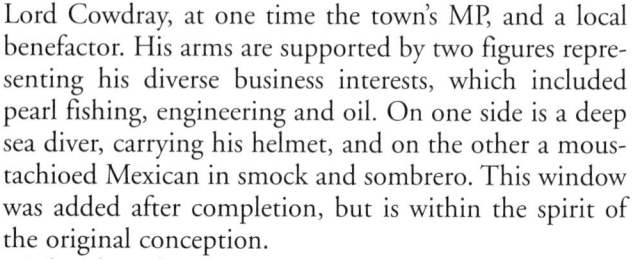

Figure 8.20
County Hall, Wakefield. Stained glass on the grand staircase. (Photo: Albert Booth)

Lord Cowdray, at one time the town's MP, and a local benefactor. His arms are supported by two figures representing his diverse business interests, which included pearl fishing, engineering and oil. On one side is a deep sea diver, carrying his helmet, and on the other a moustachioed Mexican in smock and sombrero. This window was added after completion, but is within the spirit of the original conception.

The three big round-headed windows in the moot hall, which form such a feature both internally and externally, also contain historical matter. The central window of the three has the theme of Queens of England and those to either side show the history of the borough before and after the Conquest, arranged around portraits of Edward the Elder and Richard I.

Thus, in Colchester Town Hall, the internal decoration, art and enrichment continues a pattern that is prevalent on the outside of the building, too. As, perhaps, the archetypal Edwardian civic building, Colchester makes great use of iconography, allegorical figures and pictorial representation to link it to its region and to remind the local populace that it is not only *their* building, but the embodiment of the locality and of its culture. The architectural and artistic precedent is from the gothic revival, through the arts and crafts movement. It began to be lost when the influence of the *beaux-arts* style, inherited from American practice, became more pronounced. By the end of the Edwardian period it had virtually gone, and has hardly been revived. It seems unlikely that it will, as it is perhaps too naïve and self-conscious in an electronic age where the populace is bombarded with images, and public life is anything but pure and selfless.

CHAPTER NINE

Technology

Edwardian architecture was heavily reliant upon the rapidly developing and innovative technology of the period. It was, however, not a techtonic architecture. Contemporary accounts, except those in specialist journals, seem to gloss over the nuts and bolts and concentrate on architectural effects, finishes, fittings and works of applied art. Technology was not important as a generator of style and form as it may have been, for instance, in the design of early mills or modern movement buildings of the 1920s and 1930s. From this point of view, some critics have viewed Edwardian building with disfavour as vain, pretentious and shallow.

Edwardian architects, however, cared deeply about technological issues. In the main, they did not see these as great architectural significance, especially in the design of civic buildings where symbolism, imagery and propriety were of primary concern. In some respects, too, any moralizing about the necessity for buildings to be truthful reminded them of the preceding generations who had come under the influence of Pugin and Ruskin.

These theorists had linked design to morality and religion in no uncertain terms. Buildings, they said, must represent themselves honestly in structural and functional terms and should not attempt to be less than truthful. In many ways this was admirable – but the theories became inextricably linked with dogma that insisted that only certain very specific kinds of architecture would do in certain circumstances. There were even aesthetic police in the form of critics who lost no time in condemning what they considered to be impure. Although this dogma fell out of favour by the 1870s, some of the ideas were retained in the arts and crafts movement which had a continuing effect throughout the Edwardian period. Nevertheless, mainstream architecture, as we have seen, became a more visual art, revitalizing the tradition of the picturesque strand running throughout English work. Designers who were grateful to see the diminution and then the end of Ruskin's influence, however, had a fairly brief respite before being swallowed up by modernism.

Such was the rapid development of constructional and environmental technology in the nineteenth century, that it may have been difficult to impose narrow theories about the relationship between materials and form by the end of the Victorian era, given the plethora of opportunities that arose from these innovations. Indeed, W.H. Preece wrote that 'the spirit of our present age is the rule of science over mere aestheticism'.[1] Perhaps it was inevitable, though, that a new controlling aesthetic should be introduced. The two great constructional systems of the twentieth century were nearing practicability by the 1890s. Metal structural frames – notably of cast iron – were made common by the Industrial Revolution, but the use of steel in a regular frame with members of standardized section was perfected in the United States where steel mills owned by magnates such as Carnegie were able to cater for the demand imposed by America's burgeoning cities. The speed of erection and the transfer of skill from the building site to the drawing office and the factory, were issues that became concerns for British architects during the Edwardian era.

It was during the 1880s that steel had become a viable material to use in place of wrought iron, when it was 'now relatively cheaper and more reliable'.[2] In Britain, centres of manufacture for structural steelwork were located on Teesside, where Dorman Long had a factory at Middlesbrough, and in Scotland where Redpath, Brown and Company were established. 'I' sections and compound girders were produced by these concerns, and from 1900 Dorman Long were involved in the design and erection of complete structures. Although the first buildings in the country using steel exclusively as a framework were constructed in the 1890s, it was really the revolution brought about by American practice, and, most notably the work of the engineer Sven Bylander, in the first decade of the twentieth century, that lead the way to modern, gridded steel frameworks with standardized sections.

In addition, the potential of reinforced concrete was beginning to be realized. Although its development had followed a convoluted path during the preceding eighty years or so, and was inextricably linked to the construction of fireproof floors, it was at last being systematized and was the subject of scientific investigation in both France and Germany. The outcome of these investigations was the appearance of proprietary systems which enabled engineers to design predictably in the new material. It also allowed them to perform the kind of structural gymnastics that could only have been fantasized about a few years earlier.

Of the French pioneers, it was Hennebique's system that won early popularity in Great Britain, where his agent, L.G. Mouchel, took an active role in the promotion of the material. In the late 1890s industrial buildings and civil engineering works began to be designed using reinforced concrete. Such was Mouchel's popularity that during the first decade of the new century worries about monopolies caused efforts to be made to spread knowledge amongst native architects and engineers. A London office specializing in the American Kahn system was also established. The use of reinforced concrete in prestigious projects was truly established, however, when Sir Henry Tanner, chief architect to the Office of Works, used it for the new General Post Office building in the City of London, begun in 1906.

Architects could not only avail themselves of these structural marvels, but had an ever expanding choice of materials with which to clad the building, line it out or roof it. Even if marble and stone were to be used in visible areas, there is little doubt that behind the scenes the latest factory-made building products would be fulfilling their functions relatively cheaply and conveniently.

During the preceding century, the complexity of buildings had increased as well as the size. Buildings may have had to fulfil several functions, and may have contained a variety of spaces – small cellular rooms for offices, for instance; large span assembly halls; long thin spaces such as hospital wards; grand, multi-level entrances; accommodation for plant and machinery. The Victorian hospital, built to serve enormous urban populations is a case in point, or large public buildings like Manchester Town Hall. The programme of the buildings in these cases, rather than theoretical issues, tends to drive the architect's solution in terms of form and spatial disposition. Increasingly new technology was there to help achieve these goals. Apart from the use of historical styles, to all intents and purposes these buildings were as modern in outlook as any built in the subsequent century.

As has been noted, much of the technological and operational change came from the United States. British architects were constantly brought face to face with the achievements of their American counterparts. Following a paper read at the Royal Institute of British Architects in November 1905 by Mr R.A. Denell on 'American Methods of Erecting Buildings',[3] the President of the Institute, John Belcher, peevishly commented 'I must say I often get tired of hearing of American methods ...'. However, by the time that the subsequent discussion had concluded he was able to say that 'He thought that they had learned two lessons from the paper: one that they must not lag behind; and the other that they must take every advantage of all the improved methods they could, consistent with the production of good work. In the steel frame work they had a very serious problem ... they should all have to become engineers instead of architects ...'.[4]

Although this sounds like panic, and perhaps is, the architectural profession had not been negligent in the discussion of new technology over the years as it came along. Papers and reviews of books on iron and steel construction, fireproof construction, reinforced concrete, electric power and improved methods of heating and ventilation were frequent, with the amount of material on reinforced concrete increasing considerably after the turn of the century. Developments at home and in Europe were noted, and although the older generation of Edwardian architects may have looked ahead with some dread at the prospect of having to cope with technologies for which they did not have a 'feel' and business practices which demanded American efficiency, engineering accuracy in drawings and little chance to explore the delights of the craft of building, they manfully faced up to the future and many were able to accommodate change.

These new developments form an undercurrent to the purely architectural developments that were also going on as the buildings described in this book were being planned and executed. It should be remembered, though, that building processes were also changing, and these had an effect on site operations. The numbers of men required in site construction declined drastically, and some trades diminished, whilst others retained their strength. Machinery was used more and more to help in excavation and construction. At first it was steam powered, but electricity was introduced, particularly to power cranes and hoists. R.W. Postgate notes that the period between 1900 and 1910 saw a rapid expansion in new processes and machinery that threw numbers out of employment. Joinery, for instance, was made both on and off site with machinery, and large joinery factories were established, such as Shannon Factory at Dalston in London, designed by Edwin Otto Sachs, fully powered by electricity and fire resisting. It was opened in 1902. Plumbers' work was lost through the expanding use of asphalt roofing, through the replacement of gas lighting by electricity and through the provision of factory-made ceramic sanitary ware (as opposed to lead-lined sinks, for instance). 'But the most important change in the period', says Postgate, 'was the great extension of the use of concrete ... it replaced masonry and brickwork in the vast majority of important jobs ...'.[5] All of this was set against a background of decline in the industry and a contraction that lasted from 1901 for ten years.

This may be generally true of the industry, but nearly all of the civic buildings described in this book, despite relatively advanced environmental and services systems (see below), seem to have restricted themselves to a very straight-forward approach in terms of structure and construction. Furthermore, the outer skin of the building envelope is usually in a material appropriate to its status or locality, and stone tends to predominate. Terracotta, a useful facing material, was, it appears, reserved for humble public or commercial buildings. It was, anyway, out of favour by the Edwardian period, from an aesthetic point of view, having been overused by a preceding generation of architects like Alfred Waterhouse. Furthermore, reinforced concrete, despite Postgate's comments, seems to have found employment for commercial, industrial and office buildings, rather than those concerned with civic status. In Henry Tanner's General Post Office, constructed in the Hennebique system, the new material's capabilities were exploited to the full, with high level cantilevers, box girders and large span rooms located beneath heavily trafficked external spaces. However, the mix of accommodation – public areas, office space, sorting offices, loading bays and so on – was ideally suited to the flexibility in use of in situ concrete.

This demonstration of confidence in concrete came slightly after the main period of construction for civic purposes. In nearly all of the buildings described, neither steel nor concrete was used to full advantage, and the structural elements were normally concealed except in the most utilitarian areas, well out of the gaze of the public, councillors and officers. Perhaps, rightly, it was felt that structural systems were of little interest to them. Few of the buildings, in any case, lent themselves to the repetition and regularity of a steel framework in the same way that a speculative office block with standardized spaces would do. The largest spans would be those of roofs to, say, a council chamber or a public assembly hall, which could be adequately spanned by built-up steel trusses. In almost all examples, therefore, it seems that structure and construction did not generate the form of Edwardian civic buildings, and that structural methods were pressed into service to realize the architect's spatial intent.

County Hall, Stafford, was the work of the young and enthusiastic Henry T. Hare, and here he employed modern techniques in order to achieve his design. Steelwork, was ordered from Middlesbrough and 'joists and girders' positioned when the walls had risen to 6 feet by November 1893. All of the ground floor and first floor steelwork was in place by the January of the following year. The floors, too, used steel, with concrete in-fill, making a strong 'fireproof' construction, as specified by the building's clients. This was probably not a 'patent' fireproof floor, and seems very 'over structured' by modern standards. Nevertheless the system has stood the test of time and Hare even seems to have broken new ground, as the steel and concrete roof to the council chamber (12.8 m square) was described as the largest of its type when built. Contemporaneously, at Oxford, Hare followed similar practice, where it was requested that construction should be as fireproof as possible. It is interesting to note that two steelwork contractors were employed; Dorman, Long & Co. for the floors and William Lindsay & Co. for the roofs. Lindsay also undertook the floors at Stafford. Almost fifteen years later, the structure of Lancaster Town Hall was scarcely different.

Lanchester, Stewart and Rickards followed similar practice at Cardiff City Hall. Steel stanchions were used to support the floors, and in this two-storey building, the public assembly hall is located above the rates office, where the span is divided into three parts. The floors themselves were similar to those deployed by Hare, with steel joists embedded in concrete. The roofs, including the council chamber dome, were framed up in timber, but with a steel and concrete fireproof structure beneath. The exception was the assembly hall, where built-up steelwork was used, the heavy ornamental plasterwork of Bankart's vault being hung on a substructure of expanded metal on standard steel angles. On a smaller scale, at Henley Town Hall, Hare used similar trusses with a Mansard external profile, and a segmental internal one to carry the plaster ceiling vault. The 12 m spans were fabricated in three parts to assist in transportation.

Fireproof floors were expressly requested for Bristol Central Library in the competition document. These were supported on 'a steel skeleton of box section girders'.[6] The maximum grid size was approximately 5.5 m × 7.6 m, though this was varied according to the functions of the spaces enclosed, and is, perhaps, related to the disposition of book stacks, shelving and reading desks.

The picture of unadventurous construction for civic buildings seems to be fairly consistent. Even the greatest of them all, County Hall in London, built at the end of the period, conforms. Extensive works were required to provide a suitable platform from which the building could rise, on the south bank of the Thames. Once completed, however, construction of the superstructure followed a straight forward and, by now, traditional method. Heavy steelwork was limited to a part of the building 'where the upper floors are built above large clear spans over the boiler room'. Further to this limitation of steel construction, 'because the architectural style is of massive nature, load-bearing brickwork seemed to be the obvious choice and the idea of using steelwork generally for vertical structure was ruled out virtually from the beginning'.[7] The roof, however, was formed in built up steel girders.

As far as fireproof floors were concerned, the winner of the competition to design County Hall, Ralph Knott, suggested a patent reinforced concrete system. However, the architect to the London County Council, W.E. Riley, was against the use of the system, and insisted on the use of steel joists embedded and in-filled in concrete – similar to Hare's use of the method almost twenty years before.

An exception to this conservatism is the Wesleyan Central Hall at Westminster. It was described in *The Builder* as 'without parallel as an example of modern construction in London'.[8] The complicated programme of the building and the consequent spatial variety and disposition was resolved by the exploitation of the possibilities introduced by the use of reinforced concrete. However, the material was not used exclusively, and substantial elements of steelwork were deployed for use in conjunction with the concrete, as well as brick arches in some places. It would be a mistake to think that the construction is a 'Heath Robinson' affair, although it may be over-enthusiastic in its use of different techniques by present standards, where cost and time constraints limit often predominate.

The half of the architectural partnership that designed the hall was H.V. Lanchester. He was not only a master of planning and, perhaps, one may say, the more intellectual, and hard-headed aspects of architecture – nobly complemented by his intuitive partner, Rickards – but he had confidently exploited advanced technology in earlier projects. His brother was F.W. Lanchester, the innovative mechanical engineer and, later, a proponent of inflatable structures.

Lanchester employed concrete in a manner that exploited its plasticity and versatility, using the methods of the Kahn system. The system originated in the United States and employed shear reinforcement rigidly attached to the main tension members. The reinforcement was sold to contractors together with detailed working drawings. To modern eyes, it seems strange that the Kahn system was not used for the entirety of the structure but that there was a dual reliance upon steel as well as reinforced concrete for major structural elements. The steelwork is hidden away, covered by layers of traditional materials, but the concrete is, in places, exposed to view, through given traditional form. The most obvious example of this can be seen in the 80 feet (28.4 m) diameter dome over the conference hall, which is located at first floor levels and is the major space in the building. Here the traditional coffered appearance is due to the nature of the structure which consists of the provision of reinforced concrete radiating ribs which intersect with circumferential beams. The hall is square on plan, however, and the dome is supported over it on beams 8 feet (2.4 m) deep and 50 feet (15.2 m) long. These beams, forming an octagonal pattern and are, in turn supported on concrete girders 70 feet (21.3 m) long and 13 feet (4.0 m) deep. The whole structure, however, is suspended over 80 feet (24.4 m) from pavement level on steel lattice stanchions, of which there are eight altogether, arranged in pairs at the corners. The stanchions are founded on a 'grillage' of two layers of rolled steel joists, laid perpendicular to each other and embedded in concrete 7 feet (2.1 m) thick.

The major structural use of steel elsewhere is in the galleries of the conference hall. The rakes of these are formed in concrete, but are supported at the back on a large steel girder, and by another one towards the front. However, the concrete projects over 4 metres beyond this. Girders can also be found elsewhere where convenience dictates. Over and above this, literally, is the outer dome of Central Hall. As in the case of Wren's St Paul's Cathedral this is independent of the inner dome and is designed for its urban effect, rather than as a roof covering. It is framed up from standard steel sections and consists of inclined trusses with a curved top boom located at the angles of the drum – a square with chamfered corners. There are therefore eight trusses, held in place by a steel base plate and additional framing between. Above is a lantern with a steel skeleton, but whose profile is made up by a secondary timber structure. All of this, and the dome's lead covering and ornamentation, is for effect rather than function, serving to position the building within the urban hierarchy.

Steel in this building is therefore used as an expedient, but the reinforced concrete is integral with its nature. In the basement tea rooms, for instance, elliptical 'domes' are formed into the ceilings to relieve what would be a very large area of uniform height. The 'domes' are created with the use of reinforced concrete ribs, whose maximum elevation is 6 feet (1.8 m). This would have been difficult to achieve in any other material, and the relatively thin ground floor, above, was also made possible by the way in which the thickness of the concrete and the relative amounts of reinforcement could be varied. Similarly, the raft on which the whole structure stands is of varying thickness, and ducting for services is formed into the slab, so that pipes and cables could be run around the building neatly and unobtrusively. A final example of the way in which the opportunities afforded by the use of concrete was exploited by Lanchester, was in the columns to the ground floor, which support the underside of the conference hall above. Approximately 2 feet (0.6 m) in diameter, and 28 feet (8.5 m) long, they were cast to a profile respecting classical rules, rather than being simple piers of round or rectangular section. Thus, each had 'entasis', the subtle curve given to the sides of columns,

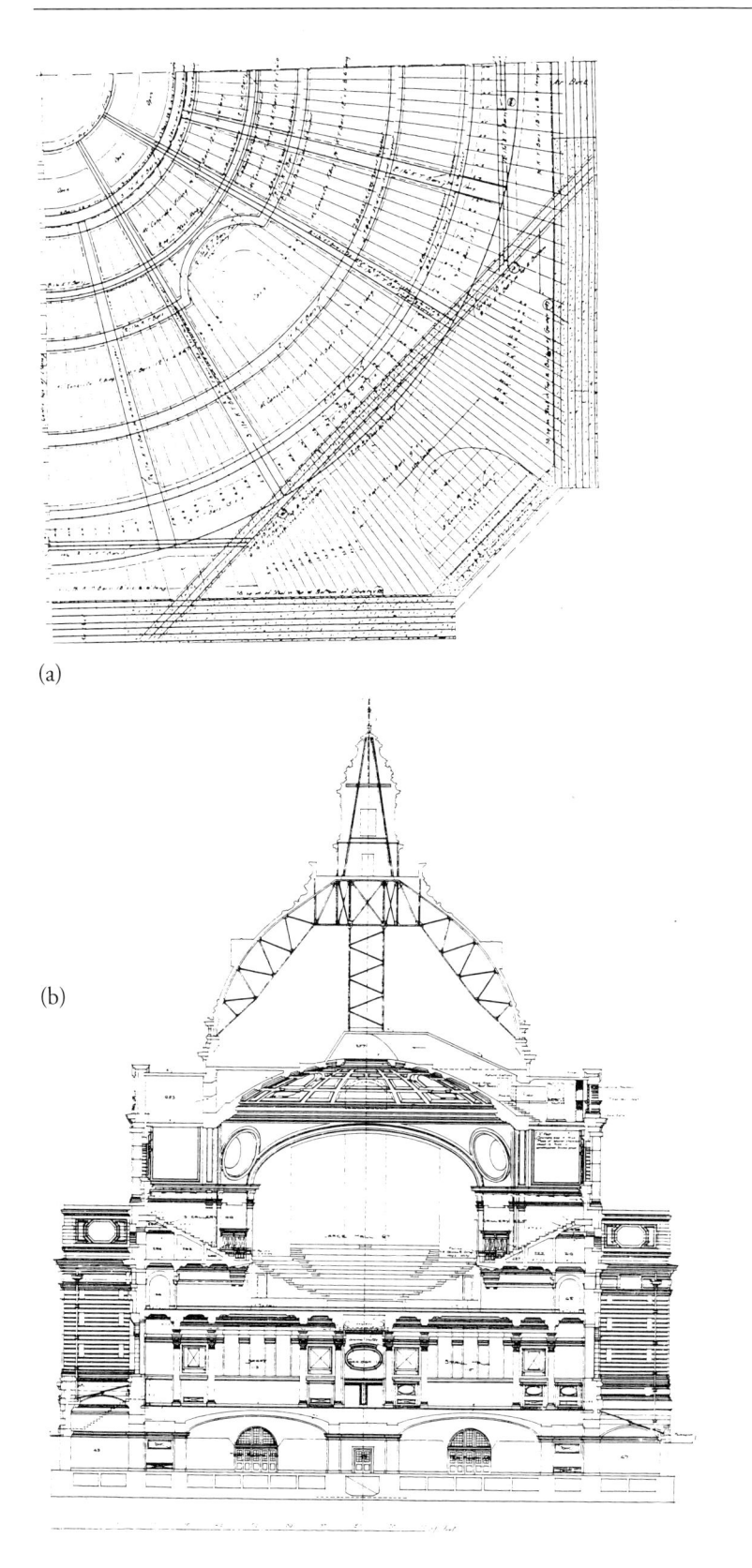

Figure 9.1
Wesleyan Central Hall. Constructional details showing, (a) part plan of the internal dome with reinforcing rod layout, (b) section through the building and (c) the built-up steel lattice stanchions supporting the reinforced concrete dome

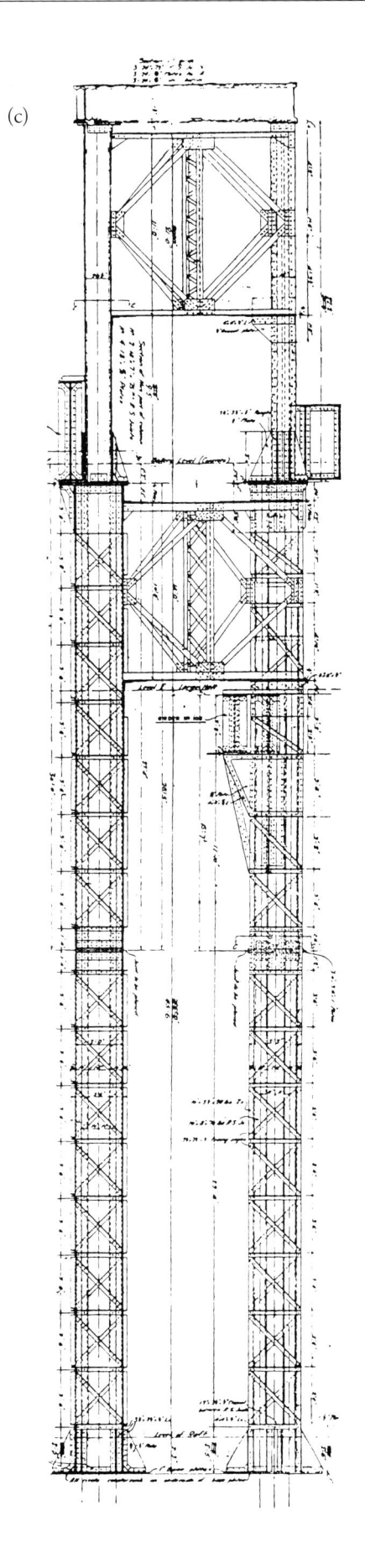

developed in ancient Greece, which prevents the visually uncouth affect of parallel sides. Plasterwork was applied to these as a finish, only 1/8 inch (3 mm) thick, rather than being employed to produce the profile on a rough base. More could be said about the structure and construction of Central Hall, but it is, to a great extent, an exception to a conservative overall picture. Where Edwardian civic buildings did exploit new technology fully was in power and services.

Even the earliest buildings noted in this book were provided with electrical power. The introduction of incandescent lamps or 'glow lamps' in 1880, and their gradual reduction in costs meant that electric light was a feasible alternative to gas, which created heat, vitiated the air and blackened ceilings and hangings. The advantages of the new developments were quickly realized, and by 1882 several important buildings in central London were illuminated by the electric light. Private companies at first set up power stations, and by 1889, for instance, Deptford had a Ferranti station on its doorstep. However, publicly generated supplies, initially transmitted at 100 volts, were to prove of more far reaching importance, and Bradford was first in the field, also in 1889. Even if a supply was not available when decisions were taken to build, then those responsible for the specification of civic buildings made provision for electricity. At Stafford, for instance, it was determined to design-in electric lighting before a local service was in existence, Stafford Corporation eventually providing power from the mains by the time the building was completed. The same was true at Wakefield, where provision for generators was made in the estimates. When power became available locally in 1896, the saving on cost was offset against the increasing outlay on construction.

Architects, as we have seen, designed appropriate light fittings to give as much illumination as possible, but effort seems to have been concentrated on the appearance of the glowing globes, rather than on the play of light over the surfaces of the interior. Prior to 1902 the carbonized filaments gave out a comparatively weak light – although contemporary observers seem to have found it extremely harsh compared to other forms of lighting – but metallic filaments were introduced at around this time, tungsten being used later on.

No doubt after several decades coping with the effects of gas tubing and gas burners of various types, architects welcomed the relative neatness of electric wiring and fittings. At Stafford, in the early 1890s the mains cable was taken into the basement, and from there to a switchboard in the porter's' box on the ground floor. From here, five circuits were established which ran to distribution boards in various parts of the building: the basement, for lighting and ventilation fans, the ground floor offices; the members' entrance hall, the committee rooms, the council chamber. Seven lamps were fed by each branch from the distribution board. Wiring was run through wooden trunking which allowed ease of replacement if necessary. This was exposed 'where the appearance of wooden casing is not objectionable', in other words in service areas and on the back stairs; elsewhere, the casing was embedded in plaster. Thus Hare's handsome light fittings were made to glow, and the concealed lighting above the glass dome in the members' entrance lobby could persuade county councillors that the sun was shining amidst winter's gloom.

Ten years later, Deptford Town Hall was also supplied with electric power. In spite of the proximity of the Ferranti power station, it was decided to generate electricity on site. The reason for this was a sensible – in modern jargon, 'sustainable' – decision. The Town Hall was constructed on land adjoining the local public baths. The extensive boiler plant had spare generating capacity, and it was decided to pipe steam through to the new building. Here, in a spick and span tiled engine room, Belliss steam engines drove two 25 kw Phoenix dynamos. Exhaust steam was used to heat the Town Hall, or returned to the baths. The output of the dynamos passed to a splendid switchboard located in the engine room, from which seven pairs of main cables emerged, rubber insulated and running in steel conduits. Storage batteries were also supplied, and excess capacity could be transferred to the baths and vice versa. The cost of the electrical installation, plant and back up gas supply came to £3,248, approximately 10 per cent of the overall building cost, and only slightly more than was spent on furniture. At Oxford Town Hall, almost a decade before, the lighting installation cost £2,354, but this was only 2.5 per cent of the overall expenditure.

Internal communications within complex buildings, dealing with important administrative matters was, needless to say, of great importance. To this end, Staffordshire County Hall was supplied throughout with the 'Homacoustic' speaking tube system. A plaintive request, made later on, for telephones, was rejected, and the county councillors were allowed only one external line, with an extension. Later, at Deptford, there were no less than three systems: that connected to the National Telephone Company; an internal intercom and 'a reply and call battery system'. Bristol Central Library also had internal and external systems. Brierley installed telephones between offices and committee rooms at North Riding County Hall; lighting, telephones and bells were all included in one tender of £851 19s 6d (£851.97p).

The other uses for electricity in civic buildings were powering fan motors, discussed below, and lifts. Stafford had Waygood lifts, as did Lancaster Town Hall, used to bring food from kitchens to the banqueting service rooms. In Bristol Central Library, though, the booklifts were manually operated, and the provision of motors was thought to be profligate. Lancaster's great organ was blown electrically.

Electricity was used extensively, though not exclusively, to power fans to move air around buildings; sometimes steam power was employed instead. The idea of 'artificial' ventilation and heating by warmed air was not new. It had been developed throughout the nineteenth century and, of course, the use of ducts to transmit heat goes back to Roman times. However, systems had gradually been developed as buildings grew in size and complexity. Unfortunately, in some cases, heating and ventilating was a matter of experiment or trial and error, rather than prediction. The most notorious instance of this was the manner in which the new Palace of Westminster was equipped, and the amount of time taken to reach a satisfactory standard of operation. By the closing decade of the century, however, and the opening of the Edwardian era, the benefits of experience were noted, new improved hardware was available, and architects were used to thinking about the integration of plant and ducting into their building designs.

In the early years of the new century, there was much debate about the 'plenum' system of heating and ventilation, and a good deal of informed comment about its operation, advantages and disadvantages. It had been in use for many years, and was chiefly employed where a deep plan was unavoidable and where large numbers of people congregated. Thus, in terms of civic buildings, it was favoured for council chambers and assembly halls. A positive pressure was created in these spaces by the forced admission of warmed or cooled air, which was then extracted, and the whole process balanced and calculated so that there were a predicted number of air changes per hour, and each occupant was provided with a known quantity of fresh air. By the turn of the century, William Henman had designed a new hospital in Belfast, the Royal Victoria Hospital, where the 'plenum' system influenced the form and planning of the building. This overturned the 'pavilion' plan, popularized by Florence Nightingale, and relying on natural ventilation, across relatively narrow blocks of building. For some commentators, this may symbolize the beginnings of modernism and the intimate and deterministic relationship between architecture and technology, rather than style, which is seen as one of the hallmarks of architectural theory later in the century.

However, even at the opening of the 1890s Hare used Ashwell and Nesbit's patent 'Leicester Plenum System' at Staffordshire County Hall as an essential element in the operation of the council chamber. Its main purpose was to provide each council member with 1000 cubic feet (28.3 m^3) of fresh air per hour, contributing, no doubt, to a high standard of debate. Fresh air was admitted from the exterior at ground floor level, and drawn by means of an electrically powered fan to a heating chamber in the basement. Here it was passed through screens covered with coconut fibre which acted as a filter to remove large

Figure 9.2

County Buildings, Stafford. The louvered oak turret above the council chamber dome through which stale air is extracted

impurities. Subsequently it passed over a battery of heating pipes, from where its path lay along wooden ducts built into the walls to the council chamber, where it was admitted through grilles, well above head height. Stale air was extracted through a separate system, whose grilles were set in the risers of steps, or through a large grille in the dome. The air was extracted by a fan located above the dome in a louvered oak turret, a feature that was to become common in Hare's work. Optionally, it could be returned by ducts to the heating chamber in the basement. In temperate conditions, of course, the heat could be turned off, and when it was hot, blocks of ice could be introduced, cooling the air which passed over them. Contemporaneously, Hare used a similar system to heat and ventilate public spaces at Oxford Town Hall.

The turret fan also sucked vitiated air from the committee rooms and library at first floor level along wooden ceiling ducts. Elsewhere, however, complex heating and ventilating methods were in use, and there were even open fires in certain rooms – though these were not the sole means of heating in those spaces. Two boilers in the basement fed low pressure steam via a distributor to the heating batteries for the plenum system, and to various other zones of the building where radiators were the main means of heat transfer. Hare located the radiators in window and wall recesses, and designed surrounds for them in Hopton Wood stone. Fresh air was admitted from outside over the radiators through grilles. These were carefully handled by the architect who provided them with stone surrounds, located just below the window cills, and forming part of the overall composition of the fenestration.

The plurality of approaches to heating and ventilation demonstrated in Staffordshire County Hall can be seen in the other buildings used as examples here. Bristol Central Library had a mixture of open fireplaces in the offices and rest rooms to the south side, with radiators in public areas. At North Riding County Hall, Brierley located a boiler house adjacent to the council chamber, but at ground level. It was big enough to enable a doubling in size of the installation, and expansion of County Hall was planned from the outset. Councillors were allowed six air changes per hour from the system driven by electric fans, but elsewhere low pressure steam warmed radiators in corridors and principal rooms. The 'Nuvacuumette' steam heating system was the patented method used, and this seems to have been popular for large installations in the Edwardian period.

'Nuvacuumette' was provided at Wesleyan Central Hall. Again, low pressure steam was used to supply heater batteries and radiators. Ashwell and Nesbit introduced the 'plenum' system into the small and large conference halls allowing all 2,700 occupants in the latter 1,000 cubic feet (28.3 m^3) per hour, as specified in the same engineers' work at Stafford. Temperature was

Figure 9.3
County Hall, Northallerton. Behind the glamour: the exterior of the council chamber, hidden from public gaze. The boiler house and plant room is attached, big enough, at the time, to allow for considerable expansion. (Photo: T Lewis. Reproduced courtesy of *Architectural Review*)

thermostatically controlled. Smaller rooms had radiators with vents and mechanical extraction. As befits the building's city centre site, the air for the ventilating system was drawn in by a centrifugal fan at roof level before being filtered and warmed.

Not all systems were successful. Despite the thought put into West Riding County Hall, the heating pipes which ran along the central corridor from the separate boiler house were said to produce conditions of 'tropical ferocity'. Apparently the temperature of the pipes was twice that specified and the contractor had miscalculated. This mistake was sufficient to cause the removal of the system and its replacement a few years after the opening of the building by a new one of a type already tried and tested elsewhere within the county's jurisdiction.

Over the years, as technology has improved in efficiency, most of the hardware associated with Edwardian heating and ventilating systems has been replaced, but quite often the boiler rooms, ducts and grilles are original. The image that remains is of sumptuous accommodation and fittings, but behind the scenes the hum of dynamos, the crackle of electricity, the glow of burnished brass and the flickering of dials, and supporting all, huge girders of steel made of plates riveted together and thick slabs of concrete bound by rods and cages of steel reinforcement.

The process of building has already been touched upon, particularly the increase in the use of machinery and the rise in productivity by using new methods and materials. By the early years of the new century, the architectural profession was left in no doubt that the lugubrious craft-based industry was about to be revolutionized by American efficiency. Everywhere, there were hints about the rapidity with which large and complex buildings could be produced on the other side of the Atlantic. This, perhaps, was more significant to the commercial sector, yet it would have an effect on building as a whole. In addition, trades disputes were rampant in the nineteen hundreds, not simply between unions and employers, but between different trades.

The architect, therefore, had a number of problems to cope with when undertaking supervision of a new building contract, and the picture is not so rosy as the modern reader may imagine. Walter Brierley's quarterly reports to the County Hall Committee of North Riding County Council may act as an example of the problems encountered by those undertaking new building work at the time, and are an illustration of their priorities.

Brierley began his reports in the second half of 1903, a tender of £25,000 being accepted for the work from Joseph Howe and Company of West Hartlepool in May, and the foundation stone laid at the end of July. His first noteworthy report in October of that year indicates a delay in provision of stone and special brick – a theme that was to recur. Brierley suggested a substitute source for the stone because the unreliability of Whitby and Farndale quarries. Nevertheless, work had progressed well on the foundations, and this continued because by January of 1904 the north and south wings were built up to first floor levels. The centre section of the building which was enriched by use of stone was, however, waiting for supplies. The first certificate, for £3,823, was issued.

As the year progressed, however, misfortune struck. Stone was again delayed, this time for the entrance hall and staircase, and this delay was compounded by a strike of masons. In addition, Mr Howe, the contractor, was ill with a disease that was to prove fatal. Notwithstanding, Brierley issued a certificate for work to the value of £8,200. All of the wall construction was finished to roof level, and half of the roof was slated, this despite a failure to deliver some of the steel principals on time. In his report, the architect noted that he had prepared designs and estimates for fittings and furnishings to the council chamber and committee rooms, and for external works. In fact, he had a model of the council chamber seating built, and the estimate of £1,500 for this room was met by the contractor. At about this time, too, questions about internal telecommunications were raised. It was felt that instruments should be installed between offices and committee rooms, which was confirmed after an inspection of West Riding County Hall at Wakefield.

At the beginning of 1905, Brierley could report that all of the plain plastering was finished, and work on provision of heating, hot water and electrical services was virtually complete. The fibrous plasterwork to ceilings was a little behind time. He also reminded the committee that all of the drawings and details were practically completed and that 'I have had a staff of assistants continually employed on this work for over two years'. Architects have always had to remind their clients that professional fees have to be paid as well as construction costs.

In October the building should have been complete, but it was about three months behind schedule. Nevertheless, the caretaker was learning how to operate the heating and ventilating system. All was not plain sailing, however, because Messrs Goodall, Lamb and Heighway Ltd of Manchester, who had the £4,000 contract for provision of furniture and fittings, had caused delays that had prompted visits from Brierley and his assistants. There was also trouble with the telephone contracts, and the General Post Office carried out the installation of the instruments in pursuit of original arrangements. Brierley was no doubt bemused near the end of his efforts to find that the council bureaucracy was making heavy weather over the labelling of doors to offices.

The building was opened on 31 January 1906, with congratulations to the architect on his production of a work that was both functional and artistic. Brierley, replying, pointed out his success of keeping within budget and noted 'I have been on the lookout for extras, with one hand on the safety valve all through the job'. It seems that his grasp of business was greater than that of mechanical engineering.

This story, with variations, must have been repeated for most of the buildings described here. Hare, for instance, suffered the bankruptcy of the general contractor at Oxford, and at Wakefield Gibson and Russell were a few months late in opening West Riding County Hall, in 1898. Embarrassingly, the date '1897' was shown throughout the building on tiles and in decorative embellishment. In general, the buildings took between two and four years to build and the problems besetting the architects would be familiar today for those working to traditional contracts. On the other hand, it seems that problems experienced on completion were usually to do with heating and ventilating systems, rather than with the failure of materials.

At the beginning of the period, the architect worked within a familiar context, from a constructional point of view. Materials were traditional, with brick and stone much in evidence; steelwork was inserted on an ad hoc basis to facilitate larger spans where necessary, and concrete was used for foundations or, in conjunction with steel, for 'fireproof floors' The art of building was understood by designer and builder alike, and the architect's intention was transmitted effortlessly to the contractor and his operatives, who knew what was required and had the experience to execute it to a high standard.

During the two decades covered, however, technology became more complex and specialized, and working methods, both in the drawing office and on the building site, changed. The introduction of electrical services became widespread, and nearly all large buildings incorporated mechanical ventilation systems combined with central heating. Steelwork practice, refined in the United States, allowed the rapid erection of complete steel frames, and reinforced concrete became a widely used material, where its capabilities were exploited by designers. All in all, the craft of building was superseded by a process that required production of accurate, fully dimensioned drawings, off-site production of major elements, and an efficient management process to ensure speedy and satisfactory construction. This change, as much as stylistic issues, signals the end of the period discussed in the book.

CHAPTER TEN

Conclusion

At its worst, there is a pompous and overblown banality about the late Victorian and Edwardian period that could be said to be reflected in its civic buildings. Images of a drum-beating, banner-waving, self-satisfied, over-ripe Empire, already on a downhill path and beyond its short phase of power and glory, may be represented in its built works. The taste of an indolent and philistine general public, mistaking quantity of ornament and detail for quality, supported an architecture that mirrored the heavy and overstuffed drawing rooms in which it played out its feeble, uneventful and hypocritical existence. Such generalizations, however, are, at best, only partial truths, and even if they do reflect justified criticism, the rumbustiousness, determination and self-confidence of the period looks distinctly attractive after a century of cynicism, bred of appalling horrors.

Setting aside questions of style and syntax, the case for Edwardian civic buildings is forcefully made by their continued presence. In the first place, most of them fulfilled the tasks dictated by their often complex programmes extraordinarily well, and certainly as successfully as later buildings which purported to be shaped by an honest response to function. This has meant that many are still carrying out the duties for which they were designed a century or more after they were opened. Even where the original purpose has changed, then quite often it is possible to make good use of them without destroying their character. Opportunities are given to the modern architect charged with conversion by the nature of the spaces contained within. In addition, the quality of construction, detailing and materials has meant that despite neglect, they are usually substantial enough to be retained, even though the cost of repairing only basic details is very high, let alone the commissioning of craftsmen to carve stone and wood, or model plaster.

Over and above this usefulness, they have performed an important symbolic public function and continue to do so. Perhaps they speak too much of civic pomp and represent the sharp divisions that were present in society, even at the relatively petty scale of provincial life. Porticoes and grand flights of stairs for the elite; corner doors and back stairs for minor functionaries and clerks. For all this, though, they seem to have attained an important place in people's lives. Local democracy, and in some cases, philanthropy, created them and they were the embodiment of local spirit. They were the places where townsfolk could meet, usually for some improving purpose. They became the symbols of towns and cities, and landmarks around which a mental map of the town was constructed. In some cases, through iconography, they portrayed the historic, geographic and commercial context of their situation, further reinforcing their local significance.

In order to satisfy these pretensions, architects employed various architectural elements, usually appropriated from suitable historical periods, to give the buildings a 'presence' and status within the urban hierarchy. Internal spaces were treated in a manner befitting their significance in terms of scale, finishes, fittings, decoration and applied art. Coinciding with the peak of the popular influence of the arts and crafts movement, the buildings became a showcase for the work of artists and craftsmen in many media. Certainly during the first decade of the period no wall or ceiling surface in major public areas seems to be untouched. Even though design became more restrained over the years, the character and quality of detail and workmanship remained very high. These buildings were palaces for the people and their democratic representatives. The local pride invested in them may seem naïve nowadays, but the buildings were seen not just as the visual representations of the 'coming-of-age' of local democracy, but often as an instrument for public improvement. This idea may be most directly related to public libraries and galleries, but it is clear, for instance, that the efforts of artists and craftsmen in civic buildings were meant to be enjoyed by all.

All too soon, the situation changed. Perhaps national cynicism was induced in the aftermath of the Great War. Councils became institutionalized and were sometimes represented as oppressive and interfering rather than beneficial bodies. Private benefactors were replaced by increased rates and taxes. At the same time as this souring of the atmosphere, architectural styles changed and became impersonal, emphasizing the alienation that was felt socially.

Fashion changed quickly in architecture, and even before the advent of high speed mass media, architects were bombarded with news of new developments, and images of the work of the profession's leaders through the relatively large number of magazines and journals that were produced. First, the bric-à-brac style of 1890 was superseded by the 'Wrenaissance'. The latter was supported by burgeoning scholarship that made the earlier style seem hopelessly whimsical, and lacking in intellectual underpinning. The 'Wrenaissance' in itself, however, was only a development of what had gone before. It was more restrained in its use of architectural language, and was suitable for both large and small scale buildings without distortion or ridiculous over-elaboration. Fundamentally, however, although the knowledge and appreciation of English baroque architecture had increased greatly, and architects knew how to use the elements of the language grammatically, it was still visually based. Designers of buildings were artist–architects, skilled at draughtsmanship, and spending much of their spare time sketching or measuring appropriate examples. The architecture was conceived pictorially; it had to look good. Other than this, there was no common system or fluency behind what was done. Sir Reginald Blomfield, a 'Wrenaissance' man *par excellence*, and then an *aficionado* of French architecture, was celebrated for his demands through a number of books, lectures and articles for the espousal of the classical grand manner, and yet, as Sir John Summerson has pointed out, 'Blomfield liked everything about classical architecture, except its classicism.'[1]

The arrival of real classical architecture spelled the end of the Edwardian period, as defined in this book, even though it began to become popular before King Edward's death. Encouraged by the growth of full-time architectural education, which demanded a teachable and systematic method of architectural design, fostered by a new respect for things that were French, and nurtured by the impression made upon Britain by the United States, the Franco-American *beaux-arts* system eliminated the 'Wrenaissance' and became the foremost style for large buildings from about 1910 up to the outbreak of the Second World War. It also paved the way for the introduction of modernism which, whilst using an alien language, had much in common with the *beaux-arts* and was initiated by those with a *beaux-arts* background.

Thus, Edwardian architecture was superseded, and with the exception of far-sighted critics such as H.S. Goodhart-Rendel, has been anathema to those involved in architectural debate ever since, if not with the general public. Essentially, though, Edwardian buildings are modern, even if past styles are used as a means of expression. They respond well to a complex programme and are functional both in this and in their use of durable and appropriate materials. Their integration of the works of artists and craftsmen into the building is enviable in an age when art, if included, is a foreign body appended to the architect's design. It would be ironic if, as we proceed into the next century, the best-respected buildings of the twentieth century are those from right at its very beginning.

Notes and references

Chapter 1

1. The term, bric-à-brac is used in H.S. Goodhart-Rendel's amusing and informative *English Architecture Since the Regency* (London, 1953).
2. Reginald Blomfield, *A History of Renaissance Architecture in England, 1500–1800*, Volume 1 (London, 1897), p. 176.
3. Roger Scruton, 'Under Scrutiny', *Perspectives,* Issue 31, Oct–Nov 1997, p. 91.

Chapter 2

1. Anon, *The Town Hall of the Borough and County Town of Lancaster: A Description and Design of the Building* (Lancaster, 1908), p. 7.
2. Anon, *Souvenir of the Opening of the Town Hall* (Deptford, 1905), p. 2.
3. Marquess of Ripon, *(Chairman's) Statement as to the Work of the Council*, West Riding of Yorkshire County Council (1892), p. 2.
4. B.J. Barker and M.W. Beresford, *The West Riding Council, 1889–1974, Historical Studies* (Wakefield, 1979), p. 107.
5. *Wakefield Express*, 22 February 1898.
6. Lord Harrowby, first Chairman of the County Council quoted in Staffordshire County Council, *An End to Picnicking: The Story of County Buildings, Stafford 1895–1995* (Stafford, 1995), p. 9.
7. Barker and Beresford, *The West Riding Council,* p. 107.
8. Letter by Brierley to building committee, 21 July 1904, North Riding of Yorkshire County Archives.
9. *Souvenir, County Hall, Northallerton*, 31 January 1906, pp. 12, 13.

Chapter 3

1. Thomas H. Mawson, *Civic Art, Studies in Town Planning, Parks, Boulevards and Open Spaces* (London, 1911), p. 225.
2. Charles M. Robinson, *Modern Civic Art, or the City Made Beautiful* (New York, 1903), quoted in David B. Brownlee, *Building the City Beautiful* (Philadelphia, 1989), p. 13.
3. William Morris, *News from Nowhere* (1890) (Nonesuch edition, London, 1948), p. 23.
4. Spiro Kostof, *The City Shaped, Urban Patterns and Meanings Through History* (London, 1991).
5. Ibid., p. 324.
6. B.J. Barker and M.W. Beresford, *The West Riding Council, 1889–1974, Historical Studies* (Wakefield, 1979), p. 107.
7. Staffordshire County Council, *An End to Picnicking: The Story of County Buildings, Stafford 1895–1995* (Stafford, 1995), p. 12
8. Derek Linstrum, *West Yorkshire Architects & Architecture* (London, 1978), pp. 358–360.
9. F.W. Lanchester, 'Cardiff City Hall and Law Courts', *Architectural Review*, Vol. 20, July–December 1906, p. 240.

Chapter 4

1. John Begg, 'The treatment of sculpture in relation to architecture', Silver medal prize essay, *Journal RIBA*, Vol. I, Series III, 1893–94, p. 327.
2. Susan Beattie, *The New Sculpture* (New Haven, CT and London, 1983), p. 56.
3. C.H. Reilly, *Representative British Architects of the Present Day* (London, 1931), p. 58.

Chapter 5

1. F.W. Lanchester, 'Cardiff City Hall and Law Courts', *Architectural Review,* Vol. 20, July–December 1906, p. 233.
2. *Schedule* to competition documents, July 1891.
3. Anon, *Wesleyan Methodist Church, Central Hall and Buildings, Westminster, S.W. Illustrated Souvenir* (Westminster, undated), p. 3.

Chapter 7

1. Reginald Blomfield, *A History of Renaissance Architecture in England, 1500–1800,* Volume 1 (London, 1897), p. 156.
2. Ibid.
3. Arthur Keen, 'The Ceilings of City Churches – II', *Architectural Review,* Jan–June 1911, Vol. 29, February, pp. 68–76, March, pp. 137–143.
4. Blomfield, opcit, p. 158.
5. David Watkin, *A History of Western Architecture* (London, 1986), p. 287.
6. Blomfield, *Renaissance Architecture in England,* p. 156.
7. Keen, 'The Ceilings of City Churches – II', *Architectural Review,* p. 71.

Chapter 8

1. Derek Linstrum, *West Yorkshire Architects & Architecture* (London, 1978), p. 356.

2. Hugh O'Neill, *Stone for Building* (London, 1956) p. 179.
3. Ibid., p. 181.
4. Supplement to *Architectural Review,* Vol. 24, 'Architects' Craftsmen. No. 1 George Jackson & Sons, Ltd', pp. 313–322.

Chapter 9

1. W.H. Preece, *Transactions of the RIBA,* Vol. VIII, New Series, p. 305.
2. Michael Stratton, 'Innovation and Conservatism: Steel and Reinforced Concrete in British Architecture, 1860–1905', in Peter Burman (ed.), *Architecture 1900* (Shaftesbury, 1998), p. 15.
3. *RIBA Journal,* Vol. XIII, Series 3, 1905, pp. 29–49.
4. Ibid., p. 29.
5. R.W. Postgate, *The Builder's History* (London, 1923).
6. A.R. Sutton, *Bristol Central Library,* unpublished ms.
7. H. Hobhouse (ed.), *County Hall,* Survey of London, Monograph 17 (London, 1991), p. 51.
8. *The Builder* (London), 11 October 1912, p. 411.

Chapter 10

1. Sir J. Summerson, *The Turn of the Century: Architecture in Britain around 1900.* W.A. Cargill Memorial Lecture, Glasgow, 1976.

Bibliography

Adshead, S.D. *Town Planning and Town Development*, London, 1923

Beattie, S. *The New Sculpture*, New Haven, CT and London, 1983

Blomfield, R.T. *A History of Renaissance Architecture in England, 1500–1800*, London, 1897

Brownlee, David B. *Building the City Beautiful*, Philadelphia, 1989

Burman, Peter (ed.), *Architecture 1900*, Shaftesbury, 1998

Champneys, A.L. *Public Libraries: a Treatise on their Design, Construction and Fittings*, London, 1907

Cunningham, C. *Victorian and Edwardian Town Halls*, London, 1981

Cusack, P. 'Reinforced Concrete in Britain: 1897–1908, unpublished PhD thesis, University of Edinburgh, 1981

Cusak, P. 'Architects and the Reinforced Concrete Specialist in Britain, 1905–1908', *Architectural History*, Vol. 29, 1986, p. 183

Dewe, M.D. 'Henry Thomas Hare (1860–1921): an Edwardian Public Library Architect and his Work', unpublished MA thesis, University of Strathclyde, 1981

Fellows, R.A. *Sir Reginald Blomfield: and Edwardian Architect*, London, 1985

Fellows, R.A. *Edwardian Architecture, Style and Technology*, London, 1995

Goodhart-Rendel, H.S. *English Architecture since the Regency: an Interpretation*, London, 1953

Gray, A. Stuart, *Edwardian Architecture: a Biographical Dictionary*, London, 1985

Hobhouse, H. (ed.) *County Hall*, Survey of London, Monograph 17, London, 1991

Kostof, Spiro, *The City Shaped, Urban Patterns and Meanings Through History*, London, 1991

Lanchester, H.V. *The Art of Town Planning*, London, 1925

Lawrence, J.C. 'Steel frame architecture versus the London Building Regulations: Selfridges, the Ritz and American Technology', *Construction History*, Vol. 6, 1990, p. 23

Linstrum, Derek, *West Yorkshire Architects and Architecture*, London, 1978

Macleod, R. *Style and Society: Architectural Ideology in Britain, 1835–1914*, London, 1971

Mawson, Thomas H. *Civic Art: Studies in Town Planning, Boulevards and Open Spaces*, London, 1911

Munford, W.A. *Penny Rate: Aspects of British Public Library History, 1850–1950*, London, 1951

Nowell-Smith, Simon (ed.), *Edwardian England, 1901–1914*, London, 1964

O'Neill, Hugh, *Stone for Building*, London, 1965

Port, M.H. *Imperial London, Civil Government Building in London 1851–1915*, New Haven, CT and London, 1995

Postgate, R.W. *The Builders' History*, London, 1923

Powell, Christopher, *The British Building Industry since 1800: An economic history*, London, 1996

Reilly, C.H. *Representative British Architects of the Present Day*, London, 1931

Saint, A. *Richard Norman Shaw*, New Haven, CT and London, 1976

Service, A. (ed.), *Edwardian Architecture and its Origins*, London, 1975

Summers, Sir J. *The Turn of the Century: Architecture in Britain around 1900*, W.A. Cargill Memorial Lectures in Fine Art, Glasgow, 1976

Thompson, P. *The Edwardians: the Remaking of British Society*, London, 1975

Specific sources

(*AR* = *Architectural Review*)

Birmingham Council House
AR Vol. 32, July–Dec 1912

Bristol Central Library
Sutton, A.R. *Bristol Central Library*, unpublished ms
AR Vol. 24, July–Dec 1908
The Builder Vol. 89, 1905

Cardiff City Hall
AR Vol. 20, July–Dec 1912

Colchester Town Hall
Green, Oliver *The Town Hall, Colchester,* Colchester, 1997
AR Vol. 4, June–Nov 1898
AR Vol. 6, June–Dec 1899
AR Vol. 7, Jan–June 1900
AR Vol. 12, July–Dec 1902

Deptford Town Hall
Anon. *Souvenir of the Opening of the Town Hall,* Deptford, 1905

Glamorgan County Hall
AR Vol. 32, July–Dec 1912

Henley Town Hall
AR Vol. 18, July–Dec 1905

Islington Central Library
AR Vol. 18, July–Dec 1905

Lancaster Town Hall
Anon. *The Town Hall of the Borough and County Town of Lancaster: A Description and Design of the Building,* Lancaster, 1908
AR Vol. 27, Jan–June 1910
Building News 4/12/1908

County Hall Northallerton
Anon. *Souvenir, County Hall, Northallerton, January 31st, 1906,* Northallerton, 1906
Ashcroft, M.Y. (ed.) *A History of the North Riding of Yorkshire County Council 1889–1974,* Northallerton, 1974
The Builder Vol. 88, 1904
AR Vol. 21, Jan–June 1907

Oxford Town Hall
Williams, Harold *The Town Hall, Oxford,* Oxford, 1992
Building News, 8/7/1892
Victoria County History, Oxfordshire, Vol. IV

County Buildings Stafford
Staffordshire County Council, *An End to Picnicking, The Story of County Buildings, Stafford 1895–1995,* Stafford, 1995
Staffordshire County Council, *The Guide to County Buildings, Stafford, On its Centenary 1895–1995,* Stafford, 1995
The Builder 6/8/1893
British Architect 8/5/1896

Stockport Town Hall
The Builder Vol. 85, 12 Dec 1903

County Hall Wakefield
Barker, B.J. and Beresford, M.W. *The West Riding County Council, 1884–1974, Historical Studies,* Wakefield, 1979
The Builder Vol. 64, 1893
The Builder Vol. 70, 1896
The Builder Vol. 71, 1896

Wesleyan Central Hall
Anon. *Wesleyan Methodist Church, Central Hall and Buildings, Westminster, S.W. Illustrated Souvenir,* Westminster, undated.

General issues

Transactions of the RIBA 1890–1892
Journal of the RIBA 1893–1910

Index

Page numbers in bold italic indicate picture reference only

Adam, Robert and James, 102
Adams, Holden and Pearson, 17
Alma-Tadema, Lawrence, 40
Anderson, John MacVicar, 19, 106
Architectural Review, 3
Art Workers' Guild, 40, 104
Arts and crafts movement, 1, 3–5, 20, 33, 39–40, 93–94, 109, 111, 121
Ashburnham House, 103
Ashley, H.V., 13, 49–50, 61, *49*
Ashmolean Museum, Oxford, *4*
Ashton Memorial, Lancaster, 11
Ashwell and Nesbit: Leicester Plenum System, 117–119
Aumonier, William, 47, 103–106

Bangor, University College, 5
Bankart, George Percy, 101–103, 113, *102*, *103*
Barry, Charles, 2, 7
Bates, Harry, 40
Bath, Guildhall, 12
Beattie, Susan, 40
'*Beaux-arts*', 1, 5–6, 22, 49, 52, 82, 110, 122, *16*, *49*, *50*
Belcher, John, 1–2, 10–11, 19–20, 32–33, 40–42, 46–47, 57, 75–77, 80, 82, 89, 112, *10*, *32*, *41*, *58*, *75*, *83*, *91*, *109*
Belfast City Hall, 35, *108*
Birmingham Council House, 13, 49–50, 61, *49*
Bishopsbarn, York, 101
Blomfield, Reginald, 2–4, 20, 47–48, 84–85, 90, 103–104, 122, *3*, *4*, *85*
Bovril Ltd., Headquarters, *77*
Bradford, 7, 116
Bradford, St George's Hall, 84
Bradford Town Hall, 12, 34, *33*
'Bric-à-brac', 2, 24, 30, 46–47, 122, *82*

Brierley, Walter H., 19–20, 48, 55, 70–71, 81, 88–89, 100–101, 116, 118–120, *15*, *48*, *56*, *71*, *80*, *88*, *91*, *103*, *118*
Bristol Public Library, 17–18, 20, 42–44, 64–65, 68–69, 90–92, 101, 104, 109, 113, 116–118, *18*, *43*, *64*, *68*, *69*, *92*
Brodrick, Cuthbert, 7
Bromsgrove Guild, 44, 101, 105
Brydon, J.M., 12
Bylander, Sven, 111

Cardiff, City Hall, 16, 20, 38–39, 44, 52, 58–61, 84, 90, 99, 101, 107–108, 113, *37*, *44*, *53*, *91*, *101*, *102*
Cardiff, Glamorgan County Hall, 16, 38, 50, 52–55, 82, *16*, *50*, *54*
Carnegie, Andrew, 5, 17–18, 111
Carnegie Corporation, 63
Caythorpe Court, Lincs., 4
Champneys, Basil, 30
Churches, 84–88, 90–92, *85*, *86*
Clayton and Bell, 109–110, *109*
Colchester Town Hall, 10, 19–20, 31–33, 42–44, 46, 55–57, 75–77, 80, 82, 89, 109–110, *10*, *32*, *41*, *58*, *75*, *83*, *91*, *109*
Collcutt, Thomas E., 8–9, 14, 19, 24–27, *24*
Competitions, 19–21
Cooper, Edwin, 20
County Halls, *See* Town and County Halls

Denell, R.A., 112
Deptford Town Hall, 11, 20, 34–36, 42–44, 55–57, 75–77, 89–90, 107–108, 116, *35*, *36*, *42*, *57*, *74*, *91*, *103*, *107*
Dorman Long & Co., 111, 113

'Edwardian baroque', 2–3, 11, 44, 80

Edwards, F.E.P., 12, 34
Edwards, J. Vickers, 19–20, 25
Edwards, John Passmore, 17
Epstein, Jacob, 40

Fehr, H.C., 38, 41, 44–45, 96, *44, 96*
Forsyth, J. Dudley, 105
Fulton, James, *88*

General Post Office, Newgate Street, London, 112–113
'George V', 2, 6
George, Ernest, 2
Gibbons, Grinling, 18, 103
Gibbs, James, 2, *49*
Gibson, James G.S., 14, 17, 20, 25–27, 58, 97–98, 120, *14, 24, 26, 59, 72, 86, 93, 94, 95, 96, 97, 98, 99, 110*
Gibson, Skipwith and Gordon, 17
Gimson, Ernest, 101, 103
Goodall, Lamb and Heighway Ltd., 119
Goodhart Rendel, H.S., 2, 122
Gotch, J. Alfred, 2
'Gothic revival', 2, 12, 17, 34
Guildford, Guildhall, 36

Hammersmith Central Library, 18
Hampton, Herbert, 37
Hare, Henry Thomas, 4–5, 9, 11–12, 18–20, 27–31, 39, 41–42, 46–47, 57–58, 61–63, 65–66, 73–74, 79–80, 82–84, 87, 90–92, 105–107, 113, 116–118, 120, *9, 12, 27, 28, 29, 30, 31, 43, 47, 48, 59, 61, 62, 65, 73, 80, 82, 87, 91, 100, 106, 117*
Harris, E. Vincent, 16, 50, 52–55, 82, *16, 50, 54*
Harrowby, Lord, 15
Hawksmoor, Nicholas, 2, 33
Heating and ventilation, 5, 116–119
Henley Town Hall, 11–12, 57–58, 113, *12, 59*
Henman, William, 117
Hennebique system (reinforced concrete), 112–113
Holden, Charles, 17–18, 42–44, 64–65, 68–69, 90–92, 104, 109, *18, 43, 64, 68, 69, 92*
House of Commons, London, 84
Howe, Joseph, and Co., 119
Huddersfield, 7
Huddersfield Town Hall, 84
Hull School of Art, 44, 55, 75–77

Institute of Chartered Accountants, Moorgate, London, 1, 40
Islington Central Library, 18, 42, 65–66, 90–92, *43, 65*

Jack, George, 103
Jackson, George, & Sons, 103, *104*
Jackson, T.G., 30
'Jacobethan', 79–80, 87, 100, *80*
Jenkins, F. Lynn, 105

Jones, A.G., 44

Kahn system (reinforced concrete), 112, 114
Keen, Arthur, 84, 90
Kirby Hall, Northants, 25, 30, 47, *3, 47*
Knott, Ralph, 19, 90, 114
Kostof, Spiro, 23–24

Lady Margaret Hall, Oxford, Library, 90
Lancaster Town Hall, 10–11, 20, 36–37, 40–41, 48–49, 61, 70, 81–84, 89, 103, 108–109, 113, 116, *11, 36, 37, 49, 60, 81, 83, 89, 91, 110*
Lanchester, F.W., 114
Lanchester, Henry V., *See* Lanchester, Stewart and Rickards
Lanchester, Stewart and Rickards, 2, 16, 19–20, 36, 38, 41, 44–46, 52–57, 75–78, 89–90, 107–108, 113–116, *35, 36, 37, 42, 44, 45, 46, 53, 57, 67, 74, 76, 77, 91, 101, 102, 103, 107, 115*
Lean, Vincent Stuckey, 17
Leeds Town Hall, 7, 34, 84
Lethaby, William Richard, 98
Libraries, 17–19, 63–66, 90–92, 104
Lifts, 5, 116–117
Lighting, 5, 97–98, 108–109, 116
Lindsay, William H., & Co., 113
Linstrum, Derek, 34
Liverpool, St George's Hall, 84
Lockwood and Mawson, 34
London, County Hall, 6, 16, 18–20, 90, 113–114
Lowther, Charles Grange, 94–95, *94, 95*

Macartney, Mervyn, 2–3, 47
McGill, Donald, 41
Manchester Town Hall, 7, 112
Mawson, Thomas, 22
Middlesex Guildhall, 16–17
Moira, Gerald, 105
Montford, Paul, 41, 44
Moodie, Thomas A., 16,
Morris, William, 2, 22
Mouchel, L.G., 112
Mountford, Edward W., 39–41, 48–49, 61, 89, 105, 108–109, *11, 36, 37, 49, 60, 81, 83, 89, 91, 110*

Nesfield, W. Eden, 2
Newman, Winton, 13, 49–50, 61, *49*
Northallerton, North Riding County Hall, 15–16, 19–20, 48, 52, 55, 58, 70–71, 81, 88–89, 100–101, 104, 108, 116, 118–120, *15, 48, 56, 71, 80, 88, 91, 103, 118*
'Nuvacuumette' heating system, 118

Oxford, Carfax, 30–31, *30*
Oxford Town Hall, 8–10, 19–20, 27–31, 41, 46–47, 61–63, 73, 79–80, 82–84, 87, 99–100, 104, 106, 113, 116, 118, *9, 29, 30, 31, 47, 62, 80, 82, 100, 106*

Parnell & Son, Rugby, 9
Paxman, James, 42
Pibworth, Charles, 44, *43*
Pite, Arthur Beresford, 1, 33
Plasterwork, 101–106, *104*
Pomeroy, Frederick W., 37, 39–40, 49
Poole, Henry, 41, 44–46, 107–108
Port, M.H., 19
Postgate, R.W., 112–113
Powell & Sons, 109
Preece, W.H., 111
Prior, Edward S., 1, 3, 20
Pugin, Augustus, 111

'Queen Anne', 2, 14, 24–25, 27, 34, 39

Reading, Berkshire County Hall, 16
Redpath, Brown and Company, 111
Reilly, Charles H., 46
Reinforced concrete, 5–6, 112–114
Rhind, W. Birnie, 41
Rickards, Edwin, *See* Lanchester, Stewart and Rickards
Riley, W.E., 114
Ripon, Marquess of, 13, 15, 20
Royal Institute of British Architects, 19, 112
Royal Victoria Hospital, Belfast, 117
Robinson, Charles M., 22
Ruskin, John, 111
Russell, Samuel B., 14, 17, 20, 25–27, 58, 97–98, 120 *14, 24, 26, 59, 72, 86, 93, 94, 95, 96, 97, 98, 99, 110*

Sachs, Edwin Otto, 112
Schenck, Frederick E.E., 41, 79, 106
Scruton, Roger, 4
Seale, Gilbert, & Son, 49, 103, *105*
Selfridge's, Oxford Street, London, 6
Shaw, Richard Norman, 2, 12, 19, 25, 27, 34, *33*
Singer, J.W., & Sons, 108–109, *107, 108*
Smith of London (stained glass), 96–97
Stafford, County Buildings, 15, 19–21, 27–28, 31, 41, 47, 61–62, 73–74, 79, 84, 87–88, 106, 113, 116–118, *27, 28, 48, 61, 73, 87, 91, 117*

Stained glass, 96–97, 105, 109–110, *109, 110*
Steel, 5–6, 111–113, 120
Stockport Town Hall, 11, 19, 34–35, 58–61, 70, 84, 89, 99, 108 *34, 70*
Summerson, John, 122

Tanner, Henry, 112–113
Thomas, Alfred Brumwell, 19, 34–35, 108, *34, 70, 108*
Thornycroft, Hamo, 40
Town and County Halls, 8–17, 23, 51–63, 84–90, *91*
'Tudorbethan', 5, 34, 66

United Kingdom Provident Institution, Strand, London, 105–106

Vanbrugh, John, 2, 70
Ventilation, *See* Heating and ventilation
Voysey, Charles F.A., 1, 3–4, 20

Wakefield, West Riding County Hall, 13–15, 20, 24–27, 41–42, 44, 47–48, 58–61, 71–72, 84, 86–87, 93–100, 104, 108, 116, 119–120, *14, 24, 26, 59, 72, 86, 93, 94, 95, 96, 97, 98, 99, 110*
Wallace, William, 20
Waring and Gillow, 11
Warwick and Hall, 16
Waterhouse, Alfred, 7, 19, 113
Watkin, David, 85
Watts, L.J., 42
Webb, Aston, 19, 104
Webb, Philip, 2
Wesleyan Central Hall, Westminster, 19–20, 44–46, 66, 75–78, 89, 108–109, 114–116, 118–119, *45, 46, 67, 76, 115*
Westminster Presbyterian College, Cambridge, 4
Wolverhampton Public Library, 18–20, 39, 66, 73, 90
Wren, Christopher, 2, 33, 79, 83–88, 90, 114, *83, 85, 86*
'Wrenaissance', 2, 12, 16, 28, 31, 33–34, 48, 72, 79, 84, 87, 90–92, 100–101, 109, 122, *4, 10, 28, 83, 102, 103*